This Gardening Life

Jonathan Sturm

Ashwood Books

First published in Australia June 2020 by Ashwood Books
PO Box 73, Franklin, Tasmania 7113
ISBN Paperback: 978-0-9874111-0-5
ISBN Kindle: 978-0-9874111-4-3
https://ashwoodbooks.com
This edition © Ashwood Books
Text © JP Sturm 2020
Printed by Lightning Source

This book's body text is set in Palatino Linotype
Headings: Avenir Next

By the same author: *Complete Organic Gardening* 1992

Website: www.sturmsoft.com

This cabbage, these carrots, these potatoes, these onions… will soon become me. Such a tasty fact!
—Mike Garofalo

In memory of my parents: my father the gardener and my mother the Stoic.

I've had a good life, and was born to and among people I've admired and loved.
　—Wendell Berry

Contents

A Sufi Story (of sorts) i
Preamble ii
Preface v
Introduction vi
Your Garden 1
   Choosing the Land 1
   Basics 3
   Soil 6
   Plant Nutrition 11
   Major Elements 12
   Important Compounds 22
   Soil Testing 23
   Composts and Fertilisers 24
Tillage and Tools 49
   Establishing your Garden 51
   Gardening Implements 55
Extending the Growing Season 64
Weed Control 70
   Mechanical 70
   Mulching 71
Pests and Diseases 77
   Disease Control Methods 84
   Pest Control Methods 86
   Snails and Slugs 88
   Recipes for Alternative Pesticides 91
Irrigation 95
   Watering the garden 95
Individual Crops 100
   Broccoli, Brussels Sprouts, Cabbages and Cauliflowers .. 100
   Pea and Bean Tribe 112
   Alliums (the Onion Family) 118
   Tomatoes and Capsicums 125
   Vine Crops 130
   Potatoes 135
   Some Useful Perennials 139
   Celery and Celeriac 142
   Sweet Corn 143

    Scorzonera and Salsify 145
    Okra 145
    Rosella 145
    Mustard and Cress 145
    Jerusalem Artichokes 146
    Fennel 146
    Hamburg Parsley 147
    Gobo 147
    Strawberries 147
    Leaf Crops 151
    Culinary Herbs 159

Seeds and Sowing Times **164**
    Planting Distances 164
    Seed Raising Mix 166
    Sowing for Transplant 169
    Seed Raising Containers 170
    Moon Planting 174
    Maintaining Records 177

Seed Saving **180**

Storage of Vegetables **185**

The Rival Growing Systems **189**
    Albrecht 189
    Biodynamic 190
    Conventional 190
    Hydroponics 192
    Natural Farming 193
    Organic 193
    Permaculture 195

Thoughts on Commercial Production **196**
    Crop Rotation, Green manures and Cover Crops 197

A Philosophical Note **208**

About the Author **214**

Recommended Reading **223**

Resources **227**

Acknowledgements **228**

Gardening is seen as a pastime that is almost like belonging to the Church of England — a sign of maturity and wisdom and right thinking.
  —Monty Don

A Sufi Story (of sorts)

MANY YEARS AGO IN A LAND FAR AWAY, there was a little village that was famous throughout the world for the quality of its wine. For countless generations, year after year, the peasants who grew the grapes and made the wine held a harvest festival in their little church. There they would give thanks to God for blessing them with the grapes that made their wonderful wine. The priest would bless the puncheon of the very best of their wine and dispense a flagon of it to each of the peasants whose vineyards contributed to their main source of income. Each peasant would then sprinkle the contents of their flagon along the rows of grapevines as a thank you to the ancient goddess Demeter.

Then one year the village was sent a new priest to replace their rather old and tired one who had retired to Rome. This young man had been well-educated rather than a rustic like his predecessor. He knew all about science and industry having been taught such things at university. He realised that the puncheon of the best wine could be sold at Rome for a very good price and that the extra fame that this brought would doubtless mean an even better price for the village's wines in the market. Indeed this turned out to be so.

For several years the villagers benefited from the extra income they now had, but slowly, ever so slowly, the quality of their wine diminished. It no longer tasted better than every wine in the land. Eventually, it was no better than the ordinary stuff you could buy anywhere and the price they received reflected that. For while the villagers had believed they were thanking Demeter by sprinkling their best wine throughout their vineyards, they had been inoculating their grapes with a particular strain of yeast that was responsible for the extraordinary quality of their wine. Without annual refreshment following the harvest festival, that strain had gradually been replaced by inferior strains of yeast.

Do not seek to bring things to pass in accordance with your wishes, but wish for them as they are, and you will find them.
  —Epictetus

Preamble

ASKING THE QUESTION: "Why grow your own vegetables?" elicits a number of responses. The most important from my point of view is *flavour*. While the initial impetus was the idea of self-sufficiency, it was the taste of what I was growing that kept me growing vegetables until severe arthritis rendered it almost impossible to continue. You will read further on about how my peas were the cause of my taking up market gardening.

I have always enjoyed doing and making things for myself, not always successfully. Gardening is far and away the most popular recreational activity in Australia and it would not surprise me if that's true of the whole world. There's more than one aspect to this. Some enjoy the aesthetic aspect: what the results look like. Others enjoy cooking and eating. I love both of these activities and I am renowned for the excellence of my dinner parties.

Knowing how your vegetables were grown is important to many. Garlic from the supermarket may have been treated with a chemical to inhibit sprouting, the silver beet may have been forced with water-soluble nitrogen fertiliser and so be full of nitrosamines, a toxic substance. I knew one apple grower who was still using DDT 30 years after it had been banned in Australia.

Growing your own vegetables can save you a great deal of money. Not a great deal if you grow to supermarket quality, but the major purchasers of the best quality produce are gourmet chefs and they pay top dollar. I have never eaten purchased vegetables of that quality from a shop, or farmer's market for that matter, but my wife once commented while we ate a meal we had prepared: "I wonder what the poor rich people are having to eat tonight".

Gardening for 45 minutes provides the same amount of exercise as running 2.4 kilometres (1½ miles).[1] Some of us find gardening to be more fun than running and I'm not sure who'd buy the product of someone running whatever that might be! Like running, the physical activity of gardening reduces stress and relieves tension. I believe that's what diazepam (Valium) is for.

The waste from purchased food (20%) generally goes to the municipal dump where it's usually buried at the ratepayers' expense. In the vegetable gardener's case, there is no waste; we gardeners return any reject vegetable parts to the soil via the compost heap or worm farm. This is genuine environmental activism, not the virtue-signalling sort.

---

1   According to the US National Heart, Lung and Blood Institute.

A small number of readers of an early draft of this book took me to task for drawing a distinction between the environmentalism I advocate and activists in the green movement. I felt it important to distance myself from them for a number of reasons. First, bear in mind that I have been a staunch advocate for conservation for most of my life. In the 1970s I was one of many who were advocates of plantation forestry rather than logging of wilderness. We laid the groundwork for Prof Ian Lowe's "An Alternative Economic Strategy for Tasmania: A Report of Principles". One of my contributions in the 1980s when I was secretary of what was widely believed to be the greenest branch of the Australian Labor Party was a document proposing conversion of the Hydro workshops in Moonah to manufacture solar hot water systems locally rather than importing them. Widespread adoption of solar hot water systems was sufficient to eliminate the need for a small hydro-electric dam such as was being proposed at the time.

The use of aquaculture to conserve wild fish stocks, co-generation of energy, sustainable tourism and many other ideas were part of what we called a "greenprint" for the future. Unlike the greens of today, I remain very much in favour of the many proposals put forward at that time, rather than opposing them.

I am a practicing Stoic and very much have in mind Epictetus' advice: *"When you do anything from a clear judgment that it ought to be done, never shrink from being seen to do it, even though the world should misunderstand it; for if you are not acting rightly, shun the action itself; if you are, why fear those who wrongly censure you?"* I am not writing this book to make money, though I'm sure it will and if my words offend the politically correct: tough!

When you grow all, or nearly all, your own food you don't need to earn as much money. Deliberately restricting your earnings in this way means you don't need to pay as much income tax. For my 30th birthday in 1981 I was given John Seymour's "Complete Guide to Self-Sufficiency", a comprehensive how-to for living simply on the land. My future wife and I purchased our small farm eight months later, a profoundly political act inspired by Helen and Scott Nearing's book: *Living the Good Life*.[2]

When I began gardening I read everything I could on the topic and early on read FH Billington's *Farmers of Forty Centuries* from the local library. My interest in climate was piqued and I ended up studying this at university when in my fifties. I spent my early teenage years

---

[2] Unlike the Nearings, we are not communists. Our politics is best described as middle of the road and I am also strongly libertarian. The Political Compass has me in the same region as the Dalai Lama. https://www.politicalcompass.org/

suffering from what was called at the time The Big Freeze in the UK before emigrating to Australia. In my late teens, the mid-century cooling and associated drought hit Biafra and Ethiopia with severe famine making a lasting impression on me of the importance of climate change.

Cooler might very well be better for us privileged whites, but not so desirable from the point of view of subsistence farmers in sub-Saharan Africa.

Stoicism

"Stoicism... offers a strong affirmative vision of what life is for: the pursuit of virtue. Living virtuously means living by reason, and the Stoics regard reason as calling for honesty, kindness, humility, and devotion to the greater good. It also calls for involvement in public affairs — that is, in the work of helping others in whatever ways are available. Instead of living to satisfy desires, Stoics regard themselves as meant to function as parts of a whole. There is great joy to be had in this, though it is not the variety that comes from the acquisition of things or approval from others. The happiness the Stoic seeks is eudaimoniad — the good life, or well-being. Virtues bring about that type of happiness as a byproduct, and Stoics regard this as the only reliable path by which happiness can be secured."[3]

To the ancient Greeks, philosophy wasn't an arid academic subject, it was a way to live your life. Stoicism had its competitors the main one being Epicureanism. Stoicism claims that living justly and virtuously is the highest good that one can experience, and that pleasure and pain are to be treated indifferently. Epicureanism claims that we should seek to maximise our own pleasure and thus avoid pain. Both instructed us to live according to Nature where Nature is broadly defined as *the way things are*. Both are about thinking and acting rather than preaching and evangelising.

There is a problem with *the way things are*: humans are very good at disagreeing. More about that in the appendix on page 208.

"Everything we hear is an opinion, not a fact. Everything we see is a perspective, not the truth."
— Marcus Aurelius

---

[3] Farnsworth, Ward. "The Practicing Stoic: A Philosophical User's Manual", David R. Godine 2018. Kindle Edition.

Preface

IN 1992, MY FIRST BOOK: *Complete Organic Gardening* was published to wide acclaim. There were some problems with this. It wasn't quite the book I had wanted to write, it was far from "complete" (no book ever can be), and my 50% share of the profits seemed a lot smaller than the 50% claimed by the publisher — closer to 5% in fact. So it goes... This book promises to be much closer to what I wanted to write, though that too has changed over the intervening years.

Like its predecessor, the content is information that I have found useful, but scattered through several books. Having it all in the one place is a great convenience. I also provide commentary on what I have found to be reliable information and what I have found to be less applicable. It is intended to be useful both to the beginner and the experienced gardener — the home gardener and small-scale market gardener.

It's a fact of the writer's life that the enjoyable part is everything that comes before writing down one's thoughts, the research stage. Some trains of thought compel one to write — it's almost as if the piece writes itself. The hard part is writing all the bits in between to knit everything together into a coherent whole. Hardest of all is the reading and rereading to eliminate as far as possible misunderstanding, and where possible simplify the language to ease understanding.

Mostly, I write about my personal experiences, rather than at second hand. Where I do write about others, it's generally because it relates to thoughts I have had, or am having. In a word, this book is intensely personal. It also tends to ramble because topics that seem quite unrelated to the specialist seem to me quite the opposite. This will either annoy the hell out of you, or you will find it entertaining and challenging, as have the regular readers of my Internet website.

Jonathan Sturm 2 December 2011

Introduction

IN 1982 THE LOCAL PUBLICAN (Boney) offered me as much beer as I cared to drink while he ate a nine-litre (two gallon) bucket of my fresh unpodded garden peas. Now Boney was a *connoisseur* of peas. He pointed out that not only were they the finest peas he had ever tasted, the pods were all full, with every pea full size. And to top all of that, there were he said an extra two peas in every pod!

Consumed with curiosity, I visited the next-door neighbour's garden, some 50 metres (55 yards) from mine. The neighbour and his farm workers were harvesting peas. While chatting with them, I grabbed a few pods and ate the peas. Sure enough, Boney was right. My neighbour's peas were bland when compared to mine. They were starchier and less sweet. I enquired as to the variety; they were Greenfeast, the same as I was growing. I then asked where the pea seed had been bought — the same store. Finally came the crucial question: what had they been manured with?

The reply was 8:4:10 — orchard fertiliser. The peas Boney liked so much had been grown with cow manure!

In four decades of farming and gardening, the only material I have used not permitted under the official organic guidelines is the herbicide, glyphosate. The reason for growing organically has nothing to do with fear of chemicals on my part. Rather, it was initially poverty, and later because organics was working so much better than conventional.

There is a common myth that organic production levels are necessarily much lower than when using artificial fertilisers, and that organic fertilisers are more expensive. My experience and that of many other growers frequently do not support these assertions. If the first claim be true, then it's a mystery why for example the world record tomato grower according to the Guinness Book of Records grows organically. When the writer was market gardening, the cheapest nitrogen source was that in chicken deep-litter. The cheapest artificial source, sulphate of ammonia, wasn't even close. Needless to say, chicken deep-litter contains many more nutrients than nitrogen.

It is important to realise that the two growing systems, organic and conventional, are 95% the same. Most of the remaining 5% of differences are in the grower's attitude toward the soil. Organics is not merely the substitution of a natural material where a synthetic material is

---

I like the physical activity of gardening. It's kind of thrilling. I do a lot of weeding.
 —John Hurt

usually used. Plants are able to use several methods of obtaining their nutritional needs. One is to obtain them from water-soluble minerals (usually chemically processed commercial fertiliser).[1] Another is to obtain them from "insoluble" minerals when soil microbes and earthworms render the nutrients available to plants. The minerals are usually already there, in the form of silt, or may have been placed there as crushed rocks by the gardener, or farmer. Yet another source of plant nutrients is the decaying remains of plants, and/or animal manure.

It is worth pointing out that it is not only organic proponents who believe avoiding excessive amounts of water-soluble mineral fertilisers is superior. Water-soluble fertilisers generally lead to increased pest and disease problems requiring ever more potent biocides for their control, along with increased soil erosion as soil organic matter declines. Reducing their use, or avoiding them altogether, increases the plants' natural resistance to pests and disease. Eliminating or reducing water-soluble fertiliser only works in soil with an abundance of organic matter and living organisms. Such a soil is easier to till, drains better, holds more moisture and is less prone to erosion.

It's also interesting to note that in several farm trials using organic fertilisers alongside conventional artificials at half the usual rate produced results far ahead of using the usual rates of artificials alone. The benefits weren't just increased yields, but there was also a marked reduction in fungal and viral disease, and substantial increase in the quality of the produce.

As a consequence, many Tasmanian farmers and horticulturists have adopted organic techniques without necessarily converting to fully organic. I played a minor role in this and have considerable admiration for those who were adventurous enough to engage in the type of research we commenced almost forty years ago.

The apple and pear growers had set themselves the goal of reducing biocide inputs by 95% in ten years. When they reached their goal in five, I was jubilant. I saw it as a very large step in the right direction. The biggest hurdle, control of the fungal disease black spot (aka apple scab), succumbed to two organically acceptable materials: builders' lime (calcium hydroxide) and waterglass (sodium silicate). Dr James Wong of the Department of Agriculture discovered the former and I the latter solution. James' proposal was the cheaper and certainly the safest.

One of the purposes of this book is to provide sufficient practical information to be a successful gardener, organic or otherwise. While

---

1 Though not always. Raw animal manures contain water-soluble nitrogen that only becomes stabilised by composting.

the commercial organic producer is necessarily restricted to materials and technologies defined in an organic standard such as that maintained by the National Standard for Organic and Bio-Dynamic Products, no such restriction applies to the conventional grower or backyard gardener who is free to adopt whatever he or she deems appropriate.

To be a successful small-scale market gardener requires not just hard manual labour, but also a sound grasp of management principles, economics, marketing, organisation, decision-making and biology. You also need enthusiasm, self-discipline and a high level of motivation. For a decade my wife and I were market gardeners, so I touch on these topics at various points throughout the book.

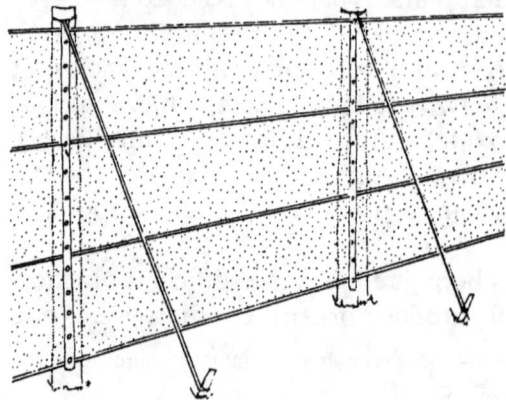

Gardens need protection from the wind. Two metres (6 foot) tall 50% shadecloth works well, but doesn't harbour predators. We used discarded lengths of black dripper line and galvanised clouts to pin the cloth to the posts. The wire stays were essential in our windy environment!

Your Garden

"Advice… advice… advice… Some of it suggests one thing and some of it says just the opposite. Most of all it is very good advice… for someone. But not all of it turns out to be good advice for you.

Why is that? It is simply because your garden and your gardening style are unique. You can't expect your work glove to fit perfectly on someone else's green thumb."

—Lois Levitan, *Improving Your Gardening with Backyard Research*, Rodale Press 1980.

Choosing the Land

Many people approach me for advice after they have purchased their land. All too often, it is not very well suited to what they want to do. However, all except the very worst sites can be improved to the point of being productive.[1]

The best soils for gardening are loams, light soils are second best and heavy soils worst though this needs some qualification. Loam is balanced soil — a mixture of sand, silt and clay. Light soils are predominantly sand making them hungry and drought-prone, but they produce crops earlier than the other two soil types, and may be worked even when wet. Heavy soils consist of mainly silt and/or clay so they tend to be very fertile, but they warm slowly in the spring, and should *never* be tilled when wet.[2] Our soil is very heavy and a friend's market garden referred to often throughout this book started out as almost pure white sand.

Vegetable gardens need shelter from strong wind. If this shelter does not already exist, then windbreaks will need to be established before you can commence gardening. Artificial windbreaks can be made, but they are rather more expensive than natural ones. As well, they do not harbour predators like a well-designed windbreak of trees and shrubs. A windbreak reduces the wind close to the ground for a distance on the leeward side equivalent to around 25 times its height. It's important to keep artificial windbreaks no higher than a couple of metres. Any taller and they have a tendency to fall over.

The aspect of the land is very important. The soil needs as much

---

1 John Jeavons started his garden in California on clay that was pH 8. If I recall correctly it had been a car park.

2 Tilling wet clays creates large, rock-like clods. Tilled when too dry, they turn to dust. Locally, our heavy soils are referred to as "Sunday soil"; there's one Sunday in the year when their moisture content is just right.

sun as you can provide and a north-easterly slope will warm quickest. In warmer districts, a north-westerly slope that warms slower might be better. Note that these recommendations are for the Southern Hemisphere.

Rainfall is another important consideration. The worst situation is too much rain. It leaches nutrients, and causes erosion and fungal disease problems. While a dry situation can be ameliorated by irrigation, the dissolved salts in groundwater can accumulate to excess in many soils, eventually poisoning them. The best situation is one of moderate rainfall with adequate supplies of water of reasonable quality to supplement the rain.

Land that is too level will create drainage problems and allows cold air to accumulate. Land that is too sloping will cause erosion unless terraces are created. Terracing is expensive and the extra effort required moving produce and compost up and down the slope consumes a great deal of energy. Land of moderate slope allows good drainage of water, and in frosty districts, cold air.

For market gardening, you will need easy access to the road and sheds. As well, you will need ready access to a market for your produce. Most important of all, you will need a source of inexpensive (that is locally sourced) compost ingredients.

When my wife-to-be and I were looking for our land, we only knew that we wanted to be within reasonable commuting distance

Gardening in raised beds makes for excellent drainage and the permanent footpaths make for comfort especially in wintertime.

of our state's capital city, the soil had to be a sandy loam and rainfall around 800 mm (32"). In the event, we discovered that good land was very hard to find. Farmers are nowhere near as stupid as city-dwellers would like to believe; they prefer to subdivide their least productive land for sale to hobby farmers. We ended up with heavy soil, rather than sand, or loam. The property is gently sloping, so it drains well (for heavy soil) and there are no frost pockets. Our water source for irrigation is at the top of the slope, so we can use gravity for irrigation, rather than expensive and unreliable pumps. Unfortunately it is a runoff dam, not on a permanent water course, or spring. One winter it failed to fill. And the following summer, we emptied it six weeks before the first autumn rains.

One potential problem for us as organic producers was spray drift from our neighbour's property. When we first moved in, we were surrounded by cattle pasture. Some two years later, our neighbour established an apple orchard on the windward side. The first time the tractor driver sprayed the young trees, I approached him and thanked him for spraying when the wind blew the spray away from our property. Ever since, he has always taken our needs into account.

A few years later, I received a telephone call from a newcomer to the district. She wanted to know what the organic sprays for apples were. I told her that organic apple production was far more than merely substituting organically acceptable sprays for those used by conventional growers. My remark appeared to upset the caller; she told me that all she wanted was what she had asked for so she could tell her neighbour what to use. I asked her who her neighbour was. When she told me, I informed her that he was using organically acceptable sprays; he was in fact already an organic farmer. "Oh, but he sprays all the time," she said, huffily, and hung up.

Basics

THERE IS A BEWILDERING NUMBER of methods of growing vegetables. Many books have been written extolling the virtues of no-dig, mulch, raised beds, circle gardens and many more. This book draws on selected aspects of many different ideas. The systems the writer advocates are based on the concept that if you are to make a profit from growing vegetables, then time management is of the essence. Even if your "profit" is "only" money saved on shop-bought produce, the same basic principles still hold. There is no single way for every gardener everywhere that's best as so many writers imply.

As an example, let's take carrots. On average, my organic fertiliser costs have been a mere 2.5% of the gross return for all crops combined, so the critical profit factors are the time consumed and yield per man-hour. Typically, 50%, or somewhat less of the time to produce a crop is spent actually growing it and 50%, or somewhat more, is spent harvesting and marketing.

There are three basic methods of growing carrots. The first is growing them in single rows spaced 30 cm (12") apart with 75 mm (3") between plants. This is the conventional method you will find in most books on vegetable gardening. It has several disadvantages. The wide row spacing is to allow the gardener room to hoe, weed and harvest the crop. The continual foot traffic between the rows compacts the soil, reducing water and air infiltration and consequently, yields. The method works particularly poorly in shallow topsoil — most varieties of carrots prefer deep soil. Heavy rains can wash the soil badly, leading to incomplete rows, and consequent topsoil and nutrient loss.

The main root mass is not the stout taproot that we consume; rather it's an almost invisible network of fine roots and root hairs that exploit uncompacted soil to obtain water, nutrients and oxygen. The compacted soil of a footpath is inimical to this. Only certain plants find tight soil a place worth growing in: typically docks, wireweed, plantain etc whose role in the ecology is to break up such compacted soil.

The second method is to grow the carrots on raised beds, 1.2 m (4') or so wide and 10–15 cm (4–6") high with 40–50 cm (16–20") wide permanent footpaths (or tractor wheel-ruts) between. The carrots are sown in rows along its length, the plants 7.5 cm (3") apart with the rows 15 cm (6") apart. The yield per unit area is higher than with the first method, because the soil that the carrots are growing in is never compacted by being walked on, and consequently water and air infiltration is unimpeded. Topsoil depth is also greater, allowing more soil for nutrient exploitation by the plants' roots. Yields are generally 50–100 % higher per unit area than with the first method.

The third method, that advocated by John Jeavons in his excellent book *How to Grow More Vegetables* (10 Speed Press), is to sow the carrots 7.5 cm (3") apart each way across the raised beds as used in method two. This has all the advantages of method two, but two disadvantages. The first of these is related to sowing. It is difficult, though not

---

Gardens are not made by singing "Oh, how beautiful," and sitting in the shade.
  —Rudyard Kipling

impossible, to sow seeds in drills 7.5 cm (3") apart. Jeavons advocates broadcasting, or sowing individual seeds on 7.5 cm centres. Broadcasting is quick, but it's very difficult to ensure the seeds are evenly covered with soil so that they germinate simultaneously, most important in close planting. If germination is staggered, the earliest plants to germinate will shade out the later germinating plants.[3] Thinning a broadcast crop is very slow. Sowing on 7.5 cm (3") centres is also slow, but means that minimal thinning is required.

The second disadvantage is that weeding cannot be done with a conventional hoe; it must be with fingers, or a custom short-handled narrow hoe. It should be pointed out that in moderately weed-free ground, that only very few finger-weedings are required as the plants quickly close up the space between, and the leaves suppress the light reaching any late germinating weed seeds. The yield from Jeavons' method is as much as 50% greater than Method Two.

While it is usually believed that Method One is the most time efficient, Method Two yields are far enough ahead in yield that it becomes difficult to justify the extra area Method One requires. Just as with Method One, the rows are readily sown with a mechanical seeding machine, and a narrow hoe is used to remove most weeds very quickly. We estimate that Method Two consumes less than 50% of the time per kilogram of carrot produced when compared to Methods One and Three.

Gardeners who like to use mulch on crops such as carrots that require a constant level of moisture will have noted that Jeavons' method is not adaptable to mulching. Jeavons' mentor, Alan Chadwick points out that the leaves of the crop plants rapidly grow to shade the soil, forming what he called "a living mulch". Method Two above, like Method One, is more conducive to mulching after seedling establishment, but also creates a living mulch as in Jeavons' Method Three, albeit somewhat more slowly.

Raised-bed gardening actually pre-dates row-gardening. Row-gardening was developed following the publication of Jethro Tull's *Horse Hoeing Husbandry* in the seventeenth century. The Tullian row cultivation method was developed for grain production, quickly supplanting the broadcast method in most British farming districts though broadcasting remained in use by poorer farmers until the late nineteenth century. Weeds that previously needed to be pulled by hand were quickly controlled by either horse, or human powered hoes. What we have done is adapt what seems the best of both

---

[3] This is particularly undesirable in commercial production where evenness of carrot size is important.

systems. In conventional row cultivation, 50% of tillage is required to undo the damage caused by soil compaction.[4] If you don't compact the soil in the first place, you've reduced tillage by half. The advantage of row-cultivation, speed of hoeing for weed control, is retained.

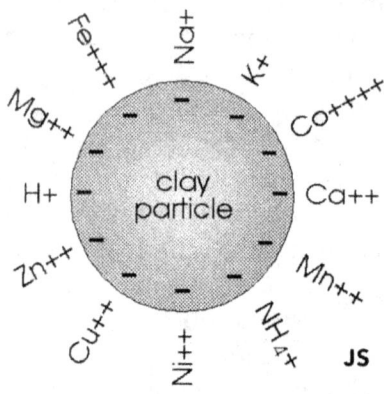

What I attempt to illustrate here is that you are not stuck with any single method. You are free to come up with your own adaptations that suit *your* needs, situation, climate and other circumstances.

Soil

SOIL CONSISTS OF A MINERAL fraction, water, air and organic matter. The ideal soil for growing crops is said to be 50% solids, 25% air, and 25% water after all excess water has drained away. The soil is then said to be at field capacity. The organic matter needs to be 5% or more of the total solids for it to be suitable for organic production. The mineral portion is subdivided into silt, sand and clay. The organic material can be subdivided into living and dead, or raw and humified.[5]

The relative proportion of the three mineral solids determines the *workability* of the soil. Silt and clay particles are very tiny. Where they predominate over sand, the soil is said to be heavy. It contains little air and holds onto a lot of water because of the huge surface area of the tiny soil particles. Tillage tends to be rather difficult because the soil is very stiff. Where coarse sand particles predominate, the soil is said to be light because it's loose and easy to till. There is an abundance of air, but little water holding capacity. The best soils from the point of view of the vegetable grower have a balanced proportion of all three mineral types and are classified as loams. However, even the most unpromising soils can be improved to the point of economic productivity. I will discuss two market gardens closely in this book. Our soil is silty clay and that of our good friends, Ian and Caryl Cairns, started out as almost pure white sand.

---

4   In an ABC Country Hour broadcast many years ago I heard of a British farm trial of tram-tracking, where the tractors tyres occupy permanent wheel ruts. The growing area between them is never compacted and the trials showed you could either double the area tilled per hour, or halve the tractor horsepower.

5   Humified means decomposed to form humus.

Clay particles are rounded, as well as very small. They pack together very tightly, and make the soil feel sticky. Clay particles carry a negative electrical charge, so they attract positively charged elements and compounds such as the essential crop nutrients: calcium, magnesium, potassium, ammonium, molybdenum and sodium. These positively charged materials are called cations (pronounced Cat-Eye-Ons). The amount of these elements a soil can contain is called its Cation Exchange Capacity (CEC) and this is an excellent measure of its potential fertility, an important aspect of capacity to produce. Cations held by the negative electrical charges on the clay particles cannot be easily leached from the soil by rainfall, or irrigation. Plants' root hairs emit positively charged hydrogen ions that displace the cations, rendering them available to be absorbed by the plant on an as needed basis.

Silt particles, while similar in size to clay particles, are flattened rather than rounded. Like clay particles, they also pack together very tightly, but make the dry soil feel silky when rubbed between the fingers as the flat plates readily move against each other. Unlike most clays, silts contain a variety of nutrients that are made available to plants through biological activity. Silt is formed by weathering, particularly the abrasive action of glaciers on rock and the bulk of silt on the planet was formed during the glacial phase of the current and previous ice ages.[6] Australia's soils are some of the oldest in the world and therefore contain less of these plant nutrients. In any event, it is rare that silt contains an ideal balance of nutrients; nutrient supplements are nearly always called for.

Sand particles are large so sand has big gaps between them when it is packed. They make the soil feel gritty when rubbed between the fingers. While sands contain negligible amounts of plant nutrients, and lack clay's ability to hold onto them, they improve the soil's drainage, air holding capacity and make it much easier to till.

Organic matter falls into two categories, living and dead. The dead material is a source of plant nutrients as it decomposes. Bacteria are able to convert raw organic matter into a material called humus. Humus acts as a sponge for water, so it improves the water holding capacity of sandy soils. By holding silt and clay particles apart, it improves the drainage and aeration of heavy soils. Heavy soils with adequate (5–10%) humus also become much easier to till. Like clay, humus also carries negative electrical charges so it increases the soil's

---

6 We are in the Holocene interglacial epoch of an ice age called the Quaternary that began 2.58 million years ago. Prior to that Earth had no ice caps at the poles. Earth has experienced at least five ice ages.

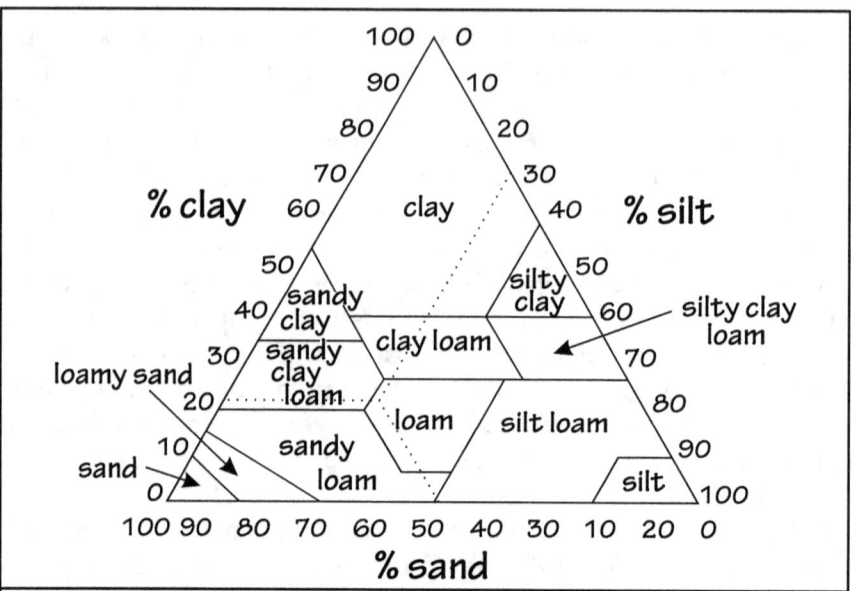

The diagram above is the USDA Soil Triangle. The dotted lines intersecting in the area labelled loam show that's for a soil consisting of 50% sand, 20% clay and 30% silt. On a small scale you can amend a soil based on using the triangle. First, you need to know the percentages of sand, silt and clay in your soil.

Gather several cupfuls of topsoil from your garden and mix thoroughly together. The idea is that they be a representative sample so take each cup from a separate location. The soil then needs to be air dried before using a kitchen sieve to remove gravel, stones, slaters etc. Take one cup (250 ml) of the remaining "fine earth" and put it into a straight-sided jar such as a canning jar with three cups of water into which you have dissolved a tablespoon of sodium hexametaphosphate.* Shake the concoction well to disperse the soil, then take a metric (mm) ruler and measure the depth of soil as it settles out. At 40 seconds you have the sand measurement, at 30 minutes the silt measurement and after 12 hours the clay measurement. Sand depth ÷ total depth × 100 = %sand. Silt depth ÷ total depth × 100 = %silt. Clay depth ÷ total depth × 100 = %clay.

The writer's soil was 50% silt and 50% clay. When he reverted to having a mere 500 square metres (600 square yards) of garden it became feasible to add sufficient sand to make the soil a clay loam rather than silty clay. It certainly made harvesting carrots *easier*!

---

* Water softener such as Calgon. Other water softeners such as trisodium phosphate (TSP) or sodium carbonate (washing soda) are not suitable. They don't disperse the soil particles before precipitating them.

(CEC). Increasing the humus level of a soil is often the only economically realistic way to improve the CEC, and consequent increase in yield potential. If marl, a mixture of clay, silt and carbonate rock is available, that will increase CEC, but not provide the many other benefits of humus.

Fungi and yeasts can also decompose organic matter. This process tends to produce alcohols and other growth inhibitors, rather than humus. One of the key differences between organic and mainstream cropping is that the organic grower endeavours to promote humification in the soil, consciously, or otherwise. Conventional growers in the past were trained to ignore soil biological processes as relatively unimportant. The best known example of humification is the process of composting. This is a major topic and so has its own chapter later in the book.

The living components of the soil include fungi, bacteria, actinomycetes, insects, plant roots, earthworms, nematodes, algae, viruses and protozoa. OK, I know that viruses aren't classified as being truly alive, but they do qualify as an intrinsic part of the living system. There is no living system that is free of virus particles, and there were new candidates for living organisms as this book was first being written: nano-bacteria. Fertile soil supports at least as much living matter within it as we can see above the soil surface. The sheer number and variety of these organisms is mind-boggling. A teaspoonful of living soil contains *billions* of microbes, most varieties of them remaining unknown to and undescribed by science. In organic production, the dynamic balance between them is the primary concern. Fortunately, we do not need to know very much about the many complex interactions — after millions of years of evolution, they are very good at managing these things for themselves. A few simple principles mastered by peasant farmers throughout the world are all that is required.

While conventional agriculture has been obsessed with the most obvious parts of the plant, the above ground parts, these are fed by a complex underground root system. The roots take up the mineral nutrients, nitrogen, phosphorus, potassium, sodium, calcium, magnesium, trace elements and water that the leaves require to convert carbon dioxide from the air into sugars, starches and other carbohydrates. The roots have short protrusions called root hairs that are

---

The only way to get positive feelings about yourself is to take positive actions. Man does not live as he thinks, he thinks as he lives.
— Rev Vaughan Quinn

responsible for nutrient uptake. Their health requires adequate moisture and air, hence the earlier prescription for healthy soil being 50% solids, 25% air and 25% water. Too much water and too little air is a common cause of ill-thrift in plants.

Many plants have fungi that live partly in the soil and partly in the root exchanging phosphorus from the soil for carbohydrate from the plant. They are called *mycorrhizae* and some plants cannot survive without their particular species of *mycorrhiza*. Many others exhibit poor productivity without them. Another example of symbiosis is that between the nitrogen-fixing bacteria called *rhizobium* and legumes. *Rhizobia* live in nodules on the roots of the *leguminosae* plant species. They convert nitrogen from the atmosphere that plants cannot use directly, into protein. The legumes include clover, Lucerne (alfalfa), beans and peas.

It was recently discovered that mycorrhizae play an important role in tomato plants' resistance to pestilence. When the plant's leaves are attacked, this generates a chemical signal that the mycorrhizae detect. The mycorrhizae then send a chemical signal to the plant to begin generating chemicals that are toxic to the insects munching on the plant's leaves. They also send a chemical signal to the mycorrhizae living on nearby tomato plants to do the same.

The single most important soil organism is the earthworm. The health and vigour of this muscular tube of protoplasm is the best indicator of overall soil health. If there are no earthworms, then plant productivity is but a small fraction of its potential. There are three main types of earthworm: the compost worm, the earthworker worm and the root-dwelling worm.[7] Compost worms require copious quantities of protein-rich organic matter and do not ingest soil. Earthworker worms require much less organic matter and ingest soil. The worms sold by worm farmers are compost worms, and are less important from the standpoint of the gardener than the earthworker worm. The root-dwelling worms include the huge Australian *Megascolides australis* that average a metre in length, but can grow to three.

The gut of earthworker worms transforms the minerals in the silt particles they ingest into usable plant food. As well their excreta, called worm-casts, are small crumbs that are just double the diameter of the length of a root hair. These crumbs are essential to the open structure of fertile soil and are easily damaged by excessive tillage. In point of fact, earthworms perform much of the tillage in organically managed soil. This concept taken to its extreme has led

---

7   Compost worms are usually tiger worms (stripy) or red wrigglers. Both exhibit considerable activity when handled while pasture worms are more sluggish.

to what is called no-dig gardening. While this is an option for the home gardener, it is generally too unproductive and costly for the commercial producer.

Even though the compost worm is relatively unimportant in the soil, it comes into its own when used for converting bulky organic matter into a rather special compost called vermicompost. This is discussed further in the chapter devoted to composting.

Plant Nutrition

WHILE CONVENTIONAL GROWERS feed the *crop*, the organic grower feeds the *soil* and the many micro- and macro-organisms living in it. These organisms then provide the crop's nutritional needs. The reasoning behind the first approach is that artificial fertilisers are said to be much cheaper than organic fertilisers. This is only superficially true. The reasoning behind the organic approach is that organic fertilisers produce healthy crops that need little if any expensive pesticide or fungicide materials usually considered essential by conventional growers. Many of the nutrients the crop needs are met by decomposition of the silt particles in the soil and they come with the land you are farming or gardening at no extra cost.

Most vegetables and fruits grown organically are tastier than their conventional counterparts; they also survive storage longer. Most consumers believe that organically grown is better for your health. Frankly, that's almost irrelevant for this organic gardener; I like the greatly enhanced flavours so there's no competition when I have a choice.[8]

The health of the living fraction of the soil is dependent on an adequate level of humus, optimally between 5 and 10%, a constant source of fresh carbohydrate and lignin (dead plant material), a much smaller constant supply of protein (such as that in animal manure and legumes), and mineral nutrients at adequate levels and in the appropriate ratio. The most important nutrients are the anions nitrogen and phosphorus, and the cations calcium, magnesium, potassium and sodium. Also of importance are the nutrients needed in only small amounts, the trace elements.

The crop nutrient in shortest supply for the plants' needs is referred to as a crop-limiting factor.

---

8 The difference in flavour between organically grown and conventional is most marked in meat. Organically raised livestock are notably healthier than their conventionally raised counterparts, hence the extrapolation to humans. There is nothing quite as dramatic as the difference in flavour of organic pork, chicken or beef.

The relative amounts of nutrients are also important from the point of view of availability. An excess of one element can inhibit, or enhance the availability of another. This is shown diagrammatically below.

Major Elements
Carbon, hydrogen and oxygen

SOMEWHAT SURPRISINGLY, you won't usually see these elements listed as crop nutrients in many books on gardening. It's surprising to me because the greatest bulk of a plant consists of these three elements. Carbon in the form of carbon dioxide (CO_2) plus hydrogen and oxygen in the form of water (H_2O) are converted by the chlorophyll in chloroplasts in green plant tissue to carbohydrates. The simpler carbohydrates are called sugars, more complex carbohydrates starches, and the most complex of the lot, cellulose. Cellulose accounts for the great bulk of plant tissue as it is the major component of plant cell walls.

While carbon dioxide levels are usually not perceived as a crop-limiting factor, greenhouse growers gain substantial increases in yields by increasing the amount of carbon dioxide available to crops. While the average background level is approximately 400 ppm, they raise the level to between 1–2,000 ppm. The elevated level of CO_2 means the pores in the plants' leaves do not need to open so wide, greatly reducing the amount of water the plants transpire. Doubling the level of CO_2 reduces a crop's water need by approximately 25%. At 1–2,000 ppm, yields of cucumbers and tomatoes are 50% higher.

In India, garden beds are surrounded by a wall of greenhouse polythene. This reduces the tendency of locally generated CO_2 to blow or drift away and results in increased crop yields. When Bill Mollison and David Holmgren were developing their Permaculture system, Bill and I discussed this while eating Vogel bread sandwiches in Salamanca Place on the Hobart waterfront. We figured that keeping chickens, or making compost in the greenhouse would provide a useful source of not only warmth in the colder months, but also CO_2 during the colder weather when keeping the greenhouse vents closed results in air being depleted of this essential nutrient.

Water is the single greatest crop-limiting factor, but not because of its nutrient content. Rather, water is the transport system for nutrients and hormones, the latter being chemical messengers that regulate the growth of all living tissue. Water is so important it is dealt with separately as a major topic.

We are what we repeatedly do. Excellence, then, is not an act, but a habit.
  —Aristotle

Phosphorus

PHOSPHORUS ENCOURAGES root development and is essential for the formation of protein in the plant. As well, it increases palatability of the plants since it promotes the formation of fats and convertible starches. By stimulating rapid cell development, phosphorus increases the plants' resistance to disease. Many plants respond to a phosphorus deficiency by showing a reddish or purple colour in their leaves. The common weed fat hen is an excellent indicator plant for this condition.[9] Heavy feeders are stunted when phosphorus is in short supply. Phosphorus toxicity symptoms include the margins and interveinal areas of older leaves dying. Younger leaves show interveinal chlorosis, particularly tomatoes, celery and sweet corn. Since this latter condition is usually caused by excessive use of superphosphate, or other water-soluble phosphorus materials the organic grower is unlikely to see it.

The most popular fertiliser source of phosphorus in recent decades has been superphosphate. The response of crops to super has declined over time, more and more being necessary to maintain satisfactory yields. On average, only 30% of the phosphorus in super becomes available to plants in the season of application. While a minute fraction leaches out of the soil through irrigation and rainfall, the bulk is locked up in the soil through chemical reaction with iron. Phosphorus from farmland appearing in rivers and streams is generally carried there through erosion of the soil, rather than phosphorus in water solution. Humic and fulvic acids, earthworms and associated beneficial bacteria and fungi in a fertile soil gradually "unlock" the phosphorus in reactive phosphate rock, superphosphate residues and silt, making it available to plants.

The fertiliser recommendations followed by most farmers results in the application of considerably more phosphorus than is removed by the crops. Consequently, many farms have built up phosphorus reserves in their soils that are sufficient for decades, and in some cases centuries, of cropping. Where low soil phosphorus levels are determined to be a genuine problem, reactive phosphate rock (RPR) is the organic alternative to super. RPR is cheaper (or should be) than superphosphate as well as containing a higher percentage of phosphorus and trace elements. Under typical soil conditions, the phosphorus in RPR is only readily available when the soil pH is around 4.5 to 5.5, somewhat lower than 6.0 to 6.5 that is optimal for most

---

9 One variety of fat hen called Good King Henry has a naturally purple tinge to its leaves, but they are apparently much larger than the ordinary sort.

crops. However, the organic acids associated with bacterial activity in a fertile soil appear to be capable of unlocking the phosphorus when the soil pH is a more acceptable 6.0-6.5.

Many, if not most Australian organic producers are exploiting the phosphorus residues locked up from their predecessors' superphosphate applications. The questions then arise: How long will those reserves last? Is there sufficient phosphorus in these residues and the silt fraction of the soil for economic, long-term production? For conventional farmers, several questions arise:
- Does it make economic sense to leave 70% of the phosphorus in superphosphate unused?
- How can farmers exploit the phosphorus reserves they have built up over many decades?
- How long will the world's fossil phosphate deposits last?

We do not have satisfactory answers to these questions at this time. Nevertheless, it should be apparent that fossil phosphate reserves will continue to dwindle, inevitably driving the price higher. As well, it would appear to be sensible to optimise the availability of any applied phosphate, rather than allowing the bulk to become chemically locked up to the detriment of the soil biology and the farmers' input costs.

Nitrogen

NITROGEN STIMULATES the production of plant tissue and influences the protein content. Nitrogen applied as nitrate produces a blue-green colour in plant leaves. When applied as protein, the colour is noticeably a more golden-green. Excessive nitrate levels are associated with increased fungal disease, delayed maturity of plants and weakening of plant tissue leading to lodging.[10] As well, nitrates in the plant sap are reduced by bacteria to nitrite that in turn is converted to nitrosamine, which is toxic to the consumer of the plant, animal, or man, particularly juveniles. Nitrogen deficiency symptoms in crops include the edges of leaves turning brown, smaller leaves and yellow-green foliage. Nitrogen toxicity symptoms include rotting of roots and delayed maturity. Young leaves are dark green and older leaves yellow with necrotic spots.

Nitrogen can be supplied as protein (rotted animal manure, legume green manure, fish, blood 'n' bone etc), or as water-soluble artificial fertiliser (Nitram, urea, ammonium sulphate etc.). It is worth noting that most raw animal manure contains much of its nitrogen as water-soluble chemicals such as ammonium carbonate. Raw animal manure is, from the point of view of the plant, very similar

---

10 Lodging is the condition where the plant stem is so weak, the plant falls over.

to artificial fertiliser in its effects, so well-rotted, or composted manure is much preferred. While a pasture can supply its own nitrogen needs through fixation of atmospheric nitrogen by clover, horticultural crops have a much higher requirement. Crops take up as little as 10% of applied water-soluble nitrogenous fertilisers. The remainder leaches into groundwater and streams to the detriment of the many organisms living there. While this may please the fertiliser manufacturers, it is not so great from the point of view of the farmer. As well as wasting money, the adverse impacts of leached nitrogen on the environment can lead to stiff penalties.

As protein slowly decomposes, it supplies the plants with nitrogen at the rate generally needed by the crop. Leaching becomes a non-issue. Where short-term nitrogen needs are not being met by the soil, liquid manures made from fish, comfrey leaves, or nettles are popular. Lucerne chaff tilled into the topsoil also works well, with the added advantage of containing plant growth hormones. This is particularly useful in the spring when the soil is beginning to warm up after winter dormancy.

In several field cropping experiments we applied pelletised poultry manure at a rate calculated to supply 50% of the usual artificial nitrogen application. This rule of thumb has worked well in supplying the nitrogen needs of most crops. One commercial grower applied a soil drench of 60 litres per hectare of Vitec liquid fish to a crop of broccoli. The plants responded as well as they did to artificials, even though the nitrogen content of the fish emulsion was a mere 2.8%. The artificial fertiliser salesman said to the grower: "You'd have been better off pissing on the crop than using this fish oil!" The grower responded: "Maybe that's what I'll do for the next crop!" The farmer told me it was easily the best quality broccoli crop he'd ever grown and it had been gratefully received in the Asian market.

Potassium

POTASSIUM IS ESSENTIAL for starch formation in the plant and the development of chlorophyll. Unlike phosphorus and nitrogen, which are part of the structure of the plant, potassium is more of a catalyst involved in plant processes. Deficiency symptoms include lowered resistance to disease, low yields and mottled, speckled, or curly leaves, especially older leaves. Potassium toxicity symptoms include marginal necrosis on the oldest leaves and in celery, black-heart.

How wonderful it is that nobody need wait a single moment before starting to improve the world.
   —Anne Frank

More and more growers are coming to appreciate the ability of deep rooting plants to bring potassium from deep in the subsoil to supply their crops' potassium needs. Such plants are called biological ploughs, because they serve much the same purpose as a ripper, leaving deep channels in the soil when they decompose. In pasture, New Zealand graziers use chicory varieties developed for this purpose. In China, vegetable growers use Paulownia trees, whose large succulent leaves decompose to humus when they fall in autumn. The roots of Lucerne (alfalfa) and comfrey are capable of diving two metres and more into the soil.

Potassium is used to excess in many crop fertiliser programs. For instance, the recommended application rate on potatoes is twice the amount removed from the soil. This leads to reduced availability of calcium and many trace elements. As well, the most commonly used potassic fertiliser is potassium chloride (muriate of potash). This material is deadly to earthworms, since the mineral particles burn holes in their skin. Frogs, Nature's vastly underrated pest controllers, are also devastated by its use. Continual overuse of potassium chloride can lead to toxic levels of chloride and a consequent decrease in yields. Potassium sulphate (sulphate of potash) is a much better source of potassium in this regard, particularly as it includes sulphur, which is often in short supply in Australian soils. It is unfortunate that it is much more expensive than muriate. Overseas books recommend greensand and other sources of potassium not generally available to organic growers in Australia. Wood ash is also often quoted as a good source of potassium. However, it is only the twigs that supply significant amounts potash — tree trunks are not overly endowed with this mineral. They consist of mostly lignin and cellulose.

When the I commenced organic market gardening over 30 years ago, a soil test showed a deficiency of potassium. This was "corrected" with the recommended amount of muriate[11] of potash. In the following ten years, only compost was applied, and this is regarded as only a fair source of potassium. Nevertheless, a soil test showed that the potassium level had risen to become slightly excessive. Two decades further on, potassium levels have fallen to the point where a small amount, applied as sulphate this time round is proving beneficial for crops needing especially high levels of this nutrient.

Short-term potassium deficiency can be met with liquid manure made from plants that concentrate potash, such as Lucerne, comfrey

---

11 Yes, this conflicts with what was written above. I have learned many lessons over the years and sometimes you need to go in the wrong direction to learn which is the right direction.

leaves, or bracken fern.

Seaweed is often recommended as a good potassium source. Because seaweed contains potent plant growth hormones and auxins, large amounts can temporarily reduce plant growth. This means when seaweed is used for this purpose, it is better used in the compost heap where these substances can decompose without affecting plant growth rate. In my early gardening days, we used to gather seaweed from a beach that accumulated large amounts, particularly after a southerly buster.

Calcium

CALCIUM IS USUALLY applied to the soil to release other nutrients by altering the soil acidity (pH). It is said, on this account, not to be a fertiliser. Calcium is a structural part of the walls in plant cells and deficiency is associated with poor keeping quality. As well, it is essential for the proliferation of beneficial soil bacteria. Clay soils often become sticky if there is an excess of sodium. Calcium displaces sodium attached to clay particles, and since it is a much bigger atom, holds the clay particles further apart thus making the

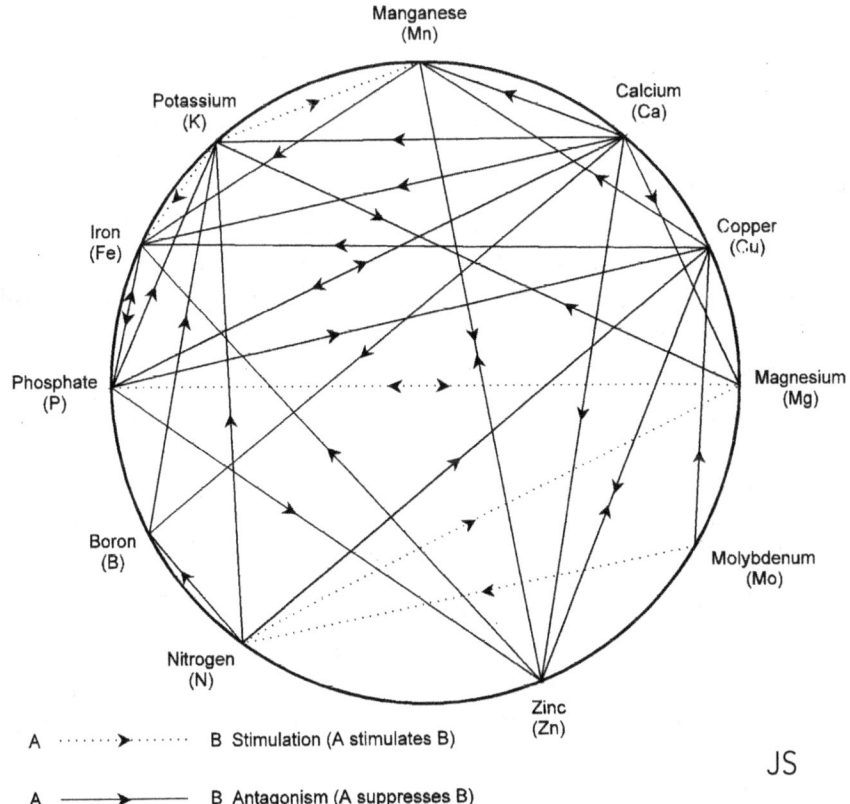

clay more friable. While gypsum (calcium sulphate) is recommended to break down sticky clay, it will only work if the cause of the stickiness is excessive sodium. If the soil is also acidic, it is cheaper to use crushed limestone (calcium or magnesium carbonate). An excess of calcium relative to magnesium is generally accompanied by insect problems in the crop.

Sap tests of potatoes grown on pelletised poultry manure showed much higher levels of calcium than those grown on artificial fertiliser. Part of the reason for this could well be the very high level of potassium in the artificial fertiliser. Excessive potassium is known to produce calcium deficiency symptoms in some crops. These include deformed terminal leaves, buds and branches, poor plant structure, such as weak stems, celery black heart, lettuce tip burn, internal browning of cabbages, cavity spot in carrots and bitter pit in apples.

Calcium is generally applied as ground limestone (calcium carbonate), or dolomite (a mixture of calcium and magnesium carbonate). As referred to elsewhere in this book, calcium and magnesium in the soil must be in appropriate ratio. Liming to merely adjust pH may lead to excess calcium, or worse, if high magnesium dolomite is used exclusively, excess magnesium.

Sometimes, builders' lime (calcium hydroxide) is used for a quick response. The bulk of this is rapidly converted to calcium carbonate when it reacts with dissolved carbon dioxide in the soil water. It is probably more economical to use very finely ground limestone where a faster response is needed.

When the soil is badly out of balance, it is not a good idea to lime heavily. This has a deleterious effect on the soil microbiology. It is much better to apply frequent, lighter applications allowing the soil biota to gradually adjust to the changing environment.

Magnesium

MAGNESIUM IS THE COMPANION to calcium in mineral deposits. The carbonates of both are used as liming materials. However, in plant nutrition it is the companion to phosphorus and stimulates the assimilation of phosphorus by plants. It is essential for the formation of chlorophyll. Magnesium deficiency causes chlorosis in plants,

---

Because work addiction keeps us busy, we stay estranged from our essential selves. An aspect of that estrangement is that we cease asking ourselves if we are doing our right work. Are we actually doing our true work, performing tasks or pursuing vocations that are good for us, for our families, for the universe?
   —Diane Fassel

analogous to anaemia in animals. An excess of magnesium relative to calcium results in too high a pH, and consequent deficiency of many trace elements. In an emergency, Epsom salts (magnesium sulphate) can be applied as a foliar source of magnesium, but this is relatively expensive. Where the use of even high magnesium dolomite will still leave an excess of calcium over magnesium, there are several suitable magnesium sources; Kieserite (16% Mg), Magnesite (25% Mg) and magnesium oxide (50% Mg).

Sulphur

SULPHUR IS A NEGLECTED element in farming. This is difficult to understand, as it's essential for the formation of chlorophyll, proteins and vitamins. Perhaps it is because we rely too much on research conducted in the Northern Hemisphere, where sulphur compounds generated as pollution by industry arrive in the rain. These compounds, sulphuric and sulphurous acids, as well as hydrogen sulphide (rotten egg gas), are a fortunate rarity in Australia's relatively unpolluted atmosphere.

Sulphur can be applied to the soil as elemental sulphur. The usual source of sulphur for Australian farmers is superphosphate that contains more sulphur than phosphorus. Perhaps it would be better named super-sulphate! However, elemental sulphur is a much cheaper source when the phosphorus is not needed.

Hopefully, more work on necessary levels in the soil for particular crops will be conducted in the future. A high level of sulphur in a soil test is generally a symptom of poor soil aeration.

Trace Elements

TRACE ELEMENTS ARE those required in minute amounts for essential plant processes. Their availability is optimised when the soil pH is between 6 and 7, the major nutrients calcium, magnesium, potassium and sodium are in balance and the soil humus level is more than 3%. Absence or deficiency of particular trace elements may mean that enzyme cycles cannot be triggered into action, resulting in reduced crop performance, or even failure. Some trace elements are required for animal and human health without having any obvious influence on plant health, or productivity.

The assessment of trace elements through soil testing is an uncertain procedure. Measured levels that have been thought to indicate deficiency have been contradicted by the measurement of adequate levels in the plant tissue, and vice versa. Part of the problem is the fact that certain elements stimulate, or suppress, other elements. This is an area of soil science that is very poorly understood, and needs much more research. While tissue and sap testing offer the potential for better assessment of crop needs, they too have their difficulties.

Trace elements are only poorly taken up by plants when they are in salt form. This has led to increasing use of chelated trace elements. Chelation (pronounced Key-Lay-Shən) means combined with an organic molecule. The compounds generally used are EDTA and ligno-sulphamate with the latter preferred. (EDTA is a suspected carcinogen). Of course, the trace elements in organic fertilisers, such as compost, pelletised poultry manure, liquid fish and seaweed, are already chelated, and often these materials, particularly seaweed and fish, contain sufficient trace elements for crop needs.

Manganese

MANGANESE IS REQUIRED in very small amounts and is very important, for without it, the production of amino acids and proteins suffer. It also works alongside magnesium in eliminating chlorosis. Soil with an excessive amount of magnesium and/or calcium locks up manganese.

Iron

IRON IS ESSENTIAL for the formation of chlorophyll in plants and the prevention of anaemia in animals. Nearly all soils contain a lot of iron, unfortunately mostly in unavailable form. Soils treated with excessive amounts of superphosphate will often have excessive available iron, which reduces the availability of other trace elements. Maintaining good humus levels is beneficial in optimising the availability of iron.

Boron

BORON IS IMPLICATED in the resistance of plants to diseases and is necessary for the formation of amino acids and protein. It is needed in only tiny amounts and many crops have benefited from the discovery that their potential was being limited by a deficiency. In the sap tests referred to earlier on potatoes grown under pelletised poultry manure, the boron levels were deemed excessive, whereas the sap tests from the conventional plot were deficient. The implications of this are unknown at this stage.

I think that most people want the word garden to be a noun which describes a place that you have set aside for your plants, so that the word gardening would be a verb that describes what you are doing when you work in your 'garden'. In my philosophy, garden is a verb; it is what you do. And, gardening is a noun that describes not what you did, but what you got when you gardened.
  —Tom Clothier

Copper, Cobalt and Zinc

THERE REMAINS MUCH to be learned about this group of trace elements. Their deficiency is implicated in a number of animal diseases, steely wool in sheep and infertility in cattle among them. Plants deficient in copper show abnormal growth and stunted young branches. Zinc is essential for the formation of chlorophyll, but copper and cobalt also play a lesser role. Zinc deficiency is implicated in poor stock fertility.

Iodine, Chlorine, Fluorine, Sodium and Lithium

IODINE, CHLORINE AND FLUORINE are all halogens. Iodine is well known as an essential ingredient in human and animal health as a regulator of metabolism. Plants readily take it up from foliar applications of liquid fish, or seaweed. It appears to have no major role in plant nutrition, or health.

Chlorine deficiency in plants is extremely rare. What is not rare is an excess caused by over-reliance on muriate of potash as a source of potassium. Excess chloride in soil tests is invariably accompanied by reduced availability of trace elements. Members of the rose family (*rosaceae* that includes pome fruit), are particularly sensitive to excessive amounts of chloride.

Fluorine is not considered essential for plant growth, but has an important role in animal nutrition. Both an excess and a deficiency are implicated in poor tooth development.

Sodium and potassium play complementary roles in plant and animal nutrition. Where potassium is deficient, sodium is absorbed in its place. Sodium is more often in excess than deficiency. Excessive sodium makes clay sticky. Gypsum (calcium sulphate) is often used to supply calcium, which displaces the sodium, allowing it to leach, making the clay more friable. Lime (calcium carbonate) is cheaper and can also be used where an increase in pH is desirable.

Lithium needs further study, but appears to be a companion to sodium and potassium. It has been applied to tobacco crops with the benefit of improving the quality of leaf grown for cigar wrappers.

Aluminium and Molybdenum

ALUMINIUM IS KNOWN more for the toxic effects of an excess than for any role in plant or animal nutrition. The conditions leading to toxicity are excessive soil acidity, reduced aeration and biological activity, and needless to say, low humus levels.

Isn't it enough to see that a garden is beautiful without having to believe that there are fairies at the bottom of it too?
—Douglas Adams

Molybdenum is essential for many plants. It serves as a catalyst in the early development of brassicas and appears to be essential in the fixation of nitrogen by bacteria. It is required in very small amounts. Excessively acid soil and low humus levels often cause deficiency. Excessive levels of molybdenum cause reproductive problems in livestock.

Cadmium and Lead

CADMIUM AND LEAD appear to play no role in plant nutrition, nor do they appear to be required for animal health. They are discussed here because they are toxic in excess, generally causing chronic disease, rather than outright poisoning. They are particularly problematic because the animal or person consuming them can only eliminate them slowly. This means that they tend to accumulate in the body over time.

Superphosphate used to be made from phosphate rock that was high in cadmium and lead. This means that soils heavily fertilised with this super can contain elevated levels of lead and cadmium and it is a cause for great concern that they are taken up by crops. The level of cadmium in sheep and beef kidneys has led to their being banned for human consumption in Western and South Australia.

In animal nutrition it is known that cadmium uptake is determined by food quality. Where the diet is deficient in zinc, cadmium absorption is increased. Other predisposing factors to increased cadmium absorption include periods of low nutrient intake and lack of high quality protein in the diet.

It is a matter for conjecture at this stage, but some organic farmers believe that increasing humus levels and bacterial activity in the soil reduces the uptake of heavy metals by crops.

Important Compounds

Enzymes

ENZYMES ARE CATALYSTS used by plants to manufacture cell tissue, trigger hormone reactions (flowering, leaf-drop etc) and take up nutrients. Most enzymes contain a trace element. An example is the use of molybdenum by the cauliflower. The enzyme requiring this element is only created in the first few days of the plant's existence. Application of molybdenum after this period has no effect on the deficiency symptom of "whip-tail" (aka "strap-leaf").

One of the most important resources that a garden makes available for use, is the gardener's own body. A garden gives the body the dignity of working in its own support. It is a way of rejoining the human race.
—Wendell Berry

Auxins

THESE PLANT HORMONES regulate cell division and elongation (i.e. plant growth and development). They are relatively unstable and are most readily created from complex organic compounds, such as those found in animal manures, fish and seaweed. They require enzymes for their formation.

Acidity

SOIL ACIDITY IS the measure of the number of hydrogen ions in the soil (pH). When there are a lot of hydrogen ions, the soil pH is a low number. When there are few, the number is high. The neutral point is 7. Thus, pH less than 7 is acid, more than 7 alkaline.

Soil that is too acid, or too alkaline, locks up essential nutrients. A soil in which the calcium, magnesium, potassium and sodium are in appropriate ratio will have a pH between 6 and 7. This level of acidity is optimum for the availability of nutrients for most crops. A few crops prefer a pH between 5 and 6 and a small number tolerate alkaline conditions.

Soil Testing

SOIL TESTING AS A METHOD of predicting crop yield is fraught with difficulty. Most soil tests used to ignore the importance of the balance between the major cations and the contribution of the organic fraction of the soil. You will find a crude organic matter figure derived by igniting the sample, but this does not reveal what proportion of that is humus. However, if you use the soil test result to bring the calcium, magnesium and potassium into balance, you will experience a long-term benefit to both the crops you grow, and the health of the consumers of your produce.

A major factor that affects humus formation is the balance of the major fertility elements calcium, magnesium, potassium and sodium. This discovery is attributed to William Albrecht who was Chairman

---

Callused palms and black fingernails precede a Green Thumb. Work — the activity that interferes with gardening. When all the chores are done, the avid gardener will invent some new ones. Gardening dissolves mental chatter in the sweat of bodily effort. How can gardening be considered a "leisure time" activity? All play and no work makes Jack a dull boy — and a pain in the neck for others. We already live in the Garden of Eden, but we now have to work to keep it growing. By the garden one knows the gardener. To dig is to discover. The toil and sweat open ourselves to fruitful possibilities. The wise gardener knows when to stop.
—Michael P. Garofalo

of the Department of Soils at the University of Missouri, and the foremost authority on the relation of soil fertility to human health until his death in 1974. The relative percentages to optimise humification and consequently protein formation in most crops are:
- Calcium: 60 – 75%
- Magnesium: 10 – 20%
- Potassium: 2 – 5%
- Sodium: 0.5 – 3%
- All other cations: 5%

We have seen soil test results that show all other cations account for 40% of the total cations. This was a dairy farm and the livestock were in extremely poor health. Bringing the major cations into better balance with each other reduced the availability of the minor cations and stock health improved quickly and dramatically. The reduction in veterinary expenses more than paid for the change in fertiliser regimen.

Composts and Fertilisers

INTENSIVE ORGANIC GARDENING requires a very high level of soil fertility, and that equates to continual inputs of large quantities of humus and mineral nutrients. The most economic source of humus is compost made on-site from raw organic materials: crop residues, sawdust, animal manures, hay, seaweed, in fact anything that was once living tissue. Composting is the controlled decomposition of the raw material and there are four main methods:
- Aerobic composting
- Anaerobic composting
- Vermicompost
- Sheet composting

All four methods require similar preconditions for success. There must be a source of cellulose (carbohydrate for energy), protein (the nitrogen source), lignin and other complex carbon compounds (the raw ingredients for humus formation) and water. The carbon to nitrogen ratio must be between 25:1 and 35:1. If there is insufficient nitrogen, the process will be too slow. If there is an excess, you will lose nitrogen in the form of the gas ammonia, readily detected by your nose.

If you grow a garden you are going to shed some sweat, and you are going to spend some time bent over; you will experience some aches and pains. But it is in the willingness to accept this discomfort that we strike the most telling blow against the power plants and what they represent.
  —Wendell Berry

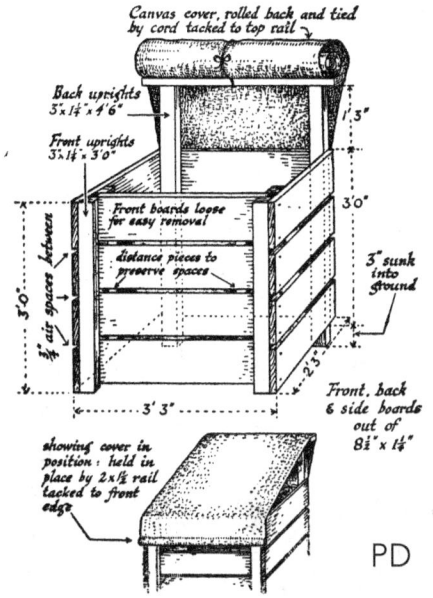
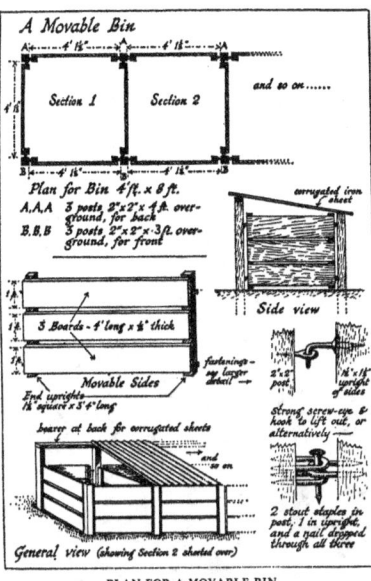

PLAN FOR A MOVABLE BIN

Aerobic Composting

AEROBIC COMPOSTING is far and away the most popular method. It has a number of advantages, chief of which are its rapidity and the development of sufficient heat to kill many weed seeds. The raw materials are placed in layers in a compost enclosure 1 – 1.5 metres (3–5 feet) square, or commercially in a windrow 1.5 – 2 metres (5–6 feet) wide and high. The length is as long as is convenient. The layers should be 25 – 50 mm (1–2 inches) thick and wetted to the consistency of a well wrung-out sponge. That is, squeezing a handful tightly, one gets the impression water is about to drip from it. If it does drip the material is too wet.

A traditional recipe is one-third animal manure, one-third fibrous material such as straw, and one-third *wilted*[12] green material. A comprehensive description of ingredients and their relevant properties is at the end of this chapter. The heap is initially invaded by the white hyphae of the fungi responsible for breaking down cellulose to simpler carbohydrates, the fuel for the thermophilic (heat loving) bacteria that subsequently take over. The temperature in the heap then rises to around 65°C. At this point, the compost is generating luxury amounts of CO_2 and it makes sense as Bill Mollison and I discussed so long ago to be piped into a greenhouse for immediate conversion back into plant tissue.

---

12 I found this essential for decomposition to commence quickly. As well, excessive amounts of unwilted greenery such as lawn clippings *can* become a slimy, maggot-infested mass according to some gardeners.

Almost anything that was once living can be composted. Meat however will attract rats.

The compost heap should be protected from rainfall, or it is liable to become too wet. While a fully roofed composting area is ideal, this is generally too expensive. Polythene covers of various sorts are frequently used, but this reduces the flow of air into the heap, so they need to be put on only in wet weather. Straw thatch allows air to enter and sheds water. When the straw becomes unusable for this purpose, it is incorporated in the next compost heap.

When the temperature of the heap begins to fall, the heap is disassembled and rebuilt, placing the material that was on the outside of the previous heap on the inside of the new heap. The temperature rises again to around 60°C and this ensures any undesirable organisms such as most weed seeds, pathogenic bacteria or antibiotics are destroyed.

Turning the heap frequently to produce finished material as soon as possible is called the Berkeley Method; turning the heap once, or twice only, the Indore Method.

The material can be used when the original ingredients are only barely recognisable. However, when the material is left for up to twelve months to mature, the humus becomes more stable and

---

The work of a garden bears visible fruits—in a world where most of our labours seem suspiciously meaningless.
—Pam Brown

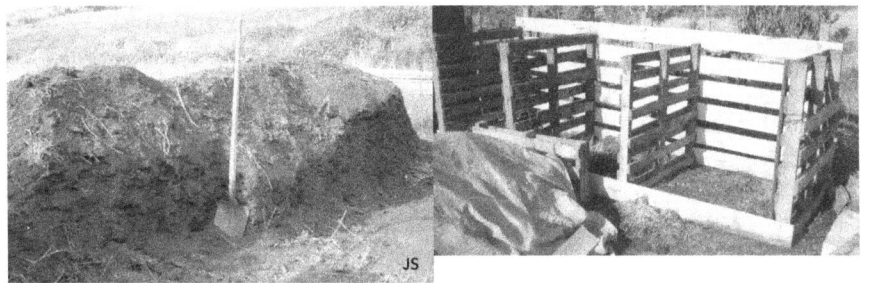

Free-form compost heap to the left and a three compartment bin above.

long-lasting in its effect. In practice, we all use much of our compost before it fully matures. Some composters believe that the compost is superior when the heap is run at the lower temperatures of 35–40°C. This would only be workable where there were few weed seeds to cause later problems. One notable common seed that survives the 60°C compost heap is that of white clover.

The temperature of the heap is controlled by altering its air content. Less air lowers the temperature — more increases it. Excessive temperatures caused by insufficient moisture can lead to scorching, or even burning of the material. Air content can be increased by inserting a perforated pipe through the centre of the heap, with, or without an air-blower attached. Decreasing air content is achieved by compressing the layers as they are built up. Improving aeration at the bottom of the heap, compacted by the weight of material above, may be achieved by using coarser material for the base, or even a simple brush-filled trench.

Insufficient moisture is indicated by excessive heat. Excessive wetness is revealed by the foul smells of anaerobic fermentation. Excessive nitrogen content is revealed by the evolution of ammonia; insufficient nitrogen by the low temperature achieved. While it would be entirely possible for you to use tables of nitrogen and carbon content of the various possible materials used in compost, I know of no one other than research scientists who would bother. In practice, we all use a fairly restricted range of materials and learn the correct ratios by trial and error. Making excellent compost is as much an art as it is a science.

When I go into my garden with a spade, and dig a bed, I feel such an exhilaration and health that I discover that I have been defrauding myself all this time in letting others do for me what I should have done with my own hands.
—Ralph Waldo Emerson

While there is a wide range of compost inoculants and activators on the market, they are almost all pretty much pointless. The spores of the bacteria and fungi needed for composting are present everywhere, especially in the soil the heap is built on. One way to test the need for them is to build one heap from raw ingredients alone and one inoculated with some finished compost and comparing the results. I did run a trial of composting chicken manure with sawdust using the Biodynamic compost preparations and a commercial inoculant. Using them definitely decreased the time required to finish though not by very much.[13] However, that would only be an issue if you needed to use the compost before allowing it to mature. As to the "special" properties of Biodynamic compost, I remain largely unconvinced.

A compost heap that should be progressing rapidly, but is nevertheless sluggish, could be for the following reasons. If the weather is very hot, the flow of air through the heap slows down. Cold air outside the heap allows what is called the chimney-effect to draw air through the heap as the hot air within rises. In typical south east Australian conditions, winter-time is best for compost-making.

The other possibility is that the ingredients are too acid. If the ingredients you regularly use fall into this category, you should dust some of the layers with very finely ground limestone, much as if you were dusting a cake with icing sugar. It is not necessary to use builders' lime (calcium hydroxide); it is rapidly converted to limestone (calcium carbonate) in contact with moisture and carbon dioxide, which are abundant in the compost heap. Do not apply the limestone directly on the animal manure or you will convert the nitrogen content to ammonia, with the distinct probability it will be lost to the atmosphere.

Compost-making is probably the most energy-consuming task for the market gardener and design of the compost area calls for some planning to make it easier. If possible, the raw materials should be accumulated at the top of a slope. The heap assembled immediately below and the rebuilt heap below that. This allows gravity to assist us. On a large scale, a scoop mounted on the front of a tractor would appear to be essential. While purpose-built machines for composting exist, they are very expensive.

Since the speed of decomposition of the component materials in the compost is dependent on their surface area, shredders are often used to pre-process the ingredients. The shredding of materials such as tree branches and cabbage stalks is probably economically justifiable if there is a sufficient amount. In any event, a heavy-duty shredder is more likely to pay for itself than the home garden variety. If

---

13 Just a few days. The compost took 12 weeks to the point of usability.

you feel you need such, you are probably already using a tractor and this makes the sort run from the tractor's PTO a better proposition. That said we acquired a home garden shredder a couple of years ago and use it to shred prunings from the orchard and decorative shrubs. This material is directed at the base of the trees and shrubs as mulch, rather than in our compost heaps.

In the home garden, cabbage, broccoli and Brussels sprouts stalks

Vic Check shows us the worm farm where he added the Biodynamic herbs and the hoofs and horns of cattle. It looked just like BD Preparation 500. Steiner had said in his lectures that hoofs of cattle were just as effective in transforming cow manure into Preparation 500 as horns, just not so suitable as containers.

can be mashed flat with a heavy hammer, or the back of an axe blade to speed their breakdown. Untreated they survive composting for a surprisingly long time.

Anaerobic Composting

It will surprise many people, but the centre of an aerobic compost heap becomes anaerobic within minutes of assembly. All the oxygen is used up. However, the aerobic portion migrates toward the outside and some part of the heap is always decomposing aerobically. Anaerobic composting is decomposition of all the ingredients in a complete absence of oxygen. This leads to foul smells, so it is just as well that the elimination of oxygen requires sealing the material within a container. In the aerobic heap, the foul smelling substances are broken down as they pass into the surrounding aerobic region. Anaerobic composting proceeds much more slowly than aerobic as it is a cold process. The temperature rise in aerobic composting requires oxygen for the thermophilic bacteria.

Having said all this, you may wonder why we are discussing anaerobic composting at all. The special purpose where you may decide to compost anaerobically is when you want the biogas (methane) that evolves for fuel. This I have never done, so I do not propose to do more than indicate it as a possibility. The finished material has higher nitrogen content than aerobic compost, but it still really needs processing through an aerobic compost heap to stabilise the nitrogen compounds as protein. I note that a lot more methane is evolved from plant material than animal manures. In India where methane is a common fuel, it's called Gobar.

Vermicomposting

This imposing word merely means the use of compost earthworms to turn your raw materials into compost. Certain materials, such as sheepskins, are difficult to process any other way. Unlike a conventional compost heap, the materials are generally placed in a container that is vermin-proof. This is a cold-composting process, so the heat generated in a conventional heap is not available to prevent vermin from invading. It is also wise to include a method of preventing the escape of the earthworms, which they are prone to do if you are not spot-on with the provision of ideal conditions for them.

My original vermicompost unit was a discarded bathtub with

The only thing that endures over time is the "Law of the Farm". You must prepare the ground, plant the seed, cultivate, and water if you expect to reap the harvest.
—Stephen R Covey

several layers of mesh over the plug-hole. The tub was covered with a sheet of marine plywood and this kept the rats and mice out. Earthworms require the ingredients to be somewhat wetter than in a normal compost heap, so the volume of material must be considerably smaller in cross-section to prevent the anaerobic condition worms will not tolerate. As well, careful attention to pH is required as earthworms have a strong aversion to acidity. Frequent additions of lime are invariably required. Two materials that worms will tolerate in only small amounts are citrus peel and onion scraps.

The vermicompost unit should be placed where it will remain between 15 and 25°C. Worms cannot tolerate temperature extremes. Light is another enemy of earthworms, so a lightproof cover is essential. A fully functioning vermicompost unit will process the addition of approximately 2.5 cm (1") of fresh material per week. To access the finished material, the fresher material on top is pushed to one side and the worm-casts removed. This material is an effective amendment to the soil at a considerably lower rate than ordinary compost.

The liquid that drains from the bathtub collects in a watering can and is used as a soil drench around hungry crops to great effect.

Sheet Composting

IN SHEET COMPOSTING, the raw ingredients are spread over the area you wish to compost. The total thickness of the material should be no more than 30 cm (12"), or it is difficult to wet thoroughly. If it is less than about 20 cm (8"), it is difficult to maintain at a high enough moisture level. While it eliminates double-handling of materials, it is harder to manage than aerobic composting in a heap. Decomposition is slower, as far less heat is generated. Weed seeds can also be a problem. In market gardening, it is most likely to be used at the beginning, before the beds are raised. We use a cover of weed mat, or discarded carpets to help retain moisture and encourage earthworms. The weed mat is attached to treated-pine half round logs to prevent it blowing away. Sadly, it also encourages slugs and snails.

Compost Ingredients and Fertilisers

ONE OF THE MOST IMPORTANT ingredients for compost is protein (for its nitrogen), and it is the most expensive. Many gardeners believe that the disease resistance of crops is enhanced more by animal protein than vegetable protein in the compost; others disagree. Nevertheless, animal manures are a staple ingredient in most compost heaps.

All gardeners need to know when to accept something wonderful and unexpected, taking no credit except for letting it be.
   —Allen Lacy

Liquid Fertilisers

SOME ORGANIC PRACTITIONERS are very much against the use of liquid fertilisers, either as soil drenches, or as foliar applications. The nitrogen in liquid manures is far more available than in regular compost and so is more akin to artificial fertiliser. They dislike foliar applications of fertiliser on the grounds that plants were designed to absorb nutrients through their roots, not their leaves.

The first point is an important one. It is entirely possible to replicate the disadvantages of artificial fertilisers with either raw animal manure, or liquid organic fertilisers. However, soil drenches of highly diluted material have effects far beyond the what the nutrient content analysis indicates. Many materials seem to have a more pronounced effect at high dilution rates than when more concentrated. Likely this is because the plant is responding to hormones, or hormone-mimics in those ingredients.

The second point is really ideological. If plants were not designed to absorb nutrients through their leaves, then it would not be possible for them to do so. Some plants, notably Spanish moss, have no roots in the soil and clearly make a living from atmospheric nutrients alone. In any event, what we apply as foliar feeds are nutrients in vanishingly small amounts. We do this not to supply the plants' needs for major nutrients, but for trace elements and the effect of these nutrients on certain micro-organisms that live on the leaves of crops and protect them from undesirable fungi and frost.

Liquid manures are easily prepared from raw ingredients by steeping them in water for a period of several days to several weeks, depending on their nature and air temperatures. On a small scale, the best vessels to use are plastic 200 litre drums with the tops cut off. Make sure that the drums you acquire were not used to store toxic materials. Plastic has pores that tend to hold on to the materials that were stored in them. Steel drums are useless, as they rapidly corrode, and the iron goes into solution.

Loosely woven bags[14] to hold the ingredients are useful to avoid later filtration, but require regular squeezing to ensure complete decomposition. The foul smells of anaerobic decomposition are reduced by regular vigorous stirring to incorporate air, which drives off the smelly nitrogenous compounds. This also reduces the nitrogen content incidentally, which somewhat takes away from the argument of the anti-brigade. The inclusion of chamomile is also said to reduce bad odours.

---

14 Synthetic cloth makes a useful material for this as natural fibres rapidly decay.

In use, the material is strained to remove particles that could block the equipment used to apply the liquid, and diluted as required. Some materials, particularly seaweed, are noticeably more effective at a dilution rate of 1000:1 than at 50, or 100:1. The optimum rates will need to be determined by trial and error, there having been little formal research at the time of writing. In any event, the ingredients you use are hardly likely to be consistent with those used by others, or even from season to season.

Animal Manures

FILL A BAG WITH ANIMAL MANURE and steep in the drum of water, squeezing daily for three to five days. Dilute to the colour of weak tea and use as a foliar application to combat fungal disease. It is also useful as a side dressing to stimulate growth in spring when the soil is still cold and biological activity sluggish, or pre-plant soil drench.

Animal manure in its raw, initial state is generally frowned upon as a soil amendment. Much of the nitrogenous content is water soluble and hence susceptible to being leached into groundwater. As well, it is caustic and can burn plant roots. Animal manure can be stacked and left to mature before use, but this risks losing much of the nitrogen through the action of denitrifying bacteria. This does not happen in a well-managed compost heap and the nitrogen is stabilised therein as bacterial protein.

There's a possible exception here and that is cow manure. One source claimed that more than 95% of nutrients were still present in cow pats some nine months after they were deposited. I suspect that this was under dry summer conditions. Cow pats on our pasture tend to be hollowed out by earthworms within three to four months.

Blood 'n' bone

THIS IS THE MOST FAMOUS of all organic fertilisers. Unfortunately it has a number of disadvantages. The nitrogen in it is quickly made available in all but very cold soil, so it is a useful side dressing. Its fibre content is nil, so it is not a substitute for compost. The bone component slowly releases phosphorus and calcium.

Bone meal is also very smelly, an issue for some. The swimming pool the writer swam in as a youth was next door to the town's bone yard.[15] Before becoming a swimming pool, it had been a sewage treatment pond!

Despite its popularity in the home garden, it is difficult to justify the expense of what would otherwise be an excellent source of phosphorus, calcium and nitrogen. The problem arises because it is such

---

15 Nuneaton, Warwickshire, UKLand.

a valuable protein source for poultry and pigs, and this generally keeps the price high. Our chickens were fed ad lib blood 'n' bone, wheat and free range pasture. They spent the night and morning in a shed where they pooped on the sawdust deep-litter that was then used in the compost. From mid-day to dusk they were free to roam until a neighbour's dog took to killing them.

Apart from my early days of gardening when I didn't know any better, I have not used blood 'n' bone as a soil amendment, nor do I recommend it. If you do use it, be aware that it needs to be incorporated into the soil rather than used as a top-dressing. Sunlight will rapidly denitrify the protein and your nitrogen will be lost as nitrogen gas.

Chicken Deep Litter

WE WERE USING TENS OF CUBIC METRES of compost a year on our market garden. At that time the cheapest source of nitrogen was chicken deep-litter from commercial grower sheds. This was a mixture of partially decomposed sawdust and chicken manure. Upon arrival at the farm it had to quickly be wetted and mixed with other compost ingredients or most of the excess nitrogen content would have gone to waste. There was also the danger of it catching fire.[16]

There are some who disapprove of this invaluable fertiliser material on the grounds that it's unkind to chickens to run them on deep litter. The writer disagrees unless the chickens are overcrowded. Our own hens loved scratching around in the deep litter and according to a rather ancient poultry keeping book I read obtain a significant amount of essential nutrients from the material.

Chicken deep litter is best mixed with cereal straw and composted. The straw will prevent the loss of valuable nitrogen and the straw decomposition products include mucins, glue-like compounds that bind soil into relatively stable crumbs.

Coal

THERE ARE SEVERAL TYPES OF COAL: lignite and anthracite are the main sorts. Anthracite is nearly all carbon and quite expensive. Lignite is also known as brown coal, the cheapest sort, and very useful in gardening. The carbon in lignite is in the form of a precursor to humic acid, the substance we create in our compost heaps. There is a grade of coal called Leonardite where the formation of humate is complete, but that is rarer than lignite. Crushed coal is then a useful soil supplement

---

16 I was told by a South Australian firefighter at a seminar the disastrous fires in South Australia at the time were started by a compost heap that spontaneously combusted. I have been corrected in this, but spontaneous combustion of compost heaps is far from unknown.

where it is cheaply available. Unfortunately that doesn't include where I live so I've never had the opportunity to try it for myself.

I have however used an extract of Leonardite called Humilac and it was a remarkable material that was applied at a very low rate to the soil where it encouraged the humification of plant remains. We used it in a number of field trials in conjunction with green manure prior to growing onions. Both the yield and quality were greatly improved when compared to green manure alone. I'm led to believe it was particularly valued by cannabis growers for it enhanced the formation of the active ingredient tetrahydrocannabinol (THC).

Comfrey and Nettles

WE HAVE USED A MIXTURE OF COMFREY AND NETTLES for the stimulation that nettles provide plants growing sluggishly in cold spring soil and the potassium content of the comfrey. We filled a plastic drum with equal parts of both and topped up with water. It smells very much like pig slurry — bloody awful! However, we find it of great benefit as a soil drench, particularly for tomatoes and pumpkins.

Compost

FILL A BAG WITH FINISHED compost and steep in the drum of water, squeezing daily for three to five days. Dilute and use as a foliar application to combat fungal disease. A trial in New Zealand when the author was just a beginning gardener gave excellent results combating apple scab (black spot).

Commercial Compost

I HAVE USED SEVERAL different commercial composts. The best was composted Lucerne (alfalfa) made locally and delivered in bulk in a ten tonne truck. I have also used bagged composted pine bark for growing in containers from the hardware store. This was successful for small crops like lettuce and strawberries, but not so effective for tomatoes and capsicums. It ran out of "oomph" before the crops were fully mature.

I have also used spent mushroom compost in the garden in conjunction with home-made fertiliser. The mushroom compost was delivered in the bags the mushrooms were grown in and used to grow several small crops of mushrooms before being consigned to the garden. Without the mushroom harvest, it's a tad expensive and most of the nutrient content has gone into the mushroom harvest. It does however provide plenty of humus for soil improvement. I note that locally at least it's made from chicken deep-litter and straw.

A thinking human, that does, is worth fifty that just eat.
—Richard Perez

Cottonseed Meal

COTTON-SEED MEAL IS VERY BULKY for its weight and so is uneconomic to transport over long distances. Where cheap transport makes the cost realistic, it is a very useful nitrogen source, both directly in the soil, or as a compost addition.

Cow Manure

THIS IS RATED SECOND ONLY to horse manure in value for the compost heap, though the author rates it above all other manures. It is just as fibrous as horse manure, but is lower in nitrogen content. In the paddock, it retains much more of its nutrient content than horse manure. Biodynamic practitioners would not dream of making compost without it.

Fish

FISH, LIKE SEAWEED IS FULL of trace elements. Fresh fish is best, rotten fish smells deplorable, but it's just as good for the compost heap. Dehydrated fish-meal is expensive. Liquid manure made from any fish you can get is probably a better use than in the compost heap. Commercial fish emulsion (liquid fish) is usually too expensive to use as a compost activator unless purchased in bulk.

Home-made fish emulsion smells even worse than comfrey and nettle. As a consequence, we use a better smelling commercial fish product. We once were given several large containers of fish meal that had not been completely cooked due to the cooker breaking down. At the time we didn't have an immediate use for it in the garden and so top-dressed an acre of extremely poor pasture with it.

The result was astonishing and the change from poor pasture to quite acceptable was rapid. Ground that had been dominated by bracken fern started producing decent grass feed instead.

Fish Emulsion

FISH EMULSION IS THE MOST useful of organic fertilisers. It is sold in a range of qualities and at a range of prices. The best we have used, Vitec, was much cheaper than liquid seaweed and unlike some fish emulsion we have used, pleasant smelling. The worst (smelliest) and most expensive we have trialled, needed filtration prior to use. It appeared to contain scallop frill (short fibres) that clogged the sprayer if not removed.

Those who see worldly life as an obstacle to Dharma see no Dharma in everyday actions; they have not discovered that there are no everyday actions outside of Dharma.
   —Zen Master Dogen

Fish emulsion applied as a soil drench at rates of around 6 ml per square metre releases many nutrients from the soil. Applied as a foliar spray at dilution rates of 50 to 1000:1, it inhibits many fungal diseases. Regular application at 10–14 day intervals is more beneficial than less frequent, more concentrated applications. One of our neighbours, a conventional apple producer, established a cherry orchard. The only fertiliser used in it was foliar fish emulsion. The flavour of the cherries were superb, but after three summers in a row of rain at harvest time,[17] he sold up and retired.

Ted Sloan and Vitec Fish Emulsion

I MET TED IN THE EARLY 1990s. He was from New Zealand where he'd been an agricultural extension officer. He decided to implement some of the advice he's been giving out by starting a kiwi-fruit (Chinese gooseberry) orchard. This was in the early days, a few years after New Zealand growers decided to rename the fruit and engage in a highly successful campaign to market this delicious and prolific fruit.

By religiously applying the advice he'd been handing out for several years, Ted succeeded in having the highest yield of any grower in his district. Unfortunately Ted discovered that wasn't sufficient to ensure financial success. His fruit had the highest break-down rate in storage!

A clue to the underlying cause of this came when he was burying the dead family cat in the home garden. Unlike the orchard, the soil was alive with earthworms and far better structured. As it happened, Ted's background was in chemical engineering and he decided that what the orchard needed was a source of organic matter that would encourage earthworm activity.

The cheapest source of organic matter to hand was fish scrap from a nearby fish processing factory. Ted set about developing a way to make applying this to the crop work. The usual methods included mechanical maceration, chemicals and/or heat. Ted decided that a biological agent was called for and he was (naturally) a little coy about the exact nature of his approach. Ted's fish emulsion was produced extraordinarily rapidly and with minimal energy input. The resultant product was inexpensive compared to many rival fish emulsions and far, far better smelling.

Vitec fish emulsion not only smelt OK. It tasted pretty good too! A Japanese food manufacturer expressed interest in using it as a raw input for their fish sauce. It was stabilised with phosphoric acid (an ingredient in many processed foods) and was readily certified

---

17 Rain on the cherries makes them split rendering them worthless. Rain covers are used but they are very expensive. Hiring a helicopter to dry the wet cherries costs a great deal also.

organic by the Biological Farmers Association.

When he used the emulsion on his kiwi-fruit orchard, the most noticeable outcome was the rapid disintegration of the fallen leaves that had hitherto collected in deep drifts. The soil came alive as the earthworms invaded and Ted's fruit stopped rotting in storage. Unfortunately for Ted, the price for kiwi-fruit dropped precipitously as the many start-up kiwi-fruit producers started to harvest the fruit. It's a phenomenally heavy cropper.

Ted realised however that he had an interesting new product from which he could make a living. Vitec worked either as a soil drench, or as a foliar fertiliser. One of the problems of pasture production is called pulling. Sheep and cattle grazing on grass in winter tend to pull the grass plants out of the soil as they eat it. This greatly reduces grass production and the gaps left tend to become populated by weeds, usually inedible ones. Vitec encouraged grasses to develop much deeper root systems and stock indicated their preference for feeding on organically-fed pasture as they have done in ever so many other places and times.

One remark that the writer recalls Ted making was that the best farmers had a similar attitude towards the soil with the best home vegetable gardeners. Lionel Pollard, the founder of Willing Workers on Organic Farms (WWOOF)[18] in Australia also made an interesting statement. He'd been a guest on a farm in East Gippsland and his host had apologised for serving a meal of roast beef without potatoes as they had run out. "But you're a potato farmer!" Lionel had remarked. "You've got acres of potatoes on the farm!"

"Oh, we wouldn't dream of eating anything we grow for the market," said the farmer, "We have run out of potatoes in the home garden." It's hard to imagine an organic farmer making such a remark.

Grass Clippings

GRASS CLIPPINGS FROM LAWNS are a good source of nitrogen. They have a tendency to form a slimy, impervious mat if layered too thick. Keep layers of grass clippings no more than about 2.5 cm (1") thick and make sure they are well-wilted before use either in the compost heap, or as a mulch.

Hay

ON THE SURFACE, HAY LOOKS like an ideal compost ingredient. It is high in fibre and lignin, and has significant protein content that cereal straw lacks. However, much hay is made with grasses at the seeding stage, so weed seeds can be a great problem. I have used

---

18 WWOOF in the UK was the acronym for Working Weekends on Organic Farms.

hay extensively, and with care, it has been invaluable. Lucerne hay is much less problematic in this regard, and it has a higher protein content than grass hay. Lucerne also contains valuable growth promoting auxins. In districts where a second hay cut is taken, the second cut contains far less seeds.

When we used hay as a mulch it we left it in "biscuits" and that made it easier to flip over when the weed and grass seeds germinated.

Hop Mark

THE MATERIAL THAT REMAINS after the hop flowers have been removed makes an excellent compost ingredient. I imagine that following the success of an organic hop growing trial at Tasmania's largest hop farm about thirty years ago, you'll be lucky to obtain any. While the production of hops organically never went anywhere at the time, the advantages of stimulating the proliferation of earthworms were manifest in the trial.

Horse Manure

HORSE MANURE IS VERY HIGH in both fibre and nitrogen content as horses are very inefficient users of the nutrients in their food. A good source of horse manure is from racing stables. As very high protein diets are fed to racehorses, their manure is also highest in nitrogen. The manure will in all likelihood come already mixed with fibre of some sort, generally sawdust, or wood shavings. Care must be taken to ensure it is not contaminated with wood preservatives, such as copper-chrome-arsenate, or the solvents and glues used in woodworking. Horse manure is generally rated number one for market gardening.

Human Manure

IT IS ILLEGAL TO USE HUMAN MANURE on the soil or in compost used to grow food for human consumption due to the possibility of contamination with several intractable human diseases. This doesn't stop people from using it. With care, long periods of decomposition, and attention to where it's used, under trees for instance, they seem to experience no difficulties.

In his garden every man may be his own artist without apology or explanation. Each within his green enclosure is a creator, and no two shall reach the same conclusion; nor shall we, any more than other creative workers, be ever wholly satisfied with our accomplishment. Ever a season ahead of us floats the vision of perfection and herein lies its perennial charm.
—Louise Beebe Wilder

Leaves

MOST TREE LEAVES ARE LOW IN NITROGEN and high in tannin, which slows decomposition. Use only moderate amounts in compost, or let them decompose in their own heaps without additives for two years or so. The resultant material, called leaf mould, is an excellent substitute for peat-moss. Eucalyptus leaves contain oils and other substances that render them somewhat less useful than European deciduous trees, so treat them with caution. The University of California recommends composting them separately and testing the effect of the resultant compost on seed germination. Pine needles contain terpenes, the raw ingredient for turpentine, so use them sparingly.

Lucerne (Alfalfa) Chaff

LUCERNE CHAFF IS LUCERNE HAY that has been chopped up small for use as stock food. It can be applied directly to the soil and lightly tilled in for a quick nitrogen boost. It also contains hormones that increase the rate of growth.

Paper

NEWSPRINT CONTAINS LIGNIN as well as cellulose so it is better than higher quality papers consist entirely of cellulose. The coating on coated paper is mostly clay. Paper should be shredded before use, to prevent it forming layers impervious to water. Many composters avoid paper printed with coloured inks as these may contain undesirable contaminants such as heavy metals. Despite the printing industry replacing many heavy metal pigments with safer ones, in 2010, 20 years later, an analysis of paper used for food packaging found lead, chrome and mercury.[19]

Pea Straw

PEA STRAW MAKES AN EXCELLENT compost ingredient, or feeding mulch being high in nitrogen. A few viable pea seeds will germinate in it when used for mulching, but they are easily removed by pulling them out by hand. Pea straw tends to be on the expensive side because it's also useful animal feed.

Phosphate Rock

THE PHOSPHATE ROCK THAT IS USED to manufacture superphosphate was all that was available in years past. Now we can buy *reactive* phosphate rock (RPR), in which the phosphorus is more readily available to crops. Phosphate rock can be applied directly by incorporating it into the soil, or via the compost heap.

---

19 Xue, M. & Wang, S. & Huang, C.. (2010). Determination of heavy metals (Pb, Cd, Cr and Hg) in printed paper as food packaging materials and analysis of their sources. Huagong Xuebao/CIESC Journal. 61. 3258-3265.

Pig Manure
PIG MANURE IS CONSIDERED little better than poultry manure, as it is devoid of fibre. Past pig-farming practice was to include a copper supplement to make the pigs grow faster. As a consequence, pig manure often had an excessive copper content and this is detrimental to earthworm health. We advise caution and make sure you know what's being fed to the pigs whose manure you are using.

Poppy Seed Meal
AS FOR COTTON-SEED MEAL above though you are unlikely to find this outside Tasmania (or Afghanistan).

Poultry Manure
LIKE HORSE MANURE, POULTRY MANURE is rated as "hot". That is, it is very high in nitrogen. Unlike horse manure, it is devoid of fibre, which is why market gardeners generally rate it last in the list of desirable animal manures. However, the writer's garden has thrived on compost made from chicken deep-litter (poultry manure mixed with sawdust) and crop residues. Poultry manure is generally free of weed seeds. Antibiotics are a common additive to poultry diets in modern intensive units. As they are very unstable compounds they generally should not be a problem in an aerobic (hot) compost heap.

Pelletised Poultry Manure
MATERIALS SUCH AS THE WELL-KNOWN *Dynamic Lifter* and *Organic Life*, consist of chicken deep-litter composted, pelletised and steam sterilised. Some products are blended with fish, seaweed, blood 'n' bone, other animal manure, or zeolite to improve the material. These products are necessarily a lot more expensive than the compost you can make for yourself. However, they do have the advantage of being much easier to handle and spread with machinery. They are generally most useful when your own composting program has fallen behind or you are a beginning gardener. This material is well-suited to direct use by incorporating it into the soil.

Rock Dusts
VARIOUS CRUSHED ROCKS CAN NOW be purchased for use in improving soil fertility. Basically, the theory is to emulate the effect of glacial action on rocks that form silt. Rather than wait for another ice age,

---

My passion for gardening may strike some as selfish, or merely an act of resignation in the face of overwhelming problems that beset the world. It is neither. I have found that each garden is just what Voltaire proposed in Candide: a microcosm of a just and beautiful society.
   —Andrew Weil

we crush the rocks containing the desired minerals and apply them either directly to the soil, or via the compost heap. To be effective the rock has to be very finely powdered so as to present as great a surface area to the soil organisms as possible. You may find that the nearest road-metal quarry will let you take the fine stuff away for free. It tends to accumulate below conveyor belts and such like. Some unscrupulous vendors mix clay with rock dust to improve their profit margins, so beware.

One enterprising quarry owner had me test the fine rock powder he was collecting and I was happy to report excellent results from inclusion in the compost. It is well-suited to direct incorporation in the soil where the crops are to grow. Being slow-acting, the effects will not be immediate and will last well beyond the first crop grown after application.

Sawdust

SAWDUST GETS A PRETTY BAD PRESS in gardening circles. However, it can be an excellent source of fibre, cellulose and lignin. Softwood sawdust contains terpenes and resins that are growth inhibitors, so we have only used eucalyptus hardwood sawdust. Sawdust from workshops may contain synthetic glue residues, so we have always used sawmill waste. Sawdust from decades old heaps is nearly all lignin, but it is generally wet, and therefore heavier and harder to move than dry, green sawdust. Sawdust must never be incorporated into the soil. Where it's used as a mulch, the soil should have compost incorporated first, or possibly blood 'n' bone. Decomposing sawdust will tie up a lot of nitrogen while it's decomposing.

Seaweed

SEAWEED CONTAINS NEITHER CELLULOSE, nor significant nitrogen. Nevertheless, it is an important ingredient in gardening. It contains the

---

Anthropocentric as [the gardener] may be, he recognizes that he is dependent for his health and survival on many other forms of life, so he is careful to take their interests into account in whatever he does. He is in fact a wilderness advocate of a certain kind. It is when he respects and nurtures the wilderness of his soil and his plants that his garden seems to flourish most. Wildness, he has found, resides not only out there, but right here: in his soil, in his plants, even in himself...
But wildness is more a quality than a place, and though humans can't manufacture it, they can nourish and husband it...
The gardener cultivates wildness, but he does so carefully and respectfully, in full recognition of its mystery.
   — Michael Pollan

full range of trace elements and is a moderate source of potassium. If you are lucky enough to be near the seaside, you can collect the material yourself where that remains legal. Bull kelp is said to be the best. Unfortunately, wet seaweed is nearly all water. Seaweed for sale is dehydrated. We have used both and the convenience of seaweed meal outweighs the inconvenience of heavy, wet, smelly seaweed half an hour's drive or more away.

Analysis of kelp meal by Mount Pleasant Laboratories of Tasmanian Department of Agriculture. File H047. Lab No 20172.

- Nitrogen: 0.750%
- Sulphur: 0.695%
- Phosphorus: 0.196%
- Zinc: 88.3 ppm
- Potassium: 1.36%
- Boron: 70.0 ppm
- Calcium: 1.08%
- Iron: 53.9 ppm
- Magnesium: 0.882%
- Manganese: 61.5 ppm
- Sodium: 2.93%
- Copper: 2.50 ppm

Some seaweed gatherers scrupulously "wash the salt off" their freshly gathered seaweed before use. Most of the salt from the seaweed has already washed off in the rain. Also it's not just sodium chloride, but many different salts. One organic grower of my acquaintance, Ray Mason, used to apply dilute seawater as a foliar spray on crops. He also gave dilute seawater to his dairy cattle. He was an excellent farmer and useful mentor when this writer was first learning the tricks of the trade forty years ago.

Seaweed Meal

SEAWEED MEAL IS AVAILABLE in various grades. The powdery sort sold as stock feed is less satisfactory than the coarser grades that are less inclined to blow everywhere in the wind. Application rates between 75 and 150 gm per square metre (2–4 oz per square yard) are ample. Rates much higher than this recommendation have the lamentable effect of depressing yield. The benefits to expect are improved trace element availability and water-holding capacity of the soil.

"You are right," said Pangloss, "for when man was placed in the Garden of Eden, he was placed there ut operaretur eum, *to dress it and keep it; which proves that man was not born for idleness."*
—Voltaire

Seaweed Emulsion
LIQUID SEAWEED IS THE SINGLE most popular liquid fertiliser. It contains substances, such as abscisic acid, the plant hormone that tells deciduous trees to drop their leaves. This material is implicated in seaweed's ability to confer disease and frost resistance to crops. Seaweed also contains plant growth hormones (auxins) that influence cell elongation and division. To cap all this off, it also contains the full range of trace elements in a form readily available to plants.

To make a liquid fertiliser with fresh seaweed, fill the drum completely and top up with water. To use seaweed meal, use about 10 kg (20 lb) or so to 200 litres (53 US gallons). Seaweed breaks down very rapidly as it contains alginate, rather than cellulose in its cell walls. We use it diluted to the colour of very weak tea.

Sewage Sludge
THIS OTHERWISE EXCELLENT SOURCE of nitrogen is often contaminated with heavy metals due to sewage and storm-water sharing the same drains. As we become more aware of the waste of this resource, the situation is hopefully going to change. Sadly, I have been saying this for more than 30 years now. Best used as compost activator where the heat will destroy most pathogens.

Sheep and Goat Manure
TO ALL INTENTS AND PURPOSES, sheep and goat manure are the same material. It is fibrous and moderately endowed with nitrogen. When we kept goats, my wife made perfect compost on her first attempt using goat manure mixed with hay the goats had refused to eat. They are very picky eaters despite a reputation for eating anything. Due to their dietary habits, these manures are nearly always full of undigested weed seeds, so careful attention to turning the heap to kill them is required.

Aged sheep manure is commonly available in wool-producing districts as large amounts accumulate under the shearing sheds. Some gardeners use it directly on the soil, but the weed seeds are a problem best avoided by incorporating sheep manure in the compost heap.

Straw (Cereal)
THIS IS A MAJOR SOURCE OF FIBRE and lignin. Except for legume straw, it has virtually nil protein content. Weed seeds are rarely a problem in straw. Decomposing cereal straw produces substances called mucins that act as a glue to improve the stability of soil crumbs. Straw should never be incorporated directly into the soil unless it's accompanied by a source of nitrogen. It makes almost perfect mulch and is excellent when composted.

Vegetable Scraps
A MARKET GARDEN WILL PRODUCE an abundance of material unsuitable for sale; leaf trimmings, pea haulm etc. The leafy material is best wilted to accelerate decomposition when composted, the denser material for vermicompost, and most can be used directly in the soil.

Weeds
WEEDS ARE WONDERFUL ACCUMULATORS of various trace elements. Before incorporating them in the compost heap, they must be wilted, or they take much too long to break down. Weeds at the seeding stage can be a source of further weed contamination if they are not heated to a sufficiently high temperature, or if their seeds can tolerate compost heap temperatures. For example, wild white clover seeds can survive 65°C.

Weeds contain a wide variety of trace elements that are useful to our crops. Biodynamic practitioners claim that making liquid manure out of your weeds and spraying it where they are a problem reduces the problem. Even if this is not true, you will be doing your crops a nutritional favour.

Wool
WE USED TO COMPOST ALL the loose bits and dags[20] after shearing our sheep flock. Wool is an excellent nitrogen source. This material can be used directly in the soil, or the compost heap.

Producing Your Own Compost Ingredients
WE HAVE PRODUCED OUR OWN HAY, goat, sheep and chicken manure. Goat manure is convenient due to the habit of goats defecating in the sheds they require for shelter from inclement weather. As well, they are very wasteful of hay and this becomes mixed with the dung. It is unfortunate that goats spend 95% or more of their intellectual abilities planning the best way to invade your garden.

We kept chickens for eggs in a shed on sawdust during the morning, allowing them free-range in the afternoons after they had finished laying their eggs. The shed was cleaned out once a year in the summer, and this material was our profit margin due to the low price for eggs and the high price of wheat at the time.

We would have liked to establish a paddock of Lucerne, far and away the best fixer of atmospheric nitrogen, but our soil is too heavy for that. An alternative would have been cow grass, a heavy yielding

---

20 The sheep's dags are the mixture of wool and faeces that accumulate around the animal's rear end. This material became far less common with the introduction of mulesing. Now that mulesing is becoming forbidden, dags are again in plentiful supply to the probable delight of the flies that lay their eggs on daggy sheep.

red clover. We do grow comfrey and stinging nettles, both being of inestimable value in compost and liquid manures as well as compost ingredients.

Using Compost

As referred to earlier, compost can be used when the original ingredients are only just barely recognisable. Compost at this stage is far from fully humified, and the nitrogen content is still susceptible to leaching by rainfall and irrigation. Consequently, it is best used on crops that are greedy feeders, such as corn, the cabbage tribe, pumpkins, lettuce and potatoes. As compost matures, it turns into a black, colloidal material in which none of the original components are recognisable. This material will last longer in the soil and is required for seed-raising mixtures.

In practice, we all use some compost before full maturity, even though we might prefer not to. The amount required depends very much on the fertility of the soil, its type and the crop. Light, sandy soils require heavier and more frequent additions of compost than heavier soils. Some crops abhor fresh compost, particularly carrots which fork. Peas and beans require little if any compost in the average garden; they are usually more than happy with what's left over from the preceding crop. Onions, like carrots, peas and beans, prefer to subsist on the compost residues from a previous crop.

A reasonably fertile loam to heavy soil will need about 25mm (1") of compost preceding a heavy feeder. This amount can be increased with benefit; there is none of the toxicity problem with overfeeding that can occur with artificial fertilisers. Availability is more of a factor than overfeeding when using compost. Compost is unique in that it allows plants to consume nutrients as they are needed and usually at the rate they require.

Compost consists of living organisms, mostly microbes that are readily killed by sunlight. Consequently, it is somewhat wasteful to use compost as mulch. It is best lightly tilled into the top 80–100mm (3–4") of soil for its optimum benefit to be realised.

Gardeners are — let's face it — control freaks. Who else would willingly spend his leisure hours wresting weeds out of the ground, blithely making life or death decisions about living beings, moving earth from here to there, changing the course of waterways? The more one thinks about it, the odder it seems; this compulsion to remake a little corner of the planet according to some plan or vision.
    —Abby Adams

The author in his market garden in 1987. The crop in the foreground is leeks.
Photo courtesy *Tasmanian Country*.

If you have built castles in the air, your work need not be lost; that is where they should be. Now put the foundations under them.
   —Henry David Thoreau

Our garden waiting to be planted out. The greenhouse is to the right out of view.

Once one knows what really matters, one ceases to be voluble. And what does really matter? That is easy: thinking and doing, doing and thinking — and these are the sum of all wisdom… Both must move ever onward in life, to and fro, like breathing in and breathing out. Whoever makes it a rule to test action by thought, thought by action, cannot falter, and if he does, will soon find his way back to the right road.
  —Johann Wolfgang von Goethe

Tillage and Tools

TILLAGE OF THE SOIL is possibly one of the most controversial areas of gardening. There are advocates for double-digging, no-dig and every shade between. The writer leans towards minimal tillage; that is the least amount required to obtain economic yields. Ignoring the special case of garden establishment, which is covered elsewhere, I follow this program. Immediately prior to establishing a deep rooting crop, such as carrots, I lever a fork through the soil to shatter it deeply, but not invert it. Then the surface is hoed with a Coleman hoe, Canterbury hoe or GR wheel-hoe to create a seedbed. When compost needs to be incorporated, it is applied immediately prior to the forking. Crops that are in the ground a long time and that are hoed frequently to control weeds are planted directly into a very coarse bed. These are referred to as cleaning crops.

Double-digging requires loosening the soil to the depth of two lengths of the blade of a digging spade (60cm or 2'). First a trench is made the width of the garden bed and the soil moved to the end of the bed where digging will finish. The soil at the bottom of the trench is manured, forked, or spaded over, then the top spit of the next trench thrown onto the loosened soil. Then you loosen the soil at the bottom of the trench... lots of work. Many places in the world the soil freezes deep enough to make this process completely redundant. In my garden, the subsoil is *very* stiff clay and the effort involved doing this every spring makes my mind spin.

One of the world's greatest advocates of zero tillage in the garden, Bill Mollison, developed his Permaculture ideas with David Holmgren here in Tasmania back in the 1970s. Our experience is that a few crops benefit from this approach, but most have much lower yield than the minimal tillage approach we have adopted.[1] The main thing is to avoid treading on the soil you have tilled, unless you place a large sheet of exterior grade plywood or something similar on the garden bed first to reduce localised compaction. One gardener contemptuously calls most gardening "farming footprints".

After several decades of using our method, occasionally pushing a long-handled garden fork deep into the soil and levering it up through an angle of around 45° followed by tilling 25 mm of compost into the

---

1 In the late 1980s and early 90s people undertaking Permaculture training in the Huon Valley south of Hobart, Tasmania were brought to my garden to experience the results of my gardening. Paradoxically, I had abandoned Permaculture techniques (as discussed with Bill Mollison in the 1970s) as unworkable in my situation by then. Tim Marshall points out that Permaculture has since moved on.

top 10 cm (4") with a small claw hoe, we don't need a trowel to make holes for transplanting. The soil is loose enough that fingers suffice.

In the early days our garden beds were free-form 1.2 metres (4') wide with very narrow footpaths between. While the narrowness of the footpaths maximised the proportion of productive land, this was a mistake. You really need sufficient space between the growing surfaces to crouch down without encroaching on an adjacent tall crop such as sweet corn, or trellised peas and beans for example. An ordinary wheelbarrow was too wide and the especially narrow sort a friend purchased in New Zealand wasn't available for love or money locally. Mostly we have used buckets. Not the ordinary sort, but large ones that previously contained about 20 litres (6 gal) of paint.

The edges of the free-form beds were under constant attack by birds seeking earthworms. The soil in the beds was scattered onto the paths. Eventually we used treated pine boards to prevent this. The birds still attack the garden beds seeking earthworms, but the soil in them tends to remain where we want it.

Keeping the paths, now 60 cm (2') wide, weed-free was a constant chore. We early on acquired a wheeled stirrup hoe and that worked well. Before that we had tried cardboard covered with green sawdust.[2] While this suppressed the weeds, slipping over in wet weather was a constant problem. Eventually we put down a layer of cheap plastic weedmat and covered that with sawdust. This works superbly and not needing to constantly hoe the paths is most welcome.

---

2   Sawdust is a very cheaply available waste material from a local sawmill.

The farm from the air. The garden is in the bottom right corner near the road and driveway. There was only one tree on the 9¾ acres when we purchased it in 1982. In the mid 1980s all of this corner of the farm was producing vegetables.

Establishing your Garden

ALMOST EVERY NEWCOMER to gardening, including myself, has bitten off far more than they can chew. A little planning and a considered approach will considerably reduce the toil and cost. For the home gardener anxious for the joys of fresh produce, a small area can be set aside to play with, but the main part of a large garden is best approached slowly and more methodically. First, decide on a crop rotation that will provide for your needs, and those of the crops you wish to grow. You will find the information you need in the section on crop rotation. An area needs to be set aside where compost can be made, raw compost materials stored, and a shed, or other storage space for tools. Next, the area needs to be fenced against marauding predators where that is necessary. Humans are the most difficult to keep away; goats and possums almost as bad. Wombats are probably impossible to control. Finally, the growing area must be cleared of unwanted vegetation.

The Compost Area

COMPOST IS BEST MADE in a shady area, sheltered from drying winds and free of weeds. In the home garden, two cubic, open-faced bins of a little over one cubic metre capacity are all that will be required unless the garden is very big. In that instance, an extra bin, or two

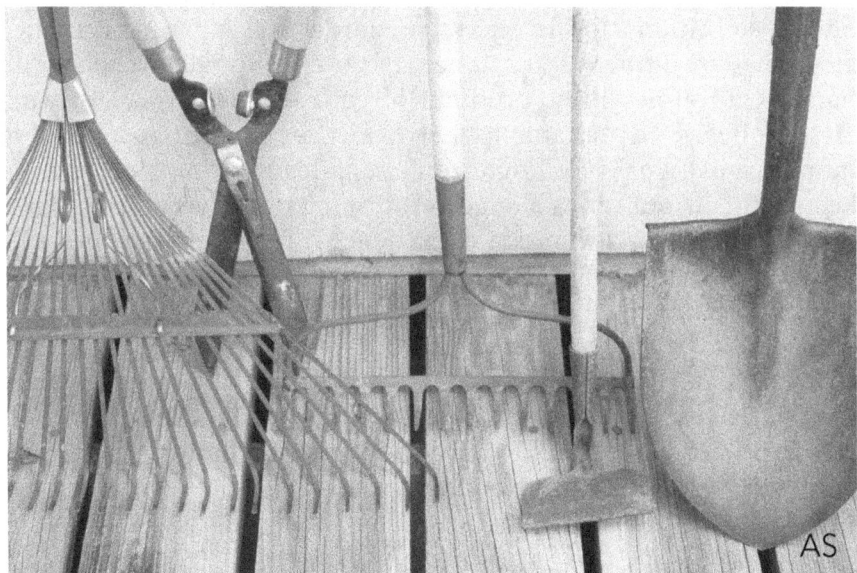

Tools need to be stored where they are out of the weather. The bow style rake is much better than the cheaper sort. Note that this is a shovel, not a garden spade.

is usually better than making the bins much bigger. For the market gardener, compost can be made in long windrows, between one and two square metres in cross-section, and as long as required. If you plan on compost materials decreasing in volume by 50%, and compost taking three months to be ready from the raw materials, you will be able to calculate how much area to set aside. A cubic metre (1.3 cubic yards) of compost will cover 40 square metres (48 square yards) to a depth of 2.5 cm (1"), the recommended amount of average compost for the average crop.

The Tool Shed

AUSTRALIAN GARDENERS ARE notorious for leaving their tools outside in the rain and sunshine. This severely reduces their useful lifespan. Providing a place where tools are protected from the elements, and are easily found can save much money and lost time. It doesn't need to be elaborate, or expensive.

Our tool shed is about a metre (3') square and almost two metres (6') tall and looks a little like a traditional outdoor dunny (toilet). It's called The Turdis because it's also similar in size and shape to Dr Who's time machine. You just need sufficient space to put your hoes, forks, spades etc.

Fences

FENCES AND FENCING are bothersome and boring, BUT they are nearly always a critical factor for successful gardening. A garden contains crops that are attractive to a variety of potential predators who will happily consume all the products of your labour if you let them. First, know your predators; what works for rabbits won't stop a human; what works for dogs won't necessarily stop goats. In fact, keeping goats out ranks alongside stopping humans and possums; they all seem able and prepared to devote all of their considerable ingenuity and skills to stealing garden produce.

Prepare your list of potential known predators, and take it to either a competent fencing contractor, or a rural supplies store that services farmers' needs. The latter can not only supply the raw materials needed, but will have literature to ensure you get the best out of what you purchase should you decide to save money by building your own fences. Skimping on fence quality is A Very Bad Decision since it means you will have to re-fence sooner rather than later. If

---

The garden suggests there might be a place where we can meet nature halfway.
   —Michael Pollan

there's one thing worse than fencing, it is the necessity to replace after a short time what should have sufficed for decades.

This isn't a fencing manual, but it's worth touching on several important fencing issues that are not apparent to the fencing neophyte. The most important part of most fences is the end assembly. Many fences are held up between the end assemblies by the tension on the wires, or wire fabric between. This reduces the cost of intermediate posts, but also withstands pressure from livestock better. Rather than gradually falling over from continuous pushing, they spring back into place following a push.

The strength of the end assembly is determined not by the diameter of the posts used to make the anchor, but their depth. An increase in depth of 30 cm (1') approximately doubles the strain that can be exerted on a post! Posts that are driven into the soil with a post-driver can take far more strain than those placed in a hole and backfilled with compacted soil or concrete.

Galvanised steel or copper-chrome-treated pine posts will last many times longer than untreated hardwood posts. Even if the hardwood posts are free, they will usually cost more in the long run as most timber decays and becomes useless in a few short years.[3] Copper-chrome[4] treated posts are much cheaper than steel, but if they burn, the fumes are toxic. Better to make sure they don't burn. If animals chew on the treated posts, look to the animals' nutritional needs rather than worrying about the possible effects of the copper and chromium! Insufficient copper and chromium in the diet should be a cause for concern and likely readily amended with kelp meal, or appropriate mineral blocks.

The electric fence on the opposite side of the road to us uses copper-chrome-arsenate posts that were originally used to trellis apple trees are still in fine fettle. They must be close to fifty years old by now with another fifty to go.

Gardens in the suburbs tend to be fenced with paling fences. They are good for keeping dogs out, less so determined humans and possums. Where possums are a problem, and that's pretty much the whole of Australia, you can put chicken-wire cages over individual

---

3 Our first fences used "free" hardwood poles from a neighbour's bush block. They had rotted off at ground level in less than ten years.

4 Note that we refer to copper-chrome treated here. One brand locally is called Ecopine. This is not to be confused with copper-chrome-arsenate (CCA). Trace quantities of arsenic are an essential dietary element in rats, goats, chickens, and presumably many other species, including humans. However, many believe that given the small quantities needed, risking excess is unwise.

garden beds, or even construct a large enclosed cage high enough to allow the gardener to walk around in. Possums are agile creatures and can leap a distance of 2.5 metres (8 feet). They are also great climbers when they can dig their claws in. They will climb a wooden fence with ease. If you have wooden fences that can be leapt onto, you can attach PVC piping to the top of the fence and grease it with some non-toxic grease. So I'm told. I was also told that attaching floppy chicken wire atop fences works too, but have met any number of gardeners who told me that didn't work for them.[5]

Soil Preparation and Maintenance

THE HOME GARDENER can mulch weedy ground, or lawn with cardboard covered with straw, or hay starting in winter. This will slowly rot the sod, leaving soil beneath that will be easily tilled the following spring. During this period, compost can be made in the bins you have made. In late spring, the largely decomposed mulch can be placed in the compost bin to start your next compost heap. The compost you have already made can be spread over the whole area you intend to garden. Do not worry if this is less than a 2.5 cm (1") cover; it is more beneficial to spread your compost over the whole area than to concentrate it on a smaller area, particularly in the early stages.

You should then till the soil to incorporate the compost and commence the lengthy task of reducing the perennial weeds and dormant weed seeds to a manageable level. The soil can be broken up initially by spading, forking, or rotary hoeing. Subsequent cultivations are better done with a hand-hoe, or wheel-hoe. By lightly tilling once every week or two, the roots of perennial weeds such as couch grass (twitch) and dock are starved and exhausted. Each pass with the hoe also encourages another batch of weed seeds to germinate and over time their numbers will decrease. Many of these weed seeds have hard seed coats, so they will continue to germinate for a number of years, but this initial phase, called a summer fallow, will make your life much easier than if you were growing a crop. The time to till is when the weed seedlings are at what is called the "white-wire" stage. This is when only the seed leaves have emerged and before, or very shortly after the first pair of true leaves.

A refinement of summer fallowing is to sow a smothering crop and till it in. Suitable crops include mustard[6] and buckwheat that

---

5   See https://www.wikihow.com/Deter-Possums-from-Your-Garden

6   Mustard is particularly beneficial if the soil is infested with nematodes. In northern Tasmania's potato growing district, there are conventional farmers sowing mustard as a green manure as the only way to control nematodes that reduce potato yields.

germinate and grow rapidly. Weeds then germinate under the heavy shade of their leaves and so their vigour is much diminished. This is only useful if there are no vigorous perennials, such as dock or twitch, sprouting from large root pieces. Mustard green manure also reduces nematode numbers so is particularly useful before a potato crop.

Gardening Implements

GARDENING IS MADE very much easier when the correct tool is selected for the job. Quality is an important issue when selecting tools. There is nothing more frustrating than to have a tool break, or more likely bend, rendering it useless. High quality steel will last for many years beyond low quality. Several of my tools are probably as old as I am or older, and still giving sterling service. Tools such as these are readily purchased at garage sales and auctions, and so need not be expensive. Expensive new tools can be cheaper than they seem. I took a costly garden fork that broke a tine back to the shop from where I purchased it 18 months before. The fork was replaced with the comment that this particular brand of fork did not break!

Maintenance of tools is important to keep them efficient and to maintain your investment. Keep them under cover when not in use and oil the steel parts with old sump oil or similar to keep them from rusting. Rubbing linseed oil into wooden handles helps to keep them tough and waterproof. Hoes and spades can be sharpened with a bastard file for ease of cutting. Scythes are best sharpened with a knife steel such as butchers use to keep their knives razor sharp.

Despite the complexity of gardening, a small range of high quality tools is all that is required. There is a plethora of gadgetry introduced onto the market each year, designed more to make money for the seller, rather than fulfilling the advertised claims. The main tools are

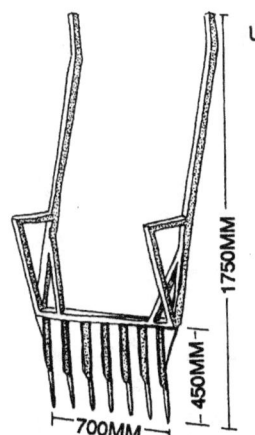

U-BAR CULTIVATES 450MM DEEP

Next page:
Dutch market gardeners' stainless steel spade and fork.

a hoe, spade, fork, rake and trowel. The spade can serve the place of a shovel if necessary, and I do own a hybrid shovel that can serve as a spade as well as a shovel. A conventional shovel makes a poor spading implement, due to its pointed shape and greater angle between the blade and handle. Using a spade as a shovel entails bending down too far and that's extra strain on the back.

Many gardeners prefer a garden fork for spading the soil. Try to use either implement to break the soil without inverting it. With the spade, this necessitates throwing the soil forward slightly, so that it breaks into its constituent crumbs. The tines of a fork can be levered through the soil to aerate it and achieve a similar result without throwing. Some growers lift the soil with the fork and gently hit the clump with the tines to break it.

Two specialised garden forks are available that implement the aeration technique superbly. The first is called the "U-bar", and its dimensions are included to allow you to have one fabricated. The second is based on a Dutch market gardener's fork and is commercially available in Australia. Also available is a more conventional garden fork with rather flattened tines. This is useful where quantities of partially decomposed compost need to be lifted and moved.

One tool I find particularly useful is the claw hoe. This is used as a substitute for the garden fork in reworking raised garden beds. It is rather quicker to use than an ordinary garden fork. The claw hoe is similar to the Canterbury hoe, but the tines are shorter and more closely spaced. Its handle is longer and lighter than that of my Canterbury hoe.

The garden rake is often used as a sort of miniature claw hoe, but most are not really sturdy enough to take this sort of punishment, nor are the teeth of the rake quite long enough. Rakes are intended to be dragged across the soil to create the final fine tilth for seed sowing and to flatten the soil surface. Also, this drags larger clumps of soil and pieces of organic material off to the side. The bow rake is generally sturdier than the more common sort.

Hoes come in several forms. They are mainly used to break the soil surface, aerating and killing weeds at the white wire stage of growth. Kept sharpened with a bastard file, they will also cut through more mature weeds and will kill most annuals. Illustrated are the conventional hoe and the Dutch hoe. The Dutch is pushed through

---

One of the maxims of the new field of conservation biological control is that to control insect herbivores, you must maintain populations of insect herbivores.
— Douglas Tallamy

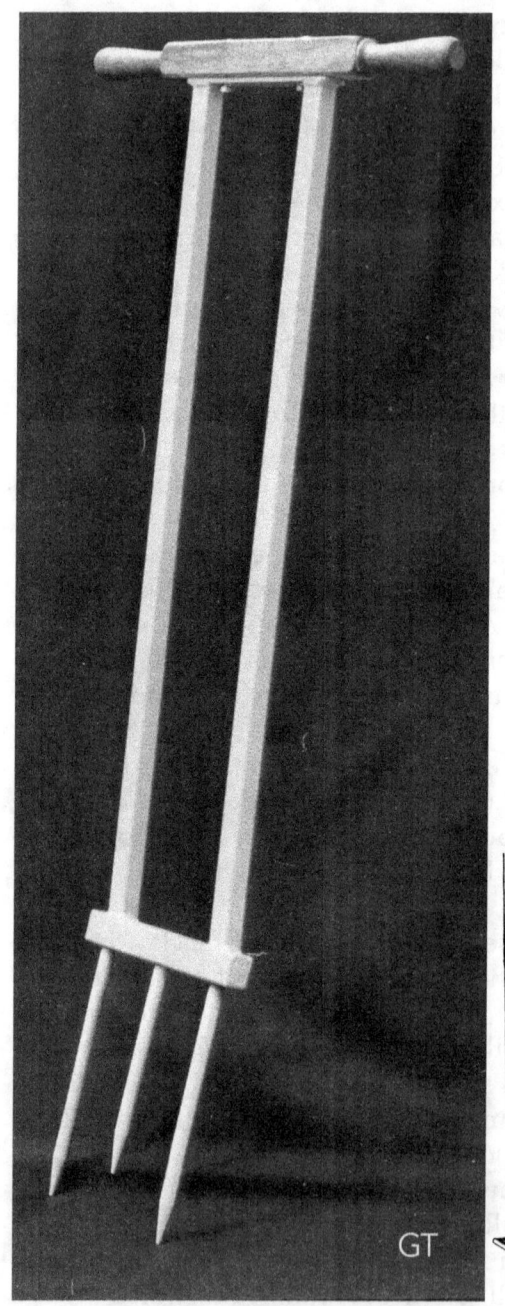

Left: Dutch market gardener's fork.
Below left to right:
Claw hoe (Canterbury hoe)
Spade
Fork
Rake
Dutch hoe (push hoe)
Draw hoe

A garden requires patient labor and attention. Plants do not grow merely to satisfy ambitions or to fulfill good intentions. They thrive because someone expended effort on them.
—Liberty Hyde Bailey

the soil, rather than the chopping action of the ordinary hoe. One also works away from the worked area, rather than into it, making for a neater result in conventional row gardening. An onion hoe is useful where hoeing between closely spaced plants is required.

Not illustrated here, I don't own one, is the stirrup hoe that works in both directions; that is when pushed, or pulled.

Scythes

SCYTHES MAKE VERY EFFICIENT mowers of long grass, particularly useful when cutting large areas for compost material. The hand grips on the snath[7] of a scythe are on a reverse screw thread (they unscrew in a clockwise direction) and can be loosened and repositioned for comfort. The appropriate way to use a scythe is best learnt from an experienced practitioner, but I will attempt to describe the method here. The blade is moved through the grass in a slicing, rather than chopping, action. Chopping is harder work and risks breaking aluminium snaths. The blade should be kept parallel to and very slightly above the ground. The effort for moving the scythe comes from a twisting action of the upper body, utilising the strong muscles of the torso as well as shoulders. A long, narrow cut is best. The blade should be kept razor sharp with a butcher's steel.

---

[7] The scythe handle is called a snath.

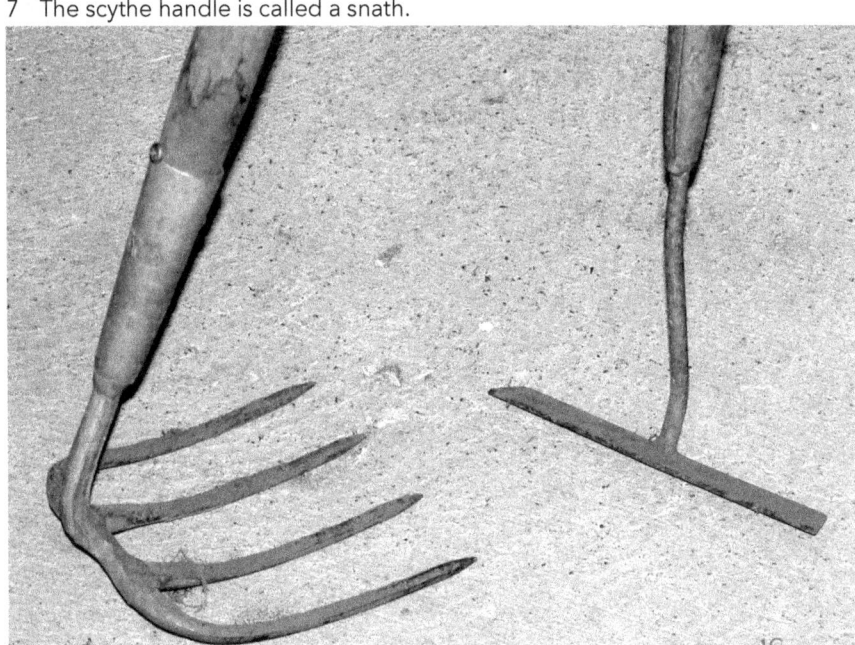

Left: The claw hoe used to till compost into the soil.
Right: The Coleman hoe that is so much easier to use than a draw hoe.

The polythene tunnel illustrated was my first venture into greenhouse production. It was mainly made with recycled material apart from the polythene. The rather large rectangular area in the lawn to the right hand side is not a shadow. This was a frosty morning in late April and that was where a crop of potatoes had been grown the year before. The extra biological activity was keeping the ground warmer than the undisturbed lawn. The shadecloth on top is to limit temperatures in the middle of the day.

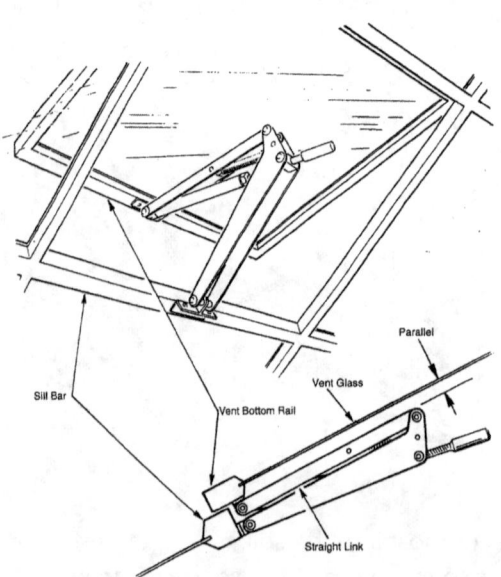

A Bayliss autovent illustrated on the left. They open up the vent by 300 mm (a foot) and can be adjusted to operate at any reasonable temperature.

Garden Tillers

WHILE A GARDEN TILLER (rotary hoe) may save labour, it is also very expensive and unlikely to return its cost to the home gardener. Tillers require the gardener to increase the area under cultivation compared to raised-bed gardening in order to produce the same amount of produce. This is not to say that they are not useful for initial preparation of the soil when beginning a garden, since this is the most labour intensive part of gardening. In use, they are remarkably tiring for a labour-saving device. Once the soil is in good heart hand tools are far less tiring. It takes about three years to achieve this happy state of affairs.

Tillers come in two forms. The smaller tillers are propelled by the action of the rotating blades in the soil. To control the forward motion, the user pushes on the handles and that increases the friction between the depth skid and the soil. They are very tiring to use on this account. The other sort has wheels driven by the motor independently of the rotating blades. The better ones also have wheel brakes or clutches to make steering easier. They are far more expensive than the blade driven hoes and much more powerful, especially those driven by a diesel motor. This sort also allows the attachment of implements other than the rotating hoe such as finger-mowers, trailers and ploughshares. They are in fact single-axle tractors and are widely used in what used to be called the Third World.

Attachments for single axle tractors include turn-wrest ploughs, potato-ridgers, disk cultivators, trailers, manure spreaders, mulch mowers, finger mowers, and sprayers. Their chief advantages over four wheel tractors include: no looking behind to monitor progress (very bad for the back), less soil compaction due to the lower weight, which in turn reduces the number of cultivations required, lower fuel consumption, lower capital cost and a smaller turning circle at the end of rows, thus using the land more efficiently. Their chief disadvantage is their slow speed but that's true of four wheel tractors, too as any motor car driver caught behind one will testify.

Rotary hoeing has one big disadvantage. Tilling at a constant depth compacts the soil at the boundary between the loosened soil and the untilled soil, creating a hard pan which plant roots find hard to penetrate. A hard pan slows water drainage, leading to water-logging. Used as hoes for mechanical weed control is justifiable, but their use

---

I have never had so many good ideas day after day as when I work in the garden.
   —John Erskine

as the main tillage implement tends to damage soil structure. As well as panning, they can pulverise the soil to create the semblance of good tilth. Rain and irrigation then caps the soil, necessitating further cultivation.

We used a small self-propelled rotary hoe during the initial preparation stage of the market garden. It self-destructed due to insufficient oil being distributed through the motor. It was a crappy design using a rotating finger to splash oil in the sump to where it was needed. The ground I was tilling was sloping and so the mechanism's efficiency was greatly reduced. Honda motors are much better designed to avoid this problem since they use an oil-pump.

A good friend lent us an ancient self-propelled Deutscher rotary hoe that did a much better job. After the rain stopped. That first October it rained every day except one! Once the garden was established, we only used hand tools for maintenance. The half an acre (0.2 Ha) of long raised garden beds aroused the curiosity of our farming neighbours. Not long after a heavy rain, one of them rushed into the garden to stop me tilling with the hoe. The soil should have been far too wet in his experience. When he saw how the excellent drainage of my system was working he exclaimed: "Aah! Now we know why you've made Jonathan's graveyard."

For the first two years on the farm, we were welcome to as much spoiled hay as we cared to take. When the neighbours saw the results we were getting from our novel ideas, the supply dried up. In those early years they were very sceptical of organic growing, but they were always respectful. As the years went by, they consulted with me more and more frequently and adopted many of the organic techniques I had demonstrated. In turn I learnt ever so much from them as their families had farmed there for more than a century.

One Christmas my neighbour Morph and I were at a party and the subject of grub[8] control came up. He asked me what an organic grower would use. I told him *Bacillus thuringiensis* (Dipel) but it was likely expensive compared to the usual chemical controls (organo-phosphates such as Malathion). It was available in commercial packages from our rural supplier. I'd purchased a 500 gm package and it was available by the kilo.

It must have been a year or two later when we ran across each other again and the subject came up. I asked Morph if he'd tried using Dipel. He was most apologetic and said he'd been meaning to thank me. He said rather than being more expensive than Malathion, it was

---

8   The larva of the Light Brown Apple Moth (LBAM or *Epiphyas postvittana*) a native "leaf-roller" moth.

a lot cheaper. The material cost was higher, but the real cost was his time on the tractor spraying. Dipel being a living organism would survive for several weeks whereas the effect of Malathion dropped off very quickly. He also noted that the effect of Dipel was immediate. The grubs stopped chewing because the stomach poison they ingested was present with the desiccated bacteria.

In the reverse direction I learnt about waterglass[9] for fungal disease control from Buck at the local pub. He said his missus used to "make it in the fireplace". Local orchardists had used it for apricot freckle control prior to the Second World War. When asked why they'd stopped using it, Buck said that "chemicals was cheaper". I noted that the reverse was now true and started my research into using waterglass for apple scab[10] (black spot) control.

---

9 Sodium silicate, used as glue in cardboard packaging, water-purification and prior to refrigeration, the preservation of eggs.

10 *Venturia inaequalis*. This disease was reputed to be impossible to control organically when Tasmanian horticultural researcher James Wong and I began our respective trials back in the late 1980s.

The twinwall polycarbonate greenhouse. It wasn't very high so that was increased by building a wooden frame to sit it on. The temperature at which the vents open is slightly different so only the left hand one is open on this cold day.

Extending the Growing Season

ONE OF THE SIMPLEST ways of obtaining better germination of seeds in the cool weather of spring is to cover the soil with a sheet of clear plastic. This warms the soil a few degrees, sufficient to allow the seeds the extra heat they need. Some sources say to use black plastic, but clear plastic works better. There is also now a translucent material made from cellulose that is placed over a growing crop. It accumulates only a little extra heat, but does not require the attention to ventilation that plastic tunnels do. It is placed loosely over, say a tomato crop, and the plants push the cloth up as they grow. It is cut where the plants are once the weather has warmed sufficiently and allowed to fall to the ground around the plants.

The most popular method of growing vegetables out of season is to use a greenhouse. Other devices, called cloches, are also used to concentrate the heat of sunlight. Traditionally, cloches were large glass vessels, open at the bottom and with a knob on top to make them easier to carry. These days, they are generally made out of polythene film stretched over some sort of framework. Greenhouses are often highly profitable, but also quite costly to build. There are a few things to bear in mind before indulging in the expense.

Glass, polythene and other plastics transmit different wavelengths of light at varying efficiencies. What this means is that the light reaching the plants has a different colour balance than ordinary, unfiltered sunlight. Research has shown that this results in differing amounts of various nutrients in the produce. Significantly, some important vitamins are present in measurably smaller amounts in greenhouse vegetables. Glass is a worse offender than polythene. Glass is opaque to several ultraviolet light frequencies as well as to infra-red. Polycarbonate appears to perform best in this regard and that's what I chose when I purchased a small greenhouse kit. It's approximately 3.5 m (12') square.

The polycarbonate is twin-wall; that is the panels consist of two sheets held apart somewhat in the manner of corrugated cardboard. This reduces heat loss overnight. It is in the nature of greenhouses to accumulate far more heat than is desirable during the day, so careful attention to ventilation is essential. Our greenhouse has automatic

---

Coffee. Garden. Coffee. Does a good morning need anything else?
 —Betsy Cañas Garmon

openers on two of the four roof vents. These use the expansion of thermal wax to open the vents and are adjusted to start working when the temperature inside the greenhouse reaches the desired level.

Before installing the openers, they are put in the fridge overnight. The following morning after fitting they are adjusted to commence opening when the appropriate temperature has been reached. They are available in different sizes to cope with different weights of ventilator and local wind conditions.

The greenhouse kit we purchased wasn't particularly cheap. The polycarbonate was high-quality from Germany because we wanted as long a lifespan as possible. Cheaper, recycled polycarbonate deteriorates quicker than we'd prefer. Nevertheless the kit wasn't as good as it could be. There were numerous small gaps where the structural members meet and they leaked air thus losing precious heat during the night. The most important improvement though was it didn't "rain" inside like the polythene tunnel did. The insulation provided by the polycarbonate panels in the new greenhouse didn't just mean the desirable higher overnight temperatures, there was no condensation either.

The original location for the greenhouse proved less than ideal and so it needed to be relocated after two years. Despite being quite large, it took remarkably little effort to move it to its new location. Greenhouses are generally used to grow a smaller range of vegetables than the open garden. This is because it is hard to justify the expense of growing low cost vegetables in them. The upshot is that it is difficult to arrange an effective, disease-preventing rotation. You can pasteurise the soil with steam, or change the soil every few seasons. Eliot Coleman showed us pictures of his greenhouse on skids. This allowed his very large greenhouse to be moved between two locations so that on alternate years the soil was exposed to the open air. This has the result of allowing better crop rotation and for the salts that build up in greenhouse soils to be washed away by rainfall.

A simpler approach is to use polythene tunnel cloches, about 1–1.2 metres (3–4') wide, to cover the growing crops in the garden. While these cannot be easily given supplementary heat, as can a conventional greenhouse, they do have several advantages. Their capital cost is much lower and they can be easily moved from place to place, not just from season to season, but during the season. An early crop of carrots can be forced in July/August, followed by sweet corn when

---

Half the interest of a garden is the constant exercise of the imagination.
  —Mrs CW Earle

the weather has warmed slightly and finally tomatoes somewhat later. You may choose a different series of crops, but the result is the earlier harvest of several crops rather than only the one. Also, the crops are covered with the device for such a short time, and removed totally before crop maturity. Consequently, the negative effects due to changes in light balance, referred to earlier, are lessened.

Other small scale devices for forcing include large plastic bottles with the bottom cut off, old car windows suspended on bricks, anything to accumulate that little extra heat around the plants. Bear in mind that many of these devices will accumulate more heat than is good for the plants, at least some of the time. The solution is to provide adequate ventilation during the hottest part of the day, closing them up as the day cools to retain heat overnight. Some people cover their polythene tunnels with old sacks on particularly cold nights, especially when frost threatens. Cold, frosty nights are generally windless so the sacks are not inclined to blow away. Rocks or cans of water inside the tunnel will also hold more heat than the soil. Water holds twice as much heat as rocks, per unit of volume. Painting the cans black will help them absorb more heat in the sun during the day and release it at night.

Greenhouses are often painted with whitewash to reduce heat gain during the hottest part of the year. Shade cloth makes a reusable alternative that does not wash off in the rain, an important point if you are in an area of high summer rainfall.

Polythene tunnels can be purchased or home-made. The frames of many of the commercial types are designed as half circles of metal that are shoved into the ground and the plastic is attached to this frame. In the illustration, you will see the details of a simple, home-made type that I have used. The prototypes were made from pine. This material was too light and they tended to blow away. Heavier timber solved this problem. They are propped up for ventilation, on the side away from the prevailing wind. Polythene becomes brittle in sunlight and when used on greenhouses lasts as little as five years. If you store your polythene tunnels out of direct sunlight when not in use, you should expect twice this lifespan and perhaps more.

The extra heat in a polythene tunnel or greenhouse means that far more attention needs to be paid to watering than in the open garden. Air circulation is poorer, so there is a significant increase in the chances of fungal disease. While more water needs to be used than

---

In almost every garden, the land is made better and so is the gardener.
  —Robert Rodale

Above: Tomato plants in the polythene tunnel greenhouse. The stakes are off-cuts of metal plasterboard lath.
Below: The new polycarbonate greenhouse. To the left of the greenhouse is a better design of cloche approximately 1 × 2 metres (3 × 6 ft).

in the open garden, try as far as possible to water with drip irrigation or flood. The idea here is to keep the plants' leaves dry because fungal disease is more prevalent in the high humidity greenhouse environment. The increased temperature also means a higher rate of metabolism in the plants. As a consequence, the humus in the soil is depleted at a much faster rate. To counter this, use about double the amount of compost that you would outdoors.

The closed environment of the greenhouse is an invitation to outbreaks of pests. The most common is the greenhouse whitefly. This relative of the aphid can be destroyed with liquid (potassium) soap (such as *Safer's*) or sticky traps. The traps consist of cardboard or plastic squares coloured yellow and coated with a non-drying, sticky substance. *Rentokil* bird repellent works fine. Place the traps no higher than the crop. The tiny parasitic wasps that predate on whitefly are caught with greatest frequency above the height of the crop.

Many vegetables need to be started in a warm place some time before they are planted out into the garden. A simple cold frame makes a good place to raise these seedlings. Even better is to provide supplementary heat. The old fashioned way is to use fresh horse manure in a pit underneath the cold frame as a source of bottom heat. Excavate the soil for a depth of 45–60 cm (1½–2') and replace all but the top 15 cm (6") with the manure. Trample it firmly or the heat will likely be excessive. The temperature will rise for some time before declining slowly.

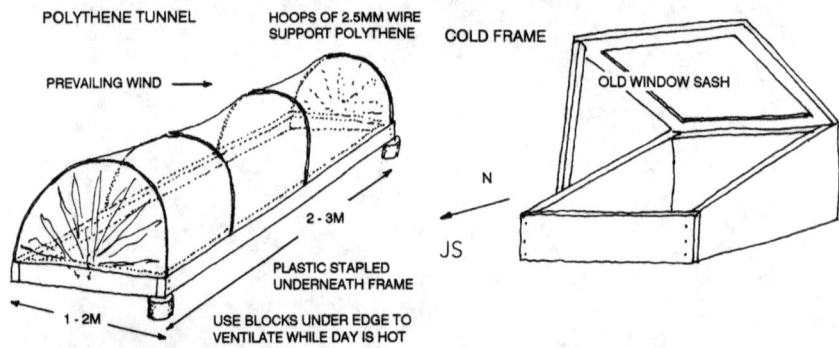

Left: Home-made tunnel cloche propped up on short rounds of timber poles. **Right:** Home-made cold frame.

But if each man could have his own house, a large garden to cultivate and healthy surroundings—then, I thought, there will be for them a better opportunity of a happy family life.
  —George Cadbury

The cold frame should be patterned along the lines of the drawing and face north.[1] Do not make the frame too deep, or the seedlings will not receive enough light. This makes them weak and spindly.

---
1 South in the northern hemisphere.

My friend Ian Cairns has loose covers that are removed during the hottest part of the day. The cover is prevented from blowing away by small concrete blocks he made with cast-in handles. His method also makes watering easier which is what he's doing here.

Weed Control

Mechanical

THERE ARE TWO MAIN METHODS of weeding: pulling the weeds out with your hands and disturbing the soil with a variety of hoe. The latter are far less time consuming than the former. There are many different types with advantages and disadvantages to each.

Tined Implements

THE TERM "HOE" CONJURES images of chopping blades for most people, but one of the most important weeding implements is the garden rake. Raking the soil before sowing a crop allows destruction of ever so many weeds while they are at the "white wire" stage. That is, the weed seeds have only just germinated and made only seed leaves. They are particularly easy to kill at this time and raking is a lot faster and less arduous than waiting until the true leaves have emerged.

Another implement designed to kill weeds at the white wire stage is the tickle weeder. This uses long stout wires that penetrate a few millimetres into the soil to kill the weeds, yet are flexible enough for the wires to be pushed aside by the established crop plants. I had one made many years ago. At that time, our garden soil was a heavy clay and silt. Except in ideal conditions, the tines didn't penetrate deeply enough. It's an implement much better suited to lighter soils.

The claw hoe you see illustrated on page 59 is more useful for tilling in compost and crop residues than it is for weed control.

Blade-type Hoes

THE MOST COMMON SORT of hoe was invented many thousands of years ago without undergoing any significant change. Then Vermont market gardener Eliot Coleman came along and rethought the process of hoeing. The wrist muscles used for the chopping motion of conventional hoeing are quite weak and the gardener tires quite quickly. The Coleman hoe also illustrated on page 59 uses an action more akin to sweeping the floor with a broom and this uses the gardener's shoulder muscles. These are much larger and stronger than those in the wrist, so hoeing with Coleman's design is much quicker and far less tiring.

The single greatest lesson the garden teaches is that our relationship to the planet need not be zero-sum, and that as long as the sun still shines and people still can plan and plant, think and do, we can, if we bother to try, find ways to provide for ourselves without diminishing the world.
—Michael Pollan

The blade of this hoe is drawn through the ground with the blade parallel to the surface and just below. Both edges of the blade are kept sharp so it can be worked either pushed or pulled. The gardening seminar that Eliot Coleman gave at my friends Ian and Caryl Cairns market garden came rather late in the writer's market gardening career. Had it come sooner we might have continued the market garden indefinitely!

Mulching

THE WORD MULCH comes from the old English word "melsc", meaning rotten hay. In modern parlance, it means any material used to cover the soil as a preventive to moisture loss and weed growth. The organic grower also prefers to use materials that will decompose and so add to the level of humus in the soil.

Rocks, hay, aluminium foil, plastic, leaves, straw, sawdust, gravel, compost, paper and grass clippings are all in common use. Each has its own advantages and disadvantages.

Rocks

ROCKS ARE FREQUENTLY used around trees. In an arid climate, water rising through the soil condenses on the underside of the rocks as they cool during the night time and take quite a while to warm up during the day. They mediate the soil temperature, protecting it from being too high or too low. In the cool climate garden, they have been

Potatoes growing in straw mulch.

used around warm climate plants, such as tomatoes and pumpkins. The heat they store during the day is released slowly at night, reducing the effect of the cool nights.

The disadvantage to rocks is that weeds grow readily between them. Since it is advantageous to use fairly big ones, moving them in order to remove weeds could prove an arduous task.

Hay

HAY IS A FEEDING MULCH. That is it contains nutrients that the plants need and they are released gradually as the plants need them. It is a relatively short-lived mulch on this account. Unfortunately, most hay contains an abundance of weed seeds. When used 30 cm (a foot or so) thick (fluffed up), this doesn't matter too much. If the layer is thin and/or compressed, then the weed seeds will germinate and take root in the mulch. Since many will be grass seeds, this could spell disaster.

We have used hay to grow potatoes successfully. The weeds where the potatoes are to grow are stomped flat, not cut. The seed potatoes are placed on the ground 30cm (12") or so apart each way. The hay is then teased apart and allowed to fall on the ground. When the hay is lightly compressed, it should be about 20–30 cm (8–12") thick. If the fertility of the soil is low, compost should be spread beforehand. The fluffing of the hay allows many seeds to fall through the hay to the ground where they will not be a nuisance until after the potatoes are harvested. The turf will by then have completely decomposed, needing much less effort to till. The potatoes all grow on the surface of the soil, protected by the hay from greening. Yields can be much higher than by the conventional method. When we first tried this technique many long years ago, we had a very wet spring. The yield for main-crop (Tasman) potatoes was well in excess of 4 kg (9lb) per plant spaced 38 cm (15") apart. In drier years, the yield was below that of conventional ridged potatoes. While the hay mulch conserves moisture well, it acts like a thatch roof that reduces the rate of water penetration. While this runoff is of little account when it is rainfall, the reduction in efficiency of irrigation water when it is in limited supply is a problem.

Success using this technique also depends upon hay quality. High quality hay, that is hay with a high protein content, will decompose quite rapidly and need topping up. Poor quality hay on the other

---

The secret of improved plant breeding, apart from scientific knowledge, is love.
    —Luther Burbank

hand will decompose much more slowly and a single application will likely be sufficient. This is certainly true when straw is substituted for hay.

Aluminium Foil
REFLECTIVE ALUMINIUM foil might seem a strange material to use, since it is quite expensive. It does have two great advantages however. It lasts a long time and it repels aphids. Apparently, the insects really dislike their habitat being brightly lit by reflected sunlight. Irrigation must be below the foil, so trickle irrigation is mandatory.

Cardboard
USED UNDER SAWDUST, this material suppresses many stout perennial weeds. We have used this on our garden paths in the past. It is also a useful mulch under young trees. We slope the cardboard inward and anchor it with rocks.

Grass Clippings
LAWNS ARE PROLIFIC producers of high quality material that needs some care in use. Put on too thickly, the grass can decompose to a fly-breeding, smelly mess and the surface a water repellent crust. Used thinly, grass clippings are a feeding mulch, being very high in nitrogen.

Leaves
LEAVES ARE WHAT NATURE uses to mulch trees and on that account have a lot to offer. Most of the nitrogen in them has been returned to the parent before leaf fall, so they are relatively long-lasting.

Paper
PAPER, PARTICULARLY NEWSPAPER, is available in large quantities for nothing. It blows away readily, and so needs covering with some other material that won't. Some people are concerned about the heavy metals used in coloured inks, so they do not use those sections of the newspaper that are printed in colour.

Plastic Film
PLASTIC, GENERALLY BLACK, is cheap, easy to apply and effective. Like aluminium foil, irrigation should be of the permanent trickle type. The main disadvantage of plastic is that it does not decompose to create nutrients; instead it falls apart under the influence of sunlight into unsightly, unecological shreds. It is somewhat more permanent

---

I grow plants for many reasons: to please my eye or to please my soul, to challenge the elements or to challenge my patience, for novelty or for nostalgia, but mostly for the joy in seeing them grow.
  —David Hobson

underneath an organic mulch of wood chips. Black plastic is also said to warm the soil, an advantage in the spring in a cool climate. However, clear plastic is far more effective. In any event, the reduction in gas exchange caused by its impermeable nature is undesirable.

Straw

STRAW IS ONE OF THE BEST mulches. It is light and easy to handle and relatively weed seed free. It is not as water repellent as hay. Being lower in nitrogen than hay, it is also a longer lasting mulch than those higher in nitrogen. Because we live a considerable distance from Tasmania's grain-growing districts, we purchase by the truckload every few years. This is where co-operation between gardeners comes in handy. Straw by the truckload is much cheaper than from the local hardware or rural supplier.

Sawdust

MANY WRITERS ABOUT gardening are somewhat unkind to sawdust. If the soil is at all lacking in fertility, then it will rob the soil of nitrogen while it decomposes. Composting before use solves the problem. It does tend to be somewhat water repellent, so do check beneath it following irrigation. Eucalypt sawdust contains growth inhibitors, which are readily decomposed by sprinkling with wood ashes or lime. My wife uses copious quantities of sawdust around the perennials in her flower and shrub garden. The coarser the sawdust, the longer lasting it is.

Be careful when using it over cardboard. Walking on it when the cardboard is very wet poses the danger of slipping and falling. The permanent footpaths in our vegetable garden were changed to sawdust over plastic weedmat on this account.

Weedmat

WEEDMAT CAN BE a useful way to prepare a garden bed following a crop. It excludes the sunlight that earthworms cannot tolerate and weeds need to grow. Laid loose on the ground it will of course blow away, so it needs to be weighed down. That illustrated below was how we used it when we had free-form garden beds. When we boxed the garden beds in, I made frames with the weedmat stretched over them. They are a little over a metre wide and two metres long (40" × 72"). This considerably lengthens the lifespan of the cloth. They're quite heavy which might seem a disadvantage, but it stops them flying away in the wind. Our farm isn't called Windfell for nothing!

My gardening neighbour Sonja using a wire-weeder (aka tickle-weeder) and a Coleman hoe.

Framed weedmat works much better than lying it loose and putting weights on it. The fabric lasts much longer.

The improved cloche is light enough to move easily, but heavy enough to not blow away.

The great men among the ancients understood very well how to reconcile manual labour with affairs of state, and thought it no lessening to their dignity to make the one the recreation to the other. That indeed which seems most generally to have employed and diverted their spare hours, was agriculture. Gideon among the Jews was taken from threshing, as well as Cincinnatus amongst the Romans from the plough, to command the armies of their countries… and, as I remember, Cyrus thought gardening so little beneath the dignity and grandeur of a throne, that he showed Xenophon a large field of fruit trees all of his own planting… Delving, planting, inoculating, or any the like profitable employments would be no less a diversion than any of the idle sports in fashion, if men could be brought to delight in them.
—John Locke

Pests and Diseases

IF THE APPROACH TAKEN by most agricultural scientists and books written by them were a guide, then pests and diseases are the result of a deficiency of pesticides and fungicides. Of course this is not so. Pests and diseases are almost always the result of plant stress. These stresses include:
- Nutritional deficiency
- Water shortage or excess
- Extremes of temperature
- Wind
- Chemical damage

Not a direct stress, but also important, is the decimation of predators caused by inappropriate pesticide use.

All of these factors are at least partially under the grower's control. If the stresses are avoided, or diminished, then many plant pests and diseases either simply do not occur, or fall below levels that justify control. The question then arises of the economic viability of avoiding plant stress versus using pesticides and fungicides. All of the stresses listed above decrease crop yields, not just through crop loss caused by the pests and diseases they encourage, but more directly.

Let's take spider mites as an example. You will probably have noticed that they are much worse in periods of hot, dry weather. Plants under stress from water deficiency are what spider mites prefer for food. Of course a plant that is suffering from water deficiency is also not going to yield as well as it would were it supplied with adequate levels of water. Is it more economical to allow crops to suffer water deficiency, thus reducing yields and use miticide, or to supply more water, thus increasing yields and eliminating the cost of the miticide?

One way to supply more water without the necessity of additional irrigation or rainfall is to improve the water-holding capacity of the soil and also the infiltration rate of water falling onto it. Increasing the humus level will accomplish this.[1] Humus is important in utilising water to its utmost. Water that runs off is not just wasted, but also carries valuable topsoil and nutrients away from the crop.

Another common pest, one that is almost ubiquitous, is the aphid. These little suckers probably cause more damage than any other insect. The first thing to consider is their nutritional needs. Aphids cannot digest complete protein; they require free amino acids (the chemical building-blocks that plants use to manufacture protein).

---
1 Soil with 4-5% humus can hold 100-150 mm of rainfall. Soil with 1.5-2% humus only 12-38 mm.

Excessive amounts of water-soluble nitrogenous fertiliser create the condition of high levels of free amino acids in plant sap, effectively a dinner invitation to aphids. Conversely, feeding protein to plants reduces the level of free amino acids and making the plants far less attractive to aphids.

Many insect problems are caused by monoculture; that is the growing of vast areas of a single crop. In a polyculture, such as a natural ecosystem, insects have the problem of finding the next plant to feed on. Not only is it likely to be some distance away, its odour, essential for insects to find it, is masked by the odours of all the other, undesirable as food plants in the insect's vicinity. Some of those other plants harbour predators on the insect, so it is more likely to be consumed in a polyculture than in a monoculture.

Insecticides, natural or synthetic, are a poor answer to the problem of excessive insect pests. This is because insect predators necessarily reproduce more slowly than their prey. If it were otherwise, then they would eat themselves into starvation. Most insecticides natural or synthetic kill pest and predator alike, so unless they are used continuously, they give pests an edge over predators. Unfortunately, continuous use is not just expensive, it leads to pesticide resistance. Then, when a pest outbreak occurs, there is one less insecticide in the arsenal to use.

Some predatory insects can be encouraged by providing attractive food sources. For instance, hover-flies whose larvae consume aphids, are attracted to flowering umbelliferous plants whose nectar they consume. Traditionally, Britain's hedgerows provided habitat for many predators on insects. It is no coincidence that the decline of hedgerows in Britain was accompanied by increasing pest problems. Many Australian farmers have discovered the virtues of leaving some bush to provide a predator reservoir, or reintroducing bush to their farms where similar problems are occurring.

Many birds are avid consumers of insects and insect larvae. In the New England Tableland, there has been an interesting study of a species of bird that consumes grass grubs. It is the female that consumes the grubs, while her male counterpart consumes the nectar of flowering gums. The females will not feed more than 150 metres (160 yards) or so from the males, so the maximum distance of pasture from trees needs to be no more than this distance for natural grub control. Growing belts of trees and shrubs on farms has other benefits

---

Insects and diseases are the symptoms of a failing crop, not the cause of it.
   —William Albrecht

apart from pest control. They keep groundwater under control and reduce evaporation of rainfall by reducing wind speed. Stock chilled by wind need to consume more feed to keep warm, so windbreaks can provide increased productivity. The shade from hot summer sun they provide reduces heat stress.

Insects that appear to be pests at first glance can also be seen in a quite different light. Japanese agricultural researcher, Masonabu Fukuoka, was trialling a pesticide to control a stem borer that afflicts rice. Much to his surprise, the first trial showed a yield decrease in the paddy treated to control the stem borer. A repeat trial also showed that killing the pest decreased rice yield. He came to the conclusion that plant density was the issue. The stem borer thinned the rice plants to produce a higher yield than when they were overcrowded. The funds for this research came from a pesticide manufacturer who forbade publication of this interesting result. After all, it would have reduced sales of their products! Fukuoka, having drawn a number of conclusions from his years of agricultural research, took up organic farming and put his then novel ideas into practice.[2]

When we look at a natural ecosystem, which by definition is devoid of synthetic pesticide and fungicide inputs, we see very little pestilence and disease. Note that there is not a complete absence, just a very low background level. Of course, such a system is not very productive from the human economic viewpoint, which is why we developed gardening and farming. What organic gardeners and farmers are attempting to do is integrate the control mechanisms of the natural system into our more productive gardening and farming systems. The problem here is that the more we improve productivity, the further removed from the natural ecosystem we get. Maintaining the mechanisms of the natural ecosystem alongside improved productivity requires considerable effort and expertise.

Peasant populations the world over have achieved this, yet we have been trained to perceive peasants as ignorant. Miguel Altieri, who coined the term agroecology, took a group of botanists and a group of peasants into a Central American forest. Each group was required to identify as many different plants as they could. The peasants won by a country mile.

The oxygen/ethylene cycle is a feedback mechanism for maintaining the balance between aerobic and anaerobic micro-organisms in living soils. Its existence was discovered in natural ecosystems and appears to be what the best organic practices can achieve.

---

2 His book *The One-Straw Revolution* is listed in the Recommended Reading at the end of this book.

Ethylene is a gas produced by ripening fruit and decomposing vegetables. When we wrap tomatoes to ripen them, we are capturing the ethylene and preventing its escape, thus accelerating the ripening process. Ripe bananas are prolific producers of ethylene, so this is why we put a banana in a bag with tomatoes to accelerate their ripening.

Disease organisms are organisms that decompose organic matter and can be looked at from two differing viewpoints. When they are attacking our living food crops they are a problem. When they are decomposing crop residues, they are converting them into food for the next generation of plants. What is it about our current agricultural practises that allow what are usually benign and/or useful organisms to run out of control? What keeps them in check under natural conditions and in organic farming? Let's look at what happens to organic matter under the systems of organic and conventional production.

Plants consist of mainly carbohydrate (starches, sugars, cellulose) and proteins. When plant matter is incorporated in the soil, it is decomposed by the soil micro-organisms. In the presence of oxygen, the carbohydrates are decomposed by fungi to generate carbon dioxide and water. The carbon dioxide displaces oxygen. These fungi are just as happy without oxygen, but now decompose the carbohydrate to alcohol and carbon dioxide. Under this condition of reduced oxygen, anaerobic bacteria come into the picture and decompose the carbohydrate to methane and ethylene. The ethylene suppresses the aerobic bacteria so they consume less oxygen. Consequently, oxygen levels increase, suppressing the anaerobic bacteria and the ethylene level then decreases. This allows the aerobic bacteria to revive and they transform the alcohol to acetic acid which dissolves nutrients from the silt. Proteins are decomposed to generate the free amino acids the bacteria require and some is converted to ammonia. Other aerobic bacteria convert ammonia to nitrate which is absorbed by plant roots. In the process these aerobic bacteria also convert oxygen to carbon dioxide. Plants convert carbon dioxide and water to carbohydrate, liberating oxygen. The plants then die to begin the cycle once more.

This is a grossly simplified view of what happens; there are over 2,000 different species of interacting micro-organisms in a healthy soil. However, this sketch is enough to give us some insight into

---

There are two spiritual dangers in not owning a farm. One is the danger of supposing that breakfast comes from the grocery, and the other that heat comes from the furnace.
— Aldo Leopold

what we can do to ensure these processes occur and what happens when our gardening practises interfere to create undesirable consequences. It illustrates the principle of the dynamics of a functioning ecosystem. Each micro-organism has a different purpose and also provides the checks and balances to maintain the system. As gardeners and farmers, we must either provide conditions that allow these processes to occur, or accept the consequences of hindering them.

What we call disease organisms are part of this ecosystem. They only become a problem when they are allowed to predominate over organisms that in a natural ecosystem keep them in check. Our gardening practices — tillage, fertilisers, pesticides, herbicides and fungicides — all affect the system. Nitrate fertilisers suppress ethylene production, the feedback mechanism for keeping fungal "diseases" in check. Many fungicides kill bacteria, and as we have seen, bacteria are an essential part of the soil ecosystem. The speed of gas diffusion is a function of soil structure. Insufficient air in the soil promotes anaerobic organisms and suppresses the aerobes. Excessive aeration leads to the rapid depletion of organic matter, the food source for micro-organisms. Herbicides are implicated in the chemical lock-up of trace elements needed by plants and micro-organisms for the formation of essential enzymes.

Does this mean we are advocating the immediate cessation of *all* synthetic inputs? Not at all! The establishment of a healthy soil ecosystem requires time and effort, which is a cost. The consequent reduced need for the supposedly necessary external inputs is a cost reduction. The difference between the two may be a profit, or a loss. For ecologically acceptable farming to be viable, a profit is essential. For a fortunate few farmers, the profit need not be monetary, but a sense of well-being engendered by not using toxic, or potentially toxic chemicals. The majority of farmers caught in the financial squeeze between high input costs and low returns must trial these techniques carefully to assess their economic viability.

When Lord Northbourne wrote about organic farming, he was writing about a closed system. A farm that's exporting food is manifestly not a closed system. Therefore the fertility elements in whatever is being exported, be it wool, milk, grain or vegetables, must be replaced. These can amount to surprisingly little. In thirty year duration soil fertilisation trials conducted in Germany and

---

Most people are more comfortable with old problems than with new solutions.
  —Anonymous

Switzerland, the researchers found that applying fertilisers to replace all the nutrients removed in the crops resulted in a 3% increase in yields. This increase did not produce enough income to pay for the fertilisers. Optimum results came from applying 50% of the nutrients removed. Since the crop residues in the trials were not returned to the soil, it should be apparent that even less fertiliser would be needed if the crop residues had not been exported off farm.

A frequently overlooked export of fertility is in the form of soil erosion. This led in the past to development of zero or low tillage systems that now rely on herbicide to kill weeds prior to sowing a crop. The most commonly used herbicide for this purpose has been glyphosate (Monsanto's *Roundup*) and it seems almost inevitable that it will like so many other agrochemicals be banned. Chemical ploughing as it's called will end and farmers will necessarily revert to mechanical ploughing and consequent increase in topsoil loss.

A further factor is change in external economic conditions. The origin of our current farm economy woes was the demand for abundant and above all cheap food. Having succeeded in supplying that demand, we now find that requirements are changing. The consumer is expecting abundant cheap food without the chemical inputs that made abundant cheap food possible in the first place. It has not yet occurred to consumers that they demand a decrease in the standard of living for farmers in order to maintain their own. We need to inform them of these and other issues vital to the well-being of farming and bring them into the decision-making process. In some European countries, where the negative impact of farm chemicals is more pressing, governments have subsidised the farm conversion process, or require the cost of damage caused by agricultural chemicals be included in the purchase price.

Another factor to take into account is the small, but growing number of consumers who are aware of the problems of agriculture and many of them are sympathetic to farmers' needs. They have shown a willingness to pay significant premiums for organically grown produce. Ian McLachlan, when he was shadow minister for primary industry, called for cooperation between farmers and the public in solving farmland degradation. Revegetation in the form of trees on farms is a cost most farmers can't meet unaided. McLachlan's suggestion was that farmers donate the 10–15% of the farm that needs

---

The greatest fine art of the future will be the making of a comfortable living from a small piece of land.
—Abraham Lincoln

to be in trees and the public provide the trees and labour. The farmer benefits from improved productivity and reduced land degradation. The public benefits in improved landscape, water quality and reduced costs of production.

In any event, while wholesale overnight change is impossible, small incremental changes are not only possible, but highly desirable. What works well on one farm does not necessarily work well on another. What may have a negative impact on profit in one location may have a positive impact at another. By proceeding slowly and sharing our experiences, we can expect to develop agricultural systems that are better and more organic than those predominating now, but they will not necessarily be identical to what we currently call organic. Current organic farming practice is not a panacea for all our agricultural problems. After all, as we discussed in the early part of this book, our pre-industrial agricultural practices were just as capable of massive land degradation as our currently much maligned conventional agriculture. It's just a lot quicker with tractors than with human or animal slaves. And it's worth noting that nature, unassisted, can take geological ages to repair the damage we can cause. If we expect to continue supporting a large human population on planet earth, we have a lot of hard decisions to make over the next few decades.

My involvement came at a time when the prevailing attitude was that organic technologies had little to nothing to offer, but a change in attitude could already be detected. An organic conference in Adelaide in 1990 brought together farmers both organic and conventional, as well as agricultural scientists. The atmosphere was one of co-operation and the speakers from overseas expressed surprise as they were more used to antagonism between two hostile camps.

While the mechanisms of pestilence and disease as we currently understand them appear complex, the solutions to them, generally speaking, are not. While we cannot create the diversity in farm ecosystems that occur in natural ones, any move towards increased diversity will help. An example from the Lockyer Valley in Queensland will illustrate. Broccoli growers adopted a number of strategies to

---

The first supermarket supposedly appeared on the American landscape in 1946. That is not very long ago. Until then, where was all the food? Dear folks, the food was in homes, gardens, local fields, and forests. It was near kitchens, near tables, near bedsides. It was in the pantry, the cellar, the backyard.
— Joel Salatin

reduce their pesticide inputs. One was the growing of a row of canola every few metres among the broccoli. The canola harbours a predator on one of the target pests and coincidentally provided some wind shelter, since it is taller growing than the broccoli. Another strategy was not growing broccoli when the market was flooded and prices so low that it wasn't really profitable to produce. This discontinuity created a feeding problem for the pests and reduced overall numbers. Dipel (Bacillus Thuringiensis) was adopted for some caterpillar control. This is a living organism, so it has the capacity to breed in the environment and infect subsequent generations of the target pest. Since the bacterial toxin is highly specific to caterpillars, only the target organism is killed. The last strategy was to rotate among a group of chemically unrelated pesticides to reduce the problems caused by target pests developing immunity to the spray, an invariable consequence of using a single pesticide continuously.

This illustrates a number of organic principles:
- An increase in biodiversity is likely to help reduce pest problems to manageable proportions;
- There are incidental benefits to the adopted strategies other than the main goal;
- Crop rotation provides pest control benefits;
- There are biological alternatives to chemical pesticides.

Disease Control Methods

AS HAS ALREADY BEEN INDICATED, organic methods are only rarely single-shot. Nearly always, a number of complementary strategies are adopted. One of the simplest ways to reduce fungal disease on leaves is to ensure that adequate sunlight and air movement occur in a crop. Most fungi thrive where there is high humidity and shade. Soil fungi are more troublesome where there is inadequate humus in the soil and poor drainage.

Another strategy almost universally adopted by organic growers is varietal selection. The more cynical organic producers believe that many modern crop varieties are promoted because of their dependence on synthetic inputs. While older varieties yield less under a conventional regime, they can outperform modern varieties in an organic context without the expensive necessity for spraying.

Nearly all fungal diseases are controlled by the stimulation of bacterial activity. Many bacteria appear to be competitors for the same ecological niches as fungi. Sclerotinia, botrytis, phytophthora, mildews and apple scab have all been controlled by applications of fish emulsion and a liquid extract made from compost. Increasing the pH of the leaf surface prevents spores of some fungal diseases from germinating. Examples of the use of this technique include control of botrytis and apple scab with applications of a 3% solution of sodium silicate, or a saturated solution of calcium hydroxide (Limil).[3] Also organically acceptable are most of the copper sprays, such as Bordeaux and Burgundy mixtures, sulphur, lime sulphur and sodium bicarbonate (baking soda). Where seed rotting is a problem, potassium permanganate (Condi's Crystals) is used as a seed dressing. Damping-off of seedlings is generally controlled by lightly dusting the soil surface with sifted wood ashes, or hydrated lime. Covering seeds with sand rather than seed raising mix also helps by improving drainage around the stem where the infection occurs. Mildews can be controlled with phosphorous acid.

Many diseases are a response to unbalanced plant nutrition. The emphasis on providing for the plants' nutritional requirements militates against most fungal diseases being a problem for the organic grower.

Research is currently under way to develop biological controls for a number of pest and disease problems. While this is laudable for its potential to reduce the level of synthetic pesticide use, this research is of more use to the users of these chemicals than to farmers whose management precludes their necessity.

Storage Diseases

ONE ASPECT OF ORGANIC production that is remarked upon with some frequency is the claim for longer shelf-life of organic produce. Opponents of organic production say that because organic produce is not protected with chemicals, it is more subject to bacterial and fungal contamination. Therefore, they say, organic produce is more hazardous to the health of the consumer than the chemical residues in conventionally grown produce. This is not borne out by scientific research.

Production Method and Storage Loss

	Conventional	Organic
Potatoes	24.5%	16.5%
Beetroot	59.8%	30.4%
Carrots	45.5%	34.5%

It is easy to see from results like these that yield could be lower in the paddock, but more produce be saleable at the all-important market end of the production process.

---

3 An incidental side-effect of this reported to me by Dr James Wong was that freshly hatched codling moth larvae fell from the fruit due to their inability to tolerate the high pH (~13) created by Limil or water-glass.

Dr Mike Walker of Watercress Valley Herbs trialled a range of fertiliser programs on parsley. Not only was the fully organic patch yielding better than the fully chemical, but the storage life of the organic herbs was way ahead. From his customers' point of view, it was more economical to purchase longer storing herbs at a higher price less frequently than to pay less and have to buy more frequently.

Pest Control Methods

HERE AGAIN THE ORGANIC grower has a multiple strategy of defence. The first line is to create as ecologically diverse an environment as possible. The few remaining pest problems can then be controlled by relatively innocuous materials. Aphids are controlled by soft soap (potassium stearate, *Safer's*), or garlic sprays, caterpillars by Bacillus Thuringiensis (Dipel), mites with potassium permanganate (Condi's Crystals) or salt solution, slugs and snails with metaldehyde baits (protected from consumption by birds, or other non-target animals) and codling moth by pheromone traps. Neem is an effective non-residual broad spectrum insecticide with pest-repellent and fungicidal properties.

The traditional organic broad spectrum insecticide, pyrethrum can be used against a wide variety of insect pests, including pear and cherry slug. Commercially, pyrethrum is almost always mixed with the synergist piperonyl butoxide. The organic standards demand that pyrethrum be used without this additive as it is a suspected carcinogen. It's not itself a pesticide but increases pyrethrum's kill rate. Other traditional broad spectrum natural materials include derris, rotenone and ryania some of which may no longer be obtainable.

One pest control method of note that is remarkably effective is making a spray from the target pest and spraying that on the crop. Caterpillars, slugs, or whatever, are finely minced in a food blender, strained and diluted. The required application rate per hectare is extremely low — around 1 kg (2 lb) of insects will treat 30 Ha (70 acres). The theories as to why this works abound, but to the best of my knowledge no work has been conducted to ascertain which is correct. They include spread of disease from the few organisms infected through the whole population, interference with breeding patterns due to spreading the

---

The only truly dependable production technologies are those that are sustainable over the long term. By that very definition, they must avoid erosion, pollution, environmental degradation, and resource waste. Any rational food-production system will emphasize the well-being of the soil-air-water biosphere, the creatures which inhabit it, and the human beings who depend upon it.

— Eliot Coleman

pests' pheromones onto all the plants in an area and repulsion due to the odour of deceased organisms of the same type.

Before predators brought the slugs under control in my market garden, I used a similar technique. Hand-picked slugs were killed by dehydration in dry sugar and the resultant slimy mess fermented for a few days in a warm place. The resultant even slimier mess was strained, diluted and sprinkled throughout the market garden area (approximately 0.4 ha or 1 acre). The slug population dropped to a tolerable level in a matter of a week or so and returned only briefly three years later. A repeat application saw no necessity for further control during a period of ten years. The effect also appeared spread beyond the area treated.

Much work is being conducted on alternative methods of pest control and most is in the field of biological control. Predators and diseases are being bred for many of the more recalcitrant pests. While this is commendable, it is important to realise that they are generally more expensive than chemical controls and often no more effective than providing a biologically diverse environment that produces its own predators and other checks on pest proliferation.

A relatively recent method involves saturating the environment with pheromones, the chemicals that insects use to find each other for the purposes of reproduction. As biotechnology increases its

efficiency, we will likely see the day when it is economical to spray a paddock with a pheromone to dramatically reduce the rate at which specific pests can reproduce. A compelling benefit of this approach is that it is highly specific to the target pest.

Snails and Slugs

SNAILS AND SLUGS WERE not included in the general pest control section, not because they are particularly difficult to control, but because of the wide range of strategies that have been adopted to control them. Also, their significance to the gardener appears to be greater than any other group of pests. The evidence for this is the amount of money that is spent on the baits generally used to control them. There are three sorts of baits, metaldehyde, iron sulphate and methiocarb. Metaldehyde breaks down to water and carbon dioxide, and so is relatively safe to use. However, it is also the most common cause of pet and wildlife poisoning. Some animals seem to develop a taste for them, so it is best to place them under cover where slugs can get them, but not birds and dogs. In any event, they fall apart and decompose less rapidly when protected. (See the chapter Recipes for Alternative Pesticides for a superior formulation). Iron sulphate is far less toxic to non-target species and so to be preferred.

Methiocarb baits are not recommended on any account. The active ingredient was used until recently as a bird repellent on fruit, particularly cherries. However, approval for this use has been withdrawn, due to its toxic nature. Strangely, it was still available for vegetable gardeners to contaminate their vegetables when I wrote this. Methiocarb is also an insecticide, and so it poisons those insects that help to control slug and snail populations.

When using baits, due to their relative ineffectiveness (the control rate is a mere 10%), many gardeners apply more than the recommended rate. This is counterproductive, as the active ingredient is a repellent when too concentrated, and the kill rate decreases. In my errant past, when using methiocarb, I noticed that my slugs' trails showed they carefully avoided going within about 10 mm of any bait. A letter to the manufacturer brought the response of a free trial pack of methiocarb spray, even though the manufacturer knew that it was not approved for use on my crops!

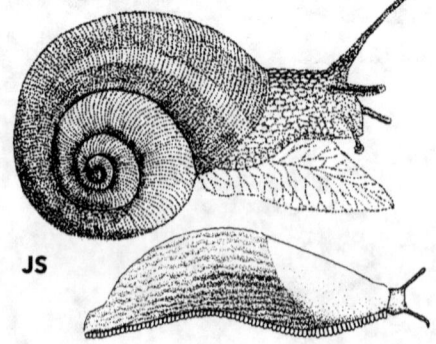

JS

Fortunately, there is a number of other strategies that will help to curb the predations of these slimy little creatures. One of the most effective is manual picking. The time to attack is dawn and dusk when conditions are moist and warm. Snails are readily crushed and are eagerly eaten by chooks if you are sensible enough to own them. Ducks are passionately fond of snails and in Indonesia you can see duck-herds who hire themselves out to farmers for the purpose of snail control. Apart from their heavy feet, ducks do little damage in the garden, unlike chooks that scratch and eat the greens.

Slugs are not so easy to pick up. The best implement is a long hat pin to spike several for transfer to a container that traditionally holds salt.[4] Some years ago, I was using this time-honoured method during a particularly wet, slug infested summer, and very pleased I was with the result. There were noticeably fewer upon each visit to the garden. However, I used sugar instead of salt, as I wanted to add their corpses to the liquid manure tub, and I was reluctant to pollute it with salt. Some weeks later, I noticed that there were almost no slugs in my garden at all, and commented to a neighbour about this. He was most surprised, his slug problems being on the increase. I subsequently discovered that fermenting slugs for a few days in water and sprinkling the resultant mess about the garden, is a Biodynamic technique for slug control. With one exception, all gardeners I have passed this on to have commented very favourably on its efficacy. Capture rates can be dramatically increased by laying down boards or similar in the garden, and looking under these from time to time.

Some gardeners report excellent results from barriers placed around plants. Sharp sand, sawdust and lime being favourites. The idea is to dramatically increase the amount of mucus the creature has to secrete to reach its food supply. I believe that softwood sawdust is best, though many books state that hardwood is the stuff to use. Apparently this was an error in translation from a Swedish book, perpetuated by writers ever since. One elaborate contraption I saw was an electric fence made by laying down lengths of rigid PVC pipe and suspending an electrified wire 5 mm above the earth return, which was in contact with the pipe. Rather than using a fence energiser, the builder employed a 12 volt car battery.

Another approach in common use is the so-called beer trap. This consists of a shallow saucer of stale beer (don't waste the good stuff), set level with the ground. Apparently home brew is much preferred by the obviously epicurean slugs. They are said to crawl in and

---
4 Or if you like a challenge you could try chopsticks.

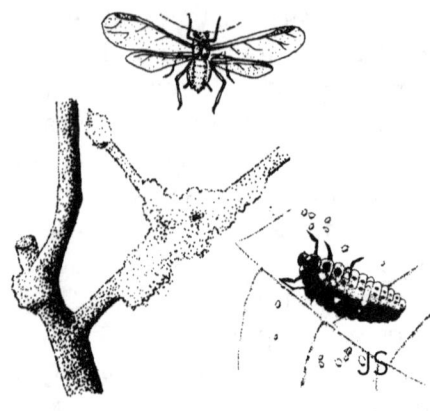

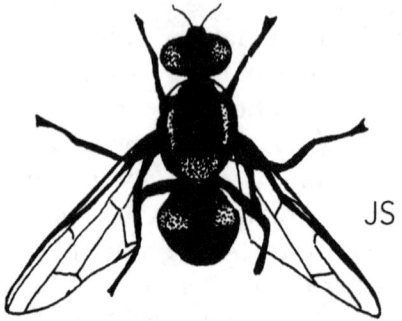

Above: The individual at the top is a whitefly. Below that are woolly aphids on an apple twig and a ladybird larva.
Below: Greenhouse whitefly, another member of the genera aphis. Commonly found on French beans in the open garden, like all aphids it can be controlled by ladybirds, or soap solution.

Above: Fruit fly, a common pest in tropical and sub-tropical Australia.
Below: European wasp. Loathed by humans, but a ferocious predator on fellow insects including many pests. They are especially fond of blowflies.

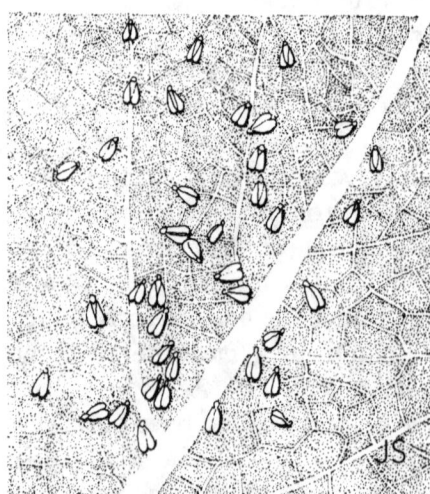

Below: Frogs are a rapidly disappearing predator on insect pests, apparently from fungal diseases.

drown. A mixture of Vegemite and water is also said to be effective, the attractant being the yeast. One disadvantage to this technique is that rain or irrigation rapidly dilutes the beer or substitute. One imagines the radius of effectiveness, and consequent kill rate would be similar to one commercial bait, the attractant being bran.

Where large areas are concerned, a dilute solution of ammonia, copper sulphate or vinegar appears to be effective. It stimulates the production of excessive amounts of mucus, dehydrating them. It would seem wisest to use this approach on the morning of a day you know is likely to be clear and sunny, to enhance its effectiveness. Frequent use of these materials is probably unwise, particularly copper sulphate. Copper build up in the soil decimates earthworm populations.

No-dig gardens seem to have greater slug problems than those gardeners who clean-cultivate. Three passes of the rotary hoe are said to kill around 75% of the slug population. The no-dig gardeners' rejoinder is that cultivation also devastates the population of soil dwelling predators, carnivorous slugs, and centipedes. Centipedes appear to eat the eggs, rather than the slugs. Slugs prefer weedy, roughly cultivated soil with lots of places where they can avoid the sun's dehydrating effects, so creating a fine tilth and keeping weeds well-controlled helps minimise the problem.

It is worth bearing in mind that one grey field slug could have 90,000 grandchildren and 27,000,000 great grandchildren, so there is something keeping the population under control other than starvation. Once again, the general advice is to encourage as much ecological diversity as possible. The more ecological niches there are, the smaller the population occupying any single niche.

Recipes for Alternative Pesticides

WHILE ORGANIC GROWERS PREFER to use no pesticides, there are times when it is a choice between no crop or using some form of poison. Some of these, such as Bacillus thuringiensis, are specific to a particular organism and harmless to man and pets. Many are very toxic and should be used with caution. The reason these latter materials have found favour with organic growers is that they break down to non-toxic materials in the garden. Until they have broken down, exercise caution with these materials.

A man has made at least a start on discovering the meaning of human life when he plants shade trees under which he knows full well he will never sit.
  —D Elton Trueblood

Borax
WHERE ANTS AND COCKROACHES are a problem, mix equal parts of borax and icing sugar. Place in shallow containers in the cupboards where these pests are a problem. This material is very poisonous, so take precautions to keep away from children.

Bordeaux Mixture
THIS IS THE COPPER SPRAY used to prevent fungal disease of fruit trees and also blight in potatoes. It must be used fresh.

Dissolve 100 gm of copper sulphate (bluestone) in 5 litres of water overnight (2½ oz per US gallon).

Mix 140 gm of slaked lime in 5 litres of water and add to the copper sulphate solution (4 oz per US gallon). Stir vigorously and use straight away. Agitate during use.

Bracken
USEFUL APHIS KILLER. Toxic to most insects.

Steep 25 gm (1 oz) dried bracken fronds in 1 litre (1 quart) of water for 24 hours. Strain and use 1 ml per litre (0.1 oz per gallon).

Bug Juice
IN THE OCTOBER 1976 ISSUE of the Rodale *Organic Gardening and Farming* magazine reported the use of "bug juice" by a commercial farmer. He reported a cost saving of $5,000 per annum on his chemical bills and that after three years no further applications were required.

1 kg (2 lb) of insects will treat 30 Ha (80 acres).

Liquefy the bugs (slugs, caterpillars etc) in a blender with about a third of the volume of water. Strain and use 4–5 ml (0.14–0.17 oz) per 100 litres (26 US gal) of water.

Fermenting slugs after killing them with dry sugar also works. The dehydrated slugs are put in a container of water in a warm place for a few days, strained, diluted and sprinkled around the garden.

Various theories abound as to why this works: natural pathogens, attraction of predators, confusion of insect communication systems (they rely a lot on pheromones which are detected by smell).

Chamomile
THIS MEDICINAL HERB is used to control fungal diseases, especially mildews. Use the generic recipe under Herbal Sprays.

I like gardening — it's a place where I find myself when I need to lose myself.
   —Alice Sebold

Coriander
A 2% EMULSION OF Oil of Coriander is an effective control for red spider mites. To make an emulsion, use a little soft soap (potassium soap, *Clensel*, *Safers* etc) in the water.

Dipel
DIPEL IS THE BRAND NAME of Bacillus Thuringiensis. In some places it is also available as *Thuricide*. It is the dehydrated bacterium mixed with a little of the toxin (a stomach poison) that you are purchasing, plus plenty of inert filler if it is a home gardeners pack. It is specific to caterpillars and completely harmless to other living things. It is expensive and can be made to go further quite cheaply. Mix a little of the powder in lukewarm milk and allow to stand for 24 hours. The bacteria multiply and a little of the mixture can be used to start a new batch. The effectiveness will probably decline over time due to genetic drift, necessitating the start of a new batch from the pure culture.

Remember that Dipel, being a living organism, prefers cool, moist conditions in the garden to work best.

Derris (Rotenone)
THIS IS A LONGER LASTING insecticide than most organic sprays persisting for 48 hours rather than 24. It kills fish as well as most insects (including predators), so use it with care.

25 gm (1 oz) derris powder
50 gm (2 oz) soft soap
10 litres (2½ US gal) water

Dissolve soap in half of the water and derris in the other half. Combine the two solutions and use.

Garlic
THIS IS USED AS an insecticide and fungal control.

100 gm (3½ oz) minced garlic
10 ml (0.4 oz) mineral oil
500 ml (1¾ cups) water
50 ml (2 oz) soft soap

Soak the garlic in the mineral oil for 2 days. Add the water and soap. Strain and store in a glass container. Use a 1% solution (1 part concentrate to 99 parts water).

Herbal Sprays
MANY HERBS CAN BE USED as insecticides and insect repellents. The formula to use is to just cover the fresh herbs with boiling water. Steep for 30 minutes. Strain and dilute with an equal quantity of water. As the potency of the herbs will vary depending on seasonal and other

conditions, exact recipes are not possible. The addition of soft soap as a wetting agent will increase the effectiveness of these materials.

Wormwood, southernwood, tansy, chamomile, rhubarb leaves, ragwort, potato leaves and lantana are all worth trying.

Milk

MOSAIC VIRUS DISEASE can be controlled with milk. Smokers should dip their fingers in milk before handling tomatoes and cucumbers.

Use equal parts of whole milk and water as a spray.

Rat Poison

A VERY EFFECTIVE RAT POISON, until the rats learn to exercise caution, which they invariably do, is as follows:

1 part cement
1 part flour
A few jelly (gelatine) crystals

The cement sets in their stomachs preventing further feeding. Another reputed sure-fire rat killer is Coca Cola. The rats bloat and die. Unfortunately it stops working when it goes flat.

Slug and Snail Baits

THE GREEN SLUG BAITS contain metaldehyde. This material breaks down to water and carbon dioxide, but until it does, is very toxic and attractive to dogs, cats and birds. The ingredients are bran and metaldehyde, so they fall to pieces quite readily in the rain. A more effective formula is:

1 part metaldehyde
1 part Limil (builders' lime/calcium hydroxide)
1 part cement
3 parts bran

This mixture lasts for a very long time indeed. Put the baits underneath boards, rocks etc where the slugs hide at night.

Soap

SOAP SOLUTION IS an effective aphid killer. The best to use is potassium soap, also known as soft soap. Being a liquid, it is easier to dissolve than bar soap. A commonly available brand available from most nurseries is *Safer's*. Use 100 ml per 2.5 litres of water.

I see in activism a kind of futility. The real power is in doing."
— Sylvia Davatz

Irrigation

Watering the garden
When to water and how much

MANY GARDEN FAILURES are due to incorrect watering, either using too much, or too little water. Too much leads to insufficient air in the soil and rotting of plant roots, called "wet feet". Too little water reduces yields and, with certain plants, leads to premature running to seed, called "bolting". Lettuces become noticeably bitter. Some perennial plants, in particular certain trees, will not respond to water applied after they have reached the stage of water stress. They will wait until the following season. Basically, leafy vegetables require as constant a supply of water as possible. Plants grown for their seeds or fruits should be watered less frequently and more deeply or they will produce foliage at the expense of fruit.

An example of the effects of watering is the humble potato. Watering prior to flowering has no noticeable effect. Watering at flowering results in an increase in the number of tubers. Watering after petal fall increases the size of the tubers. Another is peas. Watering prior to flowering can decrease yield, watering after petal fall increases yield.

Water should be applied at the appropriate time of day. Watering during the heat of the day stresses plants and can cause heat scorch due to concentration of the sun's rays by beads of water. The leaf pores that allow the plant to transpire moisture are stimulated to open by irrigation. If it is hot and/or windy, it may result in more moisture being lost than is being applied! Plant moisture use is greatest during the night, so watering in the late afternoon and early evening may be best. Where humidity and fungal disease is a problem, then watering in the morning is better.

Frequency of water application and depth of watering depend on the type of soil you have and the humus content. Well-composted soil holds more water than the same soil with insufficient compost. Sandy soil holds less water than clay, so it needs more frequent and lighter applications. Because of the faster drainage of sandy soil, over-watering is less critical than with clay soil.

Soap wasn't invented until the Romans, who also invented interesting sex. (Since my editor informs me that a gardening book is not a proper venue for discussions of interesting sex, I will go into this topic in more detail when I write my private memoirs, 'A Petunia Named Desire').
— Cassandra Danz

Sand poses an additional problem. Sand particles have a wax-like surface that repels water so irrigation water tends to have difficulty soaking in. The addition of a small amount of biodegradable detergent into the irrigation system can as much as double the efficiency of irrigation where this is a problem.

Watering too frequently leads to excessive root development near the soil surface. Under these conditions, plants become very sensitive to water shortage. Deeper, less frequent application promotes deeper rooting into soil that remains moist for longer. Sandy soil should be watered about twice a week, loamy soil about once a week and clay soil about once every ten days. The amount of water applied depends on prevailing weather conditions. Windy weather reduces soil moisture levels, and hot weather can too. Cool, still conditions reduce watering needs. The crops' level of development must also be considered. At the seedling stage, plant roots are very shallow and prone to stress from lack of adequate moisture. Somewhat later, there is little leaf area to transpire water and the plants needs are not great. When the crop has developed fully, the large leaf area transpires a lot of moisture leading to increased water loss from the soil.

The ABC Country Hour broadcasts the evapotranspiration results for many localities once a week. This is the water loss from open water in millimetres. It can be used to calculate the amount of water needed by your crops. Since rainfall can be quite localised, you will need a rain gauge to calculate the difference in rainfall between your location and that of the recording station, so you can adjust the evapotranspiration estimate.

To measure the rate of water application of your sprinklers, place three flat bottomed, straight sided jars or cans, next to a sprinkler, half way to its limit and near the limit of its throw. Turn it on for ten minutes and measure the depth of water in each of the three vessels. Add the three figures together and divide by three to get the average and divide by ten. This is the amount of water you are applying in millimetres per minute.

Odd as I am sure it will appear to some, I can think of no better form of personal involvement in the cure of the environment than that of gardening. A person who is growing a garden, if he is growing it organically, is improving a piece of the world. He is producing something to eat, which makes him somewhat independent of the grocery business, but he is also enlarging, for himself, the meaning of food and the pleasure of eating.
—Wendell Berry

Methods of Applying Water

THERE IS A WIDE VARIETY of methods of irrigating. The simplest is a bucket; the most complex (and expensive) is computer-controlled trickle irrigation. One consideration to take into account when deciding the most appropriate for you, is the nature of the soil. Sprinklers lead to considerable water wastage by evaporation and can lead to a concentration of salts from the water at the soil surface. Overhead watering can compact sensitive soils, creating a crust that seedlings find difficult to break and inhibits gas exchange between the soil and atmosphere. Flood irrigation, a sound alternative where crusting is a problem, is not possible if there is no clay sub soil. Trickle irrigation only suits widely spaced plants (you wouldn't use it for carrots, for instance), but uses the least water. Hand-held hoses allow tailoring the application to individual crop needs, but requires a lot of labour.

In my own rather large garden, a variety of irrigation methods are used. Overall watering is accomplished by butterfly sprinklers. The orifice in these is quite wide, so the water needs no filtration, an important consideration with gravity fed water from a not very high runoff dam. Filters dramatically decrease the rate of water flow and require regular cleaning. Crops that need more than the base amount of water are watered by hand held hose. The rose has a lot of tiny holes that allows a good flow of very small droplets, minimising soil compaction. Transplants are watered in by watering can. The fruit trees' needs are met by trickle irrigation. Some potatoes are grown outside the irrigated garden area and are watered by flood irrigation between the ridges. This minimises the risk of blight caused by wet leaves.

While mulching reduces water loss from the soil, reducing irrigation needs, some mulches reduce the effectiveness of watering. Hay and sawdust mulches have a marked tendency to shed water, so it is worth considering flood irrigation where these materials are used. Alternatively, trickle tape, or soaker hose can be put down prior to mulching.

Some Individual Crops

CELERY IS MOST AFFECTED by water shortage, closely followed by lettuce. Potatoes, celery, tomatoes, cucumbers, pumpkins, squash and peas are prone to fungal disease caused by wet leaves. Leeks and garlic have a much higher water requirement than their cousin, onions. Irregular water supply cracks cherries and carrots and causes blossom-end rot in tomatoes. Radishes need a constant supply of moisture or they become too strongly flavoured and woody. During one drought I ran out of water for the garden. Despite the lack of irrigation or significant rain from January until March, the garden survived thanks to the high humus level in the soil. The pumpkins failed to achieve their usual size, but they never tasted so good before or since.

Crop	Total Water Requirement	Interval
Peas (early)	35–50 mm 1½–2"	2–3 waterings between flowering and pod swell.
Peas (mid to late)	50–90 mm 2–3½"	
Beans (early)	100 mm 4"	3 applications
Beans (late)	150 mm 6"	5 applications
Onions	150 mm 6"	4–5 applications
Carrots	150–180 mm 6–7"	5–6 applications
Brassicas (early)	140 mm 5½"	4 applications
Brassicas (late)	80 mm 3"	2–3 applications
Potatoes	180–200 mm 7–8"	4 applications

Trickle irrigation

TRICKLE, OR DRIP IRRIGATION uses low-pressure, well-filtered water and a permanent network of small diameter polythene pipe. There is a wide variety of outlets to choose from. The cheapest is micro tube, also called spaghetti tube. The length of the tube determines the flow rate, which is generally adjusted to between two and four litres per hour. Moulded drippers are also available. There are two main sorts, pressure-compensating and non-pressure-compensating.

It is only our limited time frame that creates the whole "natives versus exotics" controversy. Wind animals, sea currents, and continental drift have always dispersed species into new environments... The planet has been awash in surging, swarming species movement since life began. The fact that it is not one great homogeneous tangled weed lot is persuasive testimony to the fact that intact ecosystems are very difficult to invade.
— Toby Hemenway

The latter are only suitable on short runs, or where the irrigation line slopes downward toward the end of the run. Micro sprays are available with a variety of spray patterns and outlet rates (50–90 litres or 13–24 US gallons per hour). They water an area of about 1 metre (3') diameter.

This method of irrigation has the advantage in orchards of not watering the weeds or sod between the trees. Labour is minimised and poorer quality (salt content) water can be used. A big disadvantage is the need to monitor the drippers closely, as they clog easily. Some drippers are more easily cleaned than others, so it is best to spend the few extra cents per dripper required to buy the better sort. In a drought, drip irrigation may not be sufficient to meet the trees' water needs. The trees respond to drip irrigation by creating a cluster of roots where the water enters the soil. This leads to uneven root development limiting the trees' capacity to exploit soil nutrients. Where the early part of the season is wet, followed by a prolonged period of no rain, the tree responds quite slowly to the change from overall soil moisture to the concentrated area around the dripper. Capital cost is the highest for this method of watering.

Fertigation

AN IMPORTANT PART of our pest and disease control was regular (fortnightly) applications of seaweed and fish emulsion as a very dilute foliar spray. Taking a leaf from conventional horticulture, I improvised a fertiliser injection system to add these to the irrigation water. I purchased a relatively inexpensive water filter, discarded the filter cartridge and set it up with a bypass so it could be switched between allowing the contents to be mixed with the irrigation water or not. Fish emulsion or seaweed emulsion could then be placed into the filter housing rather than needing to be sprayed onto the crops separately.

"Leaky" Pipe

There are several sorts of "leaky" pipe that supposedly ooze water through the porous pipe walls. I tried two sorts, but either due to impurities (clay particles) clogging them, or lack of sufficient pressure when filtered, neither worked sufficiently well to justify their continued use.

Only some things are worth doing well. Most things that are worth doing are only worth doing sloppily. Many things aren't worth doing at all. Anything not worth doing at all is certainly not worth doing well.
— Carol Deppe

Individual Crops

Broccoli, Brussels Sprouts, Cabbages and Cauliflowers

ALL OF THESE VERY DIFFERENT vegetables are merely different strains of one, *Brassica olereaca*, bred for the leaves, buds, or flower buds as the desired edible portion. That should not stop you eating the leaves of cauliflower, broccoli or Brussels sprouts, they too are very tasty and nutritious.

One thing the cabbage tribe all have in common is susceptibility to destruction by the caterpillars of the cabbage moth and the cabbage white butterfly. There is a bewildering variety of ingenious approaches to the problem, though Dipel a bacterial spray specific to caterpillars is probably the convenient control. Juicing the grubs in a blender, diluting and sieving the mixture to make a spray can be just as effective. A mere 35 gm (1.2 oz) of caterpillars is enough to treat a hectare (2.5 acres), though the accuracy required for toxic chemicals is not called for. Both derris dust and pyrethrum kill predators, so neither is recommended except as a last resort. Backyarders can use pantyhose to enclose the young plant and keep the caterpillars out of smaller varieties of cabbage and cauliflower. The hose stretches as the plant grows. I have seen tomato prunings, inverted eggshells on sticks and white paper cut-outs of butterflies placed on the crop as deterrents. Growing celery, dill, beetroot, or onions as companion plants is also popular. On a very small scale, hand-picking works well for cabbages and cauliflowers, though not for broccoli. The grubs hide in the loose head of flower buds.

On page 69 you will see Ian Cairns' floating row covers that keep butterflies at bay as well as providing a warmer growing environment. The covers are easily removed for weed control and watering. Note the concrete blocks with inset handles for preventing the covers from blowing away.

Beyond the harm to local wildlife, any chemicals we used in our garden might end up polluting our well, or run off the property. In a heavy rainstorm, this runoff may end up in nearby Beaver Creek, a tributary to the Brandywine Creek, which runs into the Delaware River, which flows into the Atlantic Ocean. These kinds of direct connections with the outside world exist in every garden, which is why I think we should always aim, in our gardening practices, to do the least harm and the greatest good.

— David L. Culp

Cutworms, the larvae of a nocturnal moth (*Noctuidae*) will chew off young brassica seedlings leaving the top of the plant lying on the ground adjacent to the stub of the stalk. We avoid this by planting out our brassica seedlings inside short (75–100 mm, or 3–4") offcuts of PVC drainage pipe about 75 mm (3") in diameter. We also use short lengths of plastic pipe of the same diameter obtained from a carpet layer. Prior to this we used short lengths of milk carton, but while the paper decomposes, the plastic film on it doesn't. This barrier also foils snails and slugs. The pipe can either be left in place, or removed before the plant becomes too big. By the time the plant is about 150 mm (6") high, it's too big to be killed by a cutworm.

Aphids can also be a problem, and make Brussels sprouts especially difficult to grow successfully. They attack just as their main predators (ladybirds) go to sleep for the winter. Aphids have a waxy coating to stop them from drowning in the rain. A solution of soft soap, such as *Safer's* wets them, so they drown. Soft soap is potassium stearate which is biodegradable. Apart from 100% biodegradable detergents, such as Amway Liquid Organic Cleanser (LOC), most ordinary detergents are not as good as soft soap. Also in many jurisdictions it is against the law to use any substance that has not been registered as a pesticide to control a pest. While it's unlikely that police

Young cauliflower showing PVC pipe off-cut protecting it from cutworms and slugs. The mulch is pea-straw.

will arrest the home vegetable gardener for killing aphids with the washing-up water, organic gardeners have experienced problems in the past.

Back in the 1980s, Toshi Knell a New South Wales seller of organically acceptable pesticides (garlic and herbal sprays), was charged with committing an offence. I approached the Minister for Agriculture and the appropriate officer at the Department of Primary Industry in Tasmania and asked how we could avoid such a situation arising in regard to commercial organic production here. Both assured me that the situation would not arise as they were fully behind promoting Tasmania's clean and green image.

Broad spectrum insecticides, such as pyrethrum, are not recommended for the reasons mentioned above. Aphis repellents include companion planting of calendula (English marigold), celery, garlic and hedgerows of southernwood or wormwood. The larvae of hover flies are avid consumers of aphis and are attracted by umbelliferous flowers such as those of parsley and carrot that have shallow nectar sources that are the food source for the adults.

All brassicas, including turnips and swedes, are subject to a nasty disease called club root, or finger and toe. The club root organism is present in most garden soils, but only becomes problematic when the cabbage tribe are grown in the same ground, year after year. If it is allowed to take hold, it is five years or more until you can safely grow brassicas in that ground again. To avoid this state of affairs, brassicas must be grown on a minimum of a three year rotation with unrelated crops. The only members of the family to which this does

not apply are the humble radish and mustard grown as a green manure. They are in the ground so briefly the disease doesn't have time to develop. Growing onion tribe immediately before brassicas in the rotation is supposed to assist, as does placing a piece of rhubarb stem in the hole brassica seedlings are transplanted into.

Like all crops that are usually transplanted, brassicas will do much better when sown direct. One of the main reasons for transplanting them is that they can go in immediately after a spring or summer crop has finished. Sowing them in a seedbed or flats, gains a little extra time for growing the preceding crop in the garden. Another reason for transplanting brassicas is that it makes caterpillars easier to control when the plants are concentrated in a small area. Press the soil well around brassicas transplants, they prefer firm soil, and water-in well to eliminate air pockets around their roots. A little seaweed solution and fish emulsion greatly reduce transplant shock so it's well-worth including a splash of each in the watering can.

Cabbages

THERE ARE MANY SORTS of cabbage, savoys, ball heads, conical and red cabbage are the main types. Chinese cabbage is not a cabbage, but a distant relation called *brassica pekinensis*.

The crinkly-leaved savoys are autumn and winter maturing, so they are sown in summer. They tend to be slow to bolt and hold well into the winter or even spring in very cold districts. They are pale green rather than white inside and to my mind have the best flavour of any cabbage. There used to be a couple of hundred varieties of savoys at the turn of the 19th century and they were listed in seed catalogues separately to the other cabbages. These days there seem only to be two, *Savoy King* (a hybrid) and *Vertus* available commercially. We used to save our own seed of *Carters* savoy, but sadly every seedling of the last lot of seed we saved were accidentally destroyed. I was gutted.

The conical cabbages are also known as spring cabbages and are sown in autumn and spring. They also have excellent flavour and are quicker-maturing than savoys. The most common is *Sugar Loaf*, which dates from the early nineteenth century.

The ball-head types are now the most common and nearly all are hybrids. Of the open-pollinated varieties, *Vanguard*, and *Velocity* are

---

We gardeners are healthy, joyous, natural creatures. We are practical, patient, optimistic. We declare our optimism every year, every season, with every act of planting.
— Carol Deppe

both medium size and quick-maturing types. Their flavour is superior to the hybrids, though not as fine as the conical spring cabbages or savoys. They are generally sown in spring and early summer.

AS

Red cabbage is a tougher, but tastier ball head type. It requires about twice the cooking time of conventional cabbage to become tender.

Cabbages need plenty of space to develop. Planted too close, they will form loose, rather than solid hearts. Allow 60 cm (24") between rows and 45 cm (18") between plants, or 45 cm (18") each way.

Cauliflowers

CAULIFLOWERS ARE THE GREEDIEST feeders of all the brassicas. They also have a requirement for molybdenum at the seedling stage, which can be supplied with seaweed, or seaweed meal, either in the soil or the compost. Sprays of liquid seaweed are also beneficial in this regard. Cauliflowers afflicted by molybdenum deficiency have narrow,

---

Orwell wrote easily and well about small humane pursuits, such as bird watching, gardening and cooking, and did not despise popular pleasures like pubs and vulgar seaside resorts. In many ways, his investigations into ordinary life and activity prefigure what we now call cultural studies.
    — Christopher Hitchens

strap-like leaves, giving the disease its names whip-tail or strap-leaf. The size of the curd is also greatly diminished. The molybdenum needs to be available in the first couple of weeks following seedling emergence for the creation of an essential enzyme. Afterwards, no amount of molybdenum will help. If you know there is insufficient in the soil, or seed-raising mix, then you can apply a foliar spray of sodium molybdate.

Most cauliflower varieties are very particular about sowing time. They are sown in spring through autumn and the variety determines the date of harvest. *Paleleaf*, or *Paleface* has the widest range of suitable sowing times, though it is also one of the slowest maturing. In our opinion it's also the best tasting as well as the most adaptable. There are many strains of this variety and they are identified by numbers. If you see cauliflower seed identified only by number, you will know it's a strain of this most excellent variety.

The growth of the curd takes only a few days when the plant nears maturity. Many varieties require you to tie the leaves over the developing curd to prevent discolouration from the sun. The flavour and appearance is best when the curd is still tight and not ricey.

Most cauliflower varieties need cool growing conditions at maturity. Hot weather at this time quite ruins the flavour. For warmer latitudes, hybrid varieties have been developed, but I cannot vouch for their performance having never grown them.

Cauliflowers demand plenty of growing room. A row spacing of 75 cm (30") and a similar spacing between plants is recommended. There are miniature cauliflower varieties that can be grown 15–30 cm (6–12") apart and these are generally sown direct. However, we have found these less flavoursome and less adaptable than the larger-framed, slower-growing varieties.

Broccoli

BROCCOLI IS A LOT MORE ADAPTABLE than its close cousin cauliflower and there are varieties to ensure a year round supply. Like cauliflower, broccoli is also susceptible to molybdenum deficiency, though not quite so severely. Back in 1982, I was growing three open-pollinated varieties of broccoli, *Calabrese*, *Spartan Early* and *Late Sprouting*. Sadly, only *Calabrese* is left, the hybrids having largely taken over.

Broccoli is a cut-and-come-again vegetable, forming a large central head, followed by a number of small side-heads after the central

---

The non-hybrids/heirlooms I grew equalled or out-yielded the hybrids in general, with far superior flavors and variety.
— Craig Lehoullier

head is cut. To attain the maximum possible size of the main head, broccoli needs to be pruned. Immature, developing side-shoots are cut or rubbed off until the main head is harvested.

There are three main sorts of broccoli. The oldest is sprouting broccoli and it is rarely grown these days. It doesn't make a large central head, only an abundance of small sprouts over a long period in the spring. There are white, purple and green sorts. The main type of broccoli grown nowadays has a large central head and small side heads are formed after the central head is cut. The flavour of sprouting broccoli is different to the modern type and we definitely prefer the latter. Representative of the less usual type of broccoli is *Romanesco*. Its head is similar to cauliflower, being tight rather than loose, and pale green rather than white. In flavour it does not really resemble either broccoli, or cauliflower. It's very tasty though. In very cold weather the curd develops a purple tinge that rather spoils its appearance though not its texture, or flavour.

Broccoli is usually grown at a spacing 40–50 cm (16–20") between rows and the same or a little less between plants. The closer spacing reduces the size of the main head, but increases the overall yield. Despite claims to the contrary, you can grow huge central heads on compost alone providing you supply a sufficiency. Conventional growers apply a side dressing of water-soluble N to maximise the size, but it does detract from the flavour and keeping quality.

Brussels Sprouts

BRUSSELS SPROUTS ARE SUITABLE for cold districts only. Sprouts are greatly improved in flavour by frosty mornings. The buds or sprouts grow too loose and fluffy in warm weather. Generally the first few that form at the bottom of the stem are loose and need to be removed. Modern varieties are bred to mature all at once for convenience of harvest. The home gardener prefers the older sorts that gradually mature from the bottom up over a period of several weeks. The terminal sprout looks like a miniature cabbage and is also worth eating. When the sprouts become big enough to harvest, remove the leaves below the sprouts as you harvest them leaving the stem bare. This forces more of the plant's energy into the sprouts.

Brussels sprouts prefer to grow in well-firmed soil and are usually spaced about 70 cm (30") between rows and 45–60 cm (16–24") between plants. Brussels sprouts are a difficult crop to grow well, but are well-worth the effort entailed, especially when you consider

---

The soil is the great connector of our lives, the source and destination of all.
 —Wendell Berry

how long they produce. Unless your district experiences hard killing frosts, Brussels will usually be attacked by grey aphis from late autumn onward. These are controlled with a solution of soft soap applied regularly. The aphids will attack your overwintering cabbages as well, so always check them too at this time.

Chinese Cabbage

CHINESE CABBAGE HAS much thinner leaves than European cabbage. They are more tender, slightly hairy and have an unusual flavour. They do best when sown to mature in cool weather as they are prone to bolt when it is too hot. They also should be sown direct where they are to grow. Transplanting, unless done very carefully to minimise root disturbance, results in bolting.

They are sown much closer than conventional cabbages as they have an upright habit — 60 cm (24") between rows and 30 cm (12") between plants is about right.

Varieties
Cabbage

Savoy Carters Improved	Crinkly-leaf type
Sugar Loaf	Conical spring cabbage
Velocity Ballhead	The fastest maturing, when sown direct
Red Acre	Red cabbage
Autumn/Winter Dutch	Crinkly leaf
Vanguard	Ball head
Enfield Market	Conical spring cabbage
Mammoth Red Rock	Large red cabbage
Supermarket	Medium size ball head. Holds well.
Michihili	Chinese cabbage.

Cauliflower

Open pollinated (for cool areas)	Sow	Months to maturity
Mini White	Nov–Feb	5.0
South Australian	Early Oct–Nov	5.0
Thredbo Improved	Early Oct–Nov	5.5
Phenomenal Early	Early Oct–Nov	5.5
Superstar	Early Oct–Nov	6.0
June Dark Leaf	Nov–Dec	6.0
Nortex	Nov–Dec	6.5

Channel Reef	Nov–Dec	7.0
Mill Reef	Nov–Dec	7.0
Deepheart	Nov–Dec	7.5
Paleleaf (Paleface)	Dec–Apr	8.0
Hybrids for warmer latitudes (30 & 35th parallel)	**Months to maturity**	
Snow King	4.0	
Snow Crown	4.0	
Snow Diana	4.5	
Snow March	5.0	

Broccoli

Open Pollinated	**Sow**
Calabrese (Green Sprouting)	L Winter–E Autumn
Romanesco	L Winter–E Autumn
Hybrid	
Green Duke	Spring & Summer
Corvet	Late Summer
Skiff	Mid Summer–E Winter
Premium Crop	L Wint–E Spr/Summer
Line 39	Mid Aut–L Winter

Brussels Sprouts

	Sow
Long Island	L Spr–E Summer
Rampart	L Spr–E Summer
Rasmunda	L Spr–E Summer
Royal Ruby	L Spr–E Summer
Lunet	Mid Spr–Mid Summer

Lesser Grown Brassicas and Their Near Relatives

KALE, COLLARDS, CHINESE MUSTARD spinach, mizuna, mibuna, horseradish, radishes, kohlrabi, turnips, and swedes (rutabaga).

Except for horseradish and radish, all of these members of the cabbage tribe are subject to club root. Consequently, they should not be sown in the same ground any more frequently than once every three years. Radishes left to run to seed will get club root, but when harvested at the edible stage, are not in the ground long enough. Horseradish is a perennial and appears to resist the club root. Kale, kohlrabi, turnips and swedes are all prone to attack by grey aphids, particularly in the late autumn when the ladybirds are dormant.

Thoroughly soaking the leaves with a spray of soapy water will reduce their numbers to a tolerable level, as will a hard frost. Pyrethrum works well, though it will kill any active chalcid wasps that parasitise aphids.

Except for swedes and turnips, all require well composted soil with plenty of calcium. Boron deficiency causes brownish stains inside the roots of swedes and turnips, so supplement your soil with seaweed, or seaweed meal if this happens. Foliar sprays of liquid seaweed and/or fish emulsion will help. As a last resort, borax from the pharmacy can be applied as a foliar spray.

Kale and **collards** are hardy, overwintering loose-leaf cabbages that are grown for their leaves. Kale will stand heavier frosts than almost any other garden vegetable. As well as plain green varieties of kale, there are yellow and red variegated varieties that look very attractive in the flower garden. Kale is sometimes called borecole. The leaves are much tougher than cabbage and require a longer cooking time. We quite like fried kale, but don't go out of our way to eat it. Sow the

Brussels sprouts showing the lower leaves removed, essential for control of grey aphids that infest them in all but the most favourable seasons.

seed in a seedbed or flat for transplanting in late summer, or early autumn. The plants should be in rows about 75 cm (30") apart with 50–75 cm (20–30") between plants.

Chinese mustard spinach resembles silver beet, except the thick, juicy stalks are smooth, rather than ribbed. The stalks are the main reason for growing this delectable vegetable. While celery is suggested as a substitute in Chinese recipe books written for Westerners, it is totally different in flavour, if not in texture. Unlike silver beet or genuine spinach, Chinese mustard spinach is low in oxalic acid and hence has superior flavour. The plants grow rapidly and will produce year round when sown every few weeks. The only time to avoid sowing is in the depths of winter, though plants sown earlier will be productive then. Sow the seed 10 mm (½") deep direct and allow 300 mm (12") between rows and plants.

Mibuna and **mizuna** are Japanese brassicas grown for their foliage. They have a more delicate flavour than most European brassicas and are at their best eaten raw in salads. Sow the seed 10 mm (½") deep and allow 40 cm (16") between rows and plants.

Horseradish is a perennial, though it is best dug up and replanted each winter. Roots more than a year old are too tough to use in the kitchen. Be especially careful where you establish your horseradish bed, it is very persistent, growing from even the smallest pieces of root left after harvest. Plant lateral roots about 20–30 cm (8–12") in length and at least 6 mm (¼") in diameter. Drop them into holes about 20 cm (8") deep and firm the soil around them. The plants should be 30 cm (12") apart each way. Horseradish is ready for use from midsummer on. It is a gross feeder and needs copious quantities of well-rotted manure or compost to produce tender roots of usable size.

Radishes are the quickest maturing crop apart from mustard and cress. To give of their best, they must be supplied with sufficient water for rapid growth, or they will be hot and tough. They are frequently sown with parsnip and carrot seeds to act as "markers". They germinate rapidly, indicating where the slower germinating seeds are going to arise, allowing early weed control. In heavy soils, they also break the crust that forms on the surface of the soil, inhibiting the weaker carrot and parsnip seeds. The radishes are harvested long before the

---

I plant daffodil bulbs about eight inches deep. As I mentioned before, I don't use a ruler. As a married woman, I know perfectly well what six or eight inches looks like, so it's easy to make a good estimate. This mental measurement makes planting time much more interesting than it might be otherwise.
   — Cassandra Danz

carrots or parsnips need the growing space. Sow them year round with 20 cm (8") between rows and 2.5 cm (1") between plants.

Kohlrabi is rarely grown or eaten which is a pity. It has fine flavour, somewhat resembling its cousin the turnip, but milder and to my mind tastier. Unlike the turnip, which is a swollen root, kohlrabi is a swollen stem. It matures quickly and is best eaten when no larger than tennis ball size. There are but two varieties, Purple and White. Kohlrabi prefers cool weather, so it is best sown in early spring and again in autumn. Sow in rows 40 cm (16") apart with 20 cm (8") between plants.

Turnips The humble turnip is a sadly neglected vegetable these days. Turnips are a delicious addition to soups and stews as well as a useful vegetable in their own right. In the latter case, they should be steamed lightly and still be a little crisp when brought to the table. The varieties *Gilfeather* and *Crimson Globe* are much sweeter than other sorts. The foliage of turnips is a commonly eaten green vegetable in the USA and there is no good reason why we should not follow the US lead in this. Lightly steamed, the leaves are truly delicious. Do not take too many leaves from individual plants, or you will deprive the root of the energy input it needs. Sow them in rows 30 cm (12") apart with 7.5 cm (3") between plants.

Swedes (Rutabagas) are similar to turnips, but have firmer flesh and are much slower maturing. They should be sown a few weeks earlier

Dwarf peas need little in the way of support; just a few twigs will often suffice.

to mature in cool weather. They are hardier than turnips withstanding heavier frosts. Their taste is much improved by frost, being a little too strong in flavour without it. They keep well in the garden until the lengthening days of spring send them to seed. Swede aficionados fry them like potato chips. Sow them in rows 35 cm (13") apart with 15 cm (6") between plants.

Pea and Bean Tribe
Peas and beans

PEAS AND BEANS ARE BOTH members of the same family, *leguminosae*. Legumes have an association with a particular family of bacteria (called *rhizobia*) that convert nitrogen from the air into protein. The process is called nitrogen fixation. Each species of pea or bean has its own species of rhizobium which must be present for nitrogen fixation to occur. If you are gardening where peas or beans have never grown before, you will possibly need to introduce the beneficial bacteria. All the backyarder needs to do is obtain a little soil from a garden that has them and sprinkle it about your garden.[1] Till the soil to allow the bacteria to go to work on your future crops. The market gardener will find it more economical to inoculate the seed with bacteria purchased from a rural store that supplies seed to farmers. Presumably this is a selected strain of *rhizobia*.

French beans and garden peas do not have a long enough life span to produce very much in the way of nitrogen. The Fava bean, (broad or tick bean) contributes considerably greater quantities of nitrogen and is worth growing on this count alone. Fava beans grow best in cooler weather and are generally sown in late autumn to late winter. Cow peas are also grown over the winter for the purpose of nitrogen fixation, but they contribute somewhat less nitrogen and organic matter than tick or fava beans. When grown as a green manure to be tilled into the soil in spring, they are often sown with a cereal, such as oats, rye corn or barley.

Nitrogen fixation will not occur without sufficient molybdenum in the soil. This element is required for the formation of a critical enzyme. Its availability is dramatically decreased in soil that is too acid and often liming is all that is required. If there is still insufficient molybdenum, it can be supplied as a soluble salt (sodium molybdate) as a foliar spray. Seaweed contains a small amount of molybdenum as it does of all the stable naturally occurring elements, and so can

---

[1] Do make sure though that you are not importing unwanted organisms such as white root rot of onions, or clubroot of brassicas.

be used to supply a minor shortfall, either in the compost, as a foliar spray, or applied to the growing area.

The major difference between peas and beans is that peas have a hollow stem and beans have a solid stem. There are dwarf and climbing members of both tribes. The taller varieties require support in the form of wires or trellises, if they are to produce the much heavier crops of which they are capable. Beans climb by twining around their support. Peas have little tendrils on the stem that do the twining. Poles or vertical strings make the better support for beans and horizontal strings are better for peas.

The taller sorts crop over a longer time than the dwarfs, as well as producing heavier crops. It would appear that the breeding of dwarf varieties for harvesting convenience was at the expense of flavour. Harvesting convenience is also a moving target. While the dwarfs make for more efficient mechanical harvesting, trellised plants require much less painful bending of the back than dwarfs. This largely offsets the inconvenience and expense of trellising.

Both peas and beans are classed as light feeders. They rarely need any more compost than the remnants left in the soil by the previous crop. Where the soil continually becomes more acidic, the pea and bean break is used to lime the soil. Peas and beans are quite tolerant of fresh lime and need plenty of calcium.

Trellises

DWARF BEANS NEED no support apart from being sown in double rows so that they support each other. Short peas that grow to less than a metre in height are often happy with just a few sticks placed here and there. Some gardeners use bits of wire netting. The taller peas and beans need a proper support, as shown in the illustration. We tried Jeavons' method of sowing peas all across the bed in a thick swathe. While yields are high, the peas are very hard to harvest and many are missed in the thicket. A well supported narrow row of peas is more easily harvested and the unused strip of bed can be sown to root crop, such as beetroot, or a salad crop such as lettuce.

At Eliot Coleman's suggestion, we trialled monofilament fish netting as the support, rather than wires, or strings. It is very inexpensive

---

Many gardeners will agree that hand-weeding is not the terrible drudgery that it is often made out to be. Some people find in it a kind of soothing monotony. It leaves their minds free to develop the plot for their next novel or to perfect the brilliant repartee with which they should have encountered a relative's latest example of unreasonableness.

— Christopher Lloyd

and I was told by the supplier that it lasts about seven years in full sun. We removed the fish net at the end of the season, rolled it up pea haulm and all, and put it into a compost heap to remove the crop trash. The netting has lasted a very long time indeed.

Fishermen in a nearby fishing village discard their fishing nets when repairing them is no longer viable and they become unusable for catching fish. They're more than happy to give their nets to gardeners when they reach that stage. Shark net is best having about 10 cm (4") between strings.

Peas

PEAS ARE SOWN 3–4 cm (1–1½") deep and very thickly, either in long narrow rows, or double rows with about 75 cm (30") between rows and 7.5 cm (3")between seeds or in a continuous swathe across a raised bed with 7.5–10 cm (3–4") between plants. The lower pods tend to rot on peas left to trail across the ground. There is only one pea available that grows very tall and it is referred to as a telephone pea. The variety is *Alderman* and dates back to the 19th century at least. It grows to 2 metres (6') tall and has large peas in large pods. The peas swell more slowly than other varieties, so picking requires more care than the usual varieties if you want properly filled pods.

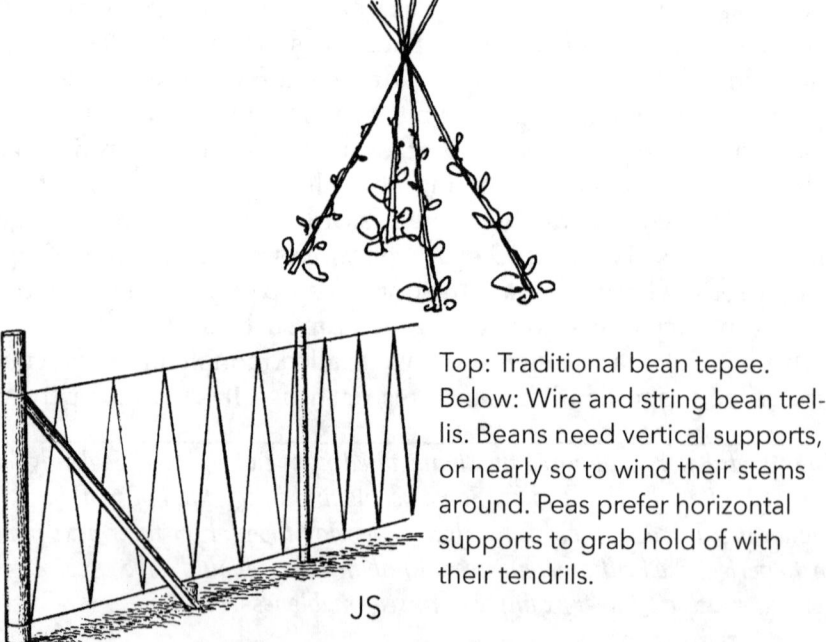

Top: Traditional bean tepee. Below: Wire and string bean trellis. Beans need vertical supports, or nearly so to wind their stems around. Peas prefer horizontal supports to grab hold of with their tendrils.

The main varieties grown these days reach to 45–150 cm (18–60") in height. The most popular is *Greenfeast*, a tasty pea that is a heavy cropper growing to well over a metre in height. *Melbourne Market (William Massey)* is a short, winter-hardy variety and the pods are much larger than *Greenfeast*. *Onward* is similar to *Greenfeast*, but crops a week or so earlier.

In recent years, the Snow Pea has become very popular because you can eat the pods without shelling out the peas while they are still flat and immature.

A more recent introduction is the *Sugar Snap* pea that is allowed to fill out before eating pods and all. These were said to be the result of an intensive breeding program in the US, but we have an heirloom

variety called *Molly's Pea*. *Molly's Pea* is not as sweet as *Sugar Snap*, but it's very winter hardy and a very early cropper. You can also eat the immature pods before the peas inside begin to swell.

Garden peas are eaten by shelling out the peas somewhat prior to full maturity, before the sugar is turned to starch. Over-mature peas have prominent veins on the pods.

Beans
French Beans

FRENCH BEANS ARE of two sorts, dwarf and climbing. *Blue Lake*, one of the climbing sorts, has the flavour to which all other beans are compared. It is a "stringless" bean and they require slightly warmer conditions than the so-called "string" beans. When conditions are too cool, the pods of beans become curved and remain small. String beans are more tolerant of cool weather, though if they are picked at the right stage of maturity before they develop strings, are just as tender. String beans have flattened pods, stringless cylindrical pods.

Climbing beans are sown 2.5–5 cm (1–2") deep in rows one metre (40") apart and 20 cm (8") between plants. Dwarf beans are sown in double rows with 45 cm (18") between rows and 10 cm (4") between plants. The double rows allow the plants to give each other some support as they are prone to wind damage. When sown in swathes across wide beds, they are sown about 15 cm (6") apart each way. This makes harvest more difficult, but yields are somewhat higher.

French beans come in a variety of colours. Butter beans are yellow, and there are streaky red, purple and green sorts. Purple beans turn green when cooked.

Runner Beans

RUNNER BEANS ARE perennial and were introduced from America along with the potato, and tobacco. They form a starchy tuber under the ground and this is reputed to be edible though we have never tried to eat any yet. Each spring, the tuber sprouts a number of stems that bear brilliant scarlet flowers. There is a bicolour and a rarer white flowered strain. As well, a dwarf variety is available in the UK.

For many years runner beans were grown in Europe only for the floral display they made. The beans have a reputation for being stringy and tough, but gourmets are aware that when picked while still young and tender, they have a unique and superb flavour.

The plants we've chosen will collect and cycle Earth's minerals, water, and air; shade the soil and renew it with leafy mulch; and yield fruits and greens for people and wildlife.
  — Toby Hemenway

Runner beans are very prolific and a few plants only are needed for the average family. The sowing requirements are the same as for the climbing French beans.

Some gardeners lift the tubers and store them in sand over the winter. The tubers are planted out in spring and this is supposed to give an earlier start. They tolerate cooler weather than French beans and intensely dislike very hot conditions. We grow both sorts in the knowledge that no matter the season, one, or the other is going to do well. Sometimes pod-set is a problem and a misting of cold water mid-morning helps.

Drying Beans

SOME BEAN VARIETIES are grown to dry for use in winter soups and so on. *Cannelini* are white, *Red Kidney* brown and *Borlotti* are speckled. *Cannelini* and *Red Kidney* are dwarfs and *Borlotti* is a climber. The pods are left on the bush to dry, before being shelled out and stored. They perform poorly in cool, humid conditions, as they are susceptible to a disease called halo blight. This complaint is a seed-borne disease and so prevents saving any French bean seed under such conditions.

Soya beans are also difficult to grow in cool districts, though *Fiskby IV* is a variety more tolerant of cool weather than others. In southern Tasmania, I was disappointed by the yield. The seed is also very small.

Broad Beans

BROAD BEANS WERE the staple diet of the ancient Egyptians and Europeans through the Middle Ages. Their strong flavour is disliked by some, but there is no other cool climate bean to rival their yield and versatility. We eat them as immature beans as if they were French beans, pods and all. Later, we eat the tender, immature beans. After they become starchy, we slip the leathery skins off after cooking them to eat the green inner portion. This makes a particularly fine soup. Finally, some are left to dry, both for seed and for winter soups.

Unlike French and runners, they are somewhat self-supporting as

---

Corn is at the core of modern agribusiness, the most important food crop in North America. In no other crop are the values of modern commercial agribusiness as thoroughly embedded. There is nothing we can do that is ultimately subversive — there is no act of gardening that is so profound a rebellion, there is no act of eating that is so potent a blow for food quality and food system sanity — as to take back the corn crop in our own backyards, and grow, breed, eat, and save seed of corn based upon an entirely different set of values.

— Carol Deppe

they have stout stems. They are however prone to wind damage and so are often sown in double or triple rows for extra support. This is all Coles Dwarf need, but stakes and strings are generally necessary for the taller varieties. They are sown 5–7.5 cm (2–3") deep 15 cm (6") apart in rows 60 cm (24") apart. Autumn and early winter are the best sowing times in most districts and late winter second best. Grown too early, they will be buffeted by strong winds, too late and they are prone to attack by aphids. At the onset of aphid attack, removal of the growing tips prevents further damage as the aphids only attack fresh new growth. These tips make a lovely substitute for spinach if you harvest them before the aphids infest them.

Broad beans and their close relatives, the tick beans, are often grown as a green manure. Since they are a long season crop, they fix copious quantities of nitrogen for use by subsequent crops. They are also very bulky, providing large quantities of organic matter to feed the soil micro-organisms.

Coles Dwarf is shorter than the other varieties and so is less prone to wind damage. *Green Windsor* has the best flavour and the beans stay tender longer, but the seed is difficult to find (we save our own). *Aquadulce Claudia* is very early. One of our favourites was *Big Ben* which is a prolific cropper, useful when the destination is the freezer. The productive period is quite short compared to others, so a succession is necessary for prolonged production in the home garden.

Alliums (the Onion Family)
Onions, leeks and garlic

THE ALLIUMS HAVE BEEN prized for many centuries. They are an almost indispensable flavouring ingredient in many recipes. It is hard to decide which is the king of vegetables, leeks, or asparagus (a close relative).

All members of the onion family are prone to a particularly nasty disease called white root rot. This malady is encouraged by growing onions in the same ground, year after year, or by bringing the infection in on affected plants, or even your boots. You can avoid it by growing onions in a minimum of a three year rotation and practising strict hygiene. Grow your own seedlings if at all possible as

---

A nuclear reactor is a proposed "solution" to "the energy problem." But like all big-technological "solutions," this one "solves" a single problem by causing many... A garden, on the other hand, is a solution that leads to other solutions. It is a part of the limitless pattern of good health and good sense.
— Wendell Berry

the disease is not carried on seeds. If you get it, it could be a decade or more until your soil recovers.

Onions

ONIONS COME IN A VARIETY of colours and maturation times. There are white, brown and red, perennials that are propagated by division, and some that do not make bulbs, called spring onions, or scallions. The white bulbing types are sometimes grown as spring onions as well.

The main crop onions that keep well are very day length sensitive. If they are sown too soon before the shortest day, they will want to bolt, or run to seed. May, June and July are the main sowing months here in Tasmania. Sown late enough, they will form very small onions that can be saved for planting out as sets in the following season. There are strains that have been developed for sowing in late winter/spring, so use these if you are a little late. *Pukekohe* is the main brown onion in this group and is an excellent keeper, possibly the best. *White Spanish* also keeps well and is the best frying onion in my opinion.

The early, non-keeping varieties can be sown from early autumn into winter. They include the extremely mild red onions, such as *Calred Early*, a very large onion. Most of this group are white, *Early Barletta, Late Flat White* and *Savages Flat White* are good examples. *Pearl Pickler* is related to leeks and is sown in the winter. Onions are

Leeks in a seedbed. They need to be about the diameter of a pencil before they are ready for transplanting.

usually sown in rows about 30 cm (12") apart with 5 cm (2") or more between plants. They can be sown in seed beds for transplanting or sown direct. The thinnings from direct sowing can be eaten as spring onions or transplanted.

Eliot Coleman told us he plants onions out in groups of four about

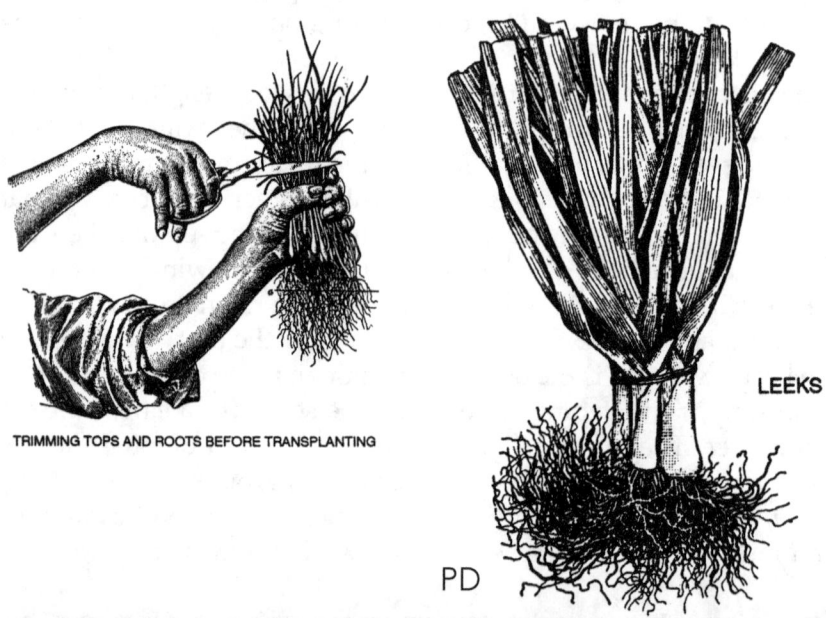

TRIMMING TOPS AND ROOTS BEFORE TRANSPLANTING

LEEKS

PD

Onions close to harvest. The tops are bent over when they start to fall over of their own accord.

15 cm (6") apart each way leaving room for easy hoeing. Each onion still gets to exploit the same area that would be the case were they equidistant, but too close for easy hoeing.

Most of the spring onions are sown all year round and have little if any bulb. They are sown in rows 30 cm (12") apart with about 1 cm (½") between plants. Some varieties will reproduce by division, even

Properly cloved for the kitchen: Jonathan Sturm with a healthy bunch of garlic. NC

The writer in 1995 demonstrating to Hobart Mercury reporter Elaine Reeves how he keeps werewolves at bay.

though they are also propagated by seed. The French shallot makes no seed and reproduces by division in spring and early summer. *Ishikuro* is a Japanese spring onion variety that grows very large, almost like a small leek.

There are several sorts of perennial bulbing onions propagated by division. The Egyptian onion, which is native to North America, reproduces by two methods. The planted bulb divides and there are little bulblets formed on the tips of the leaves. Consequently it is also known as the tree onion. The potato onion is similar, but does not have the terminal bulblets on the leaves. It is usually grown for pickling. The golden shallot is generally used for flavouring rather than for eating as a vegetable in its own right.

Onions need rich soil, though not oversupplied with nitrogen. Too much of the latter creates thick necks that allow rots to enter, greatly reducing the storage life. The early onions are often harvested before full maturity, while they are still green. Onions for storage are left until their stalks begin to fall over. The stalks on all the onions are then bent over and watering is stopped. After a week or two, they are pulled and allowed to dry on the surface of the ground, or put on racks in humid conditions. After they are fully cured in the sun, they can be put in a cool, airy place until needed. Pantyhose make excellent storage bags. Fill both legs equally and put them over a beam or line of wire or rope.

When transplanting onions, it is important not to plant them too deep; they will suffer from neck rot. Mulching too deeply also causes problems with fungal disease. Plant your onions away from the garlic. The water requirement for onions is much lower than garlic and one crop or the other will suffer if their separate needs cannot be catered for. Leeks also require copious quantities of water, though this is in autumn/winter when there is usually plenty of rainfall and a low evapotranspiration rate.

Since their foliage is so meagre, onions compete poorly with weeds. Onions are quite resistant to heat and commercial organic growers have turned to flame weeders[2] to combat emerging weed seedlings. The home gardener must be prepared for a considerable amount of hand weeding.

Leeks

LEEKS ARE GENERALLY BLANCHED in Australia. The seedlings are raised in a seed bed before being transplanted into a trench when about the

---

[2] Take care using flame near mulch. A friend new to gardening inadvertently set fire to the mulch in his garden and very nearly burnt his house down.

thickness of a pencil. The sides of the trench are then gradually filled in as the plants grow. An alternative is to make holes with a dibbler, which is a pointed stick. The holes should be about 15 cm (6") deep. The seedlings are then dropped into the holes and the ground well irrigated to wash a little soil into the holes. The leeks then grow to fill the holes.

Leeks are greedy feeders unlike the other alliums. The more well-rotted compost the better the yield. Make sure you check the soil moisture at root depth from time to time; they are very thirsty plants compared to onions. In a drier year it can be bone dry down there limiting both the size and tenderness of your leeks.

Garlic

GARLIC BULBS SELECTED FOR PROPAGATION are the biggest, best and healthiest from the previous crop. The bulb is broken into its constituent cloves immediately before planting and the biggest are used for "seed." The size of the clove has an influence on the size of the resultant bulb, so the smaller cloves are rejected. Or, thanks to Joyce Wilkie, are grown closely and used as spring garlic just like we use immature white onions as spring onions. The individual cloves are then planted at a depth of 2.5 to 5 cm (1–2"), unmulched. When mulched, the cloves can be planted on the surface and thickly covered with mulch.

The most favourable planting time is autumn after the soil has cooled to below 10°C. In general, the longer the crop is in the ground, the heavier it will become. The latest I have attempted to plant garlic is October, the earliest February. The garlic was mature in February and January respectively, only 6–8 weeks' difference, despite the 8 month difference in planting times. This is because garlic is daylength as well as temperature sensitive. You can trick garlic into

---

Mrs Loudon was even more successful than her husband thanks to a single work, Practical Instructions in Gardening for Ladies, *published in 1841, which proved to be magnificently timely. It was the first book of any type ever to encourage women of elevated classes to get their hands dirty and even to take on a faint glow of perspiration. This was novel almost to the point of eroticism.* Gardening for Ladies *bravely insisted that women could manage gardening independent of male supervision if they simply observed a few sensible precautions – working steadily but not too vigorously, using only light tools, never standing on damp ground because of the unhealthful emanations that would rise up through their skirts.*

— Bill Bryson

sprouting early by storing the bulbs in the fridge for a few weeks before planting out the cloves. Bulbing will not occur until some time after the shortest day.

Planting too close to the longest day can lead to small bulbs without separate cloves. They can make useful planting material however as they are larger than average single cloves.

Varieties
Onions

White	Sow	Comments
Late Flat White	Apr–May	Use fresh.
Savages Flat	Mar–Aug	Use fresh.
Lockyer White	Apr–May	Use dry or fresh.
SA White Globe	May–Sep	Use dry or fresh.
White Sweet Spanish	Aug–Sep	Use dry. Late sowing only.
White Spanish	May–Jul	Good keeper. Our favourite frying onion.
Southport White Globe	Jun–Aug	Use dry.
Prizetaker	Aug–Sep	Use dry. Very late.
Gladalan White	May–Aug	Use dry or fresh.

Brown	Sow	Comments
Manifold	Jun–Jul	Heavy yields.
Ailsa Craig	Aug	Big mild bulb. Moderate keeper.
Australian Brown	June	Long keeper. Pungent.
Gladalan Brown	Apr–May	Earliest. Heavy yield.
Odorless	May–Jul	Matures L Spr–E Summer
Pukekohe	Jun–Jul	Best quality. Keeps well.
Di Onno	Apr–Jun	Early.
Lockyer Brown	Apr–Jun	Early.
Rossvale	Apr–Jun	Use dry or fresh.
Creamgold	Jul–Sep	Good keeper.
Prizetaker	Aug–Sep	Very late.

Red	Sow	Comments
Red Italian	Jul–Aug	Large and tender.

Calred Early	May–Jul	Mild, can be used immature.
Odorless Globe	May–Aug	As described.
Red Italian Torpedo	May–Jul	Distinctive shape. Very high yields.

Spring	**Sow**	**Comments**
Straight Leaf	All year	Non bulbing.
White Lisbon	All year	Slight bulbing. Best cool areas.
Evergreen Long White Bunching	All year	Will reproduce vegetatively if thinned to 15cm (6").
Winter Straight Leaf	Aut	Good winter variety.

Leeks	**Sow**	**Comments**
Musselburgh	L Win–L Spr	Mid season.
Elephant	Spr–E Sum	Late Season.

Garlic	**Sow**	**Comments**
Italian Purple	Aut–Spr	Good flavour
Russian (Elephant)	Aut–Spr	Poor flavour, large cloves. Very decorative.
California Early	Aut–Spr	Medium cloves, mild.
Japanese Purple	Aut–Spr	Large cloves, strong flavour. Early maturing.
South Australian White	Aut–Spr	Small cloves, excellent flavour.

Tomatoes and Capsicums
Tomatoes
TOMATOES ARE THE MOST WIDELY GROWN vegetable by the backyard gardener. There is a simple explanation for this. Commercially grown tomatoes are nearly always tasteless and since they are prolific croppers, produce a worthwhile harvest from a small area. Where conditions are warm enough, or in the green house, the tomato's close relative the capsicum is well worth growing. Not so much on the grounds of vastly improved flavour, but because of the high price asked for capsicums.

The commercial tomato grower starts his or her disservice by growing varieties that are tough. They must be able to take all the handling required between the producer and consumer. Secondly, the tomato is one bred to be prolific, rather than tasty. Third, they are picked green and ripened artificially with ethylene gas. To add insult to all this, they are often grown with the system called hydroponics, all of which taken together is almost guaranteed to remove any potential for flavour that the genes in the tomato originally had.

The backyard gardener takes the opposite approach. Through experience, and possibly by breeding, which is easy, the gardener selects for flavour. The tomatoes are grown with good compost humus, and allowed to ripen on the vine. Even where they need to be ripened indoors at the end of the season, they are superior in every way to the tasteless, odourless (ignoring the preservative chemicals), monstrosities purveyed to an ignorant public.

Taking varieties first, it is important to distinguish between the hybrid and open-pollinated types. There are more varieties of tomato than any other vegetable so there is no need to purchase the hybrid types. Hybrids are more expensive, have a poorer germination rate, and are almost invariably inferior in flavour. There are two main sorts of tomatoes, determinate and indeterminate. The determinate are often called bush and the indeterminate, staking. The bush varieties require no pruning; the staking varieties are pruned to one, two, or three leaders, depending on the vigour and fruit size. Left to grow indiscriminately, the fruit size will be small.

Pruning entails the removal of the laterals that grow from the junction between leaf and stem, as shown in the diagram. Some bush varieties will need staking, due to their size, but little if any pruning.

Tomatoes are best raised from seed at home. A warm, sunny window ledge and a few small pots are all that is required by the average home gardener. Sow the seeds 6–8 weeks before you anticipate planting them out, about three to a pot. Thin the seedlings to the most vigorous plant. Do not be tempted to plant out any earlier than is usual for your district (ask your gardening neighbours). Tomatoes exposed to even brief bouts of cool weather will sulk and never be as productive as those planted out later. Frost will kill the plants. Before planting out, they must be hardened off. That is, exposed to increasing periods outdoors until, after about a fortnight, they are acclimatised to the vagaries of weather.

Unlike many other plants, tomatoes will benefit from being

You will realize that those round, pinkish red things that are available in the stores bear no resemblance at all to the real tomato.
— Craig Lehoullier

planted considerably deeper in the garden than they were in the pot. The buried portion of stem will produce extra feeding roots and the increased depth will help reduce the plants' susceptibility to drought. The tomato also benefits from being slightly root-bound in the pot before planting out. The reason for this is that the plant responds to this condition by producing flowers, and hence fruit, much earlier.

Excessive levels of nitrogenous fertiliser will delay the onset of fruiting, and consequently reduce yield. Try to plant into soil high in humus from a previous crop and give copious side dressings of potash-rich liquid fertiliser. Comfrey tea is the traditional brew. Fill a container with comfrey leaves, top up with water and leave to ferment in a warm place for a fortnight. Strain, dilute and sprinkle around your plants. The addition of a liquid seaweed preparation, such as *Seasol* or *Maxicrop* is also beneficial.

Some growers remove leaves from around the fruits in the mistaken belief that sunlight ripens them. It is heat that ripens, so do not get into this foolish habit which weakens the plant, reducing your harvest. You also run the risk of sun scorch on the fruit.

Tomatoes hate wet leaves, so water from below, if at all possible. In humid conditions, they are susceptible to a variety of fungal diseases. Watering in the morning and occasional foliar sprays of

Peppers in the greenhouse.

liquid seaweed will help prevent these. Smokers should probably be banned from wherever tomatoes are grown. Tobacco mosaic virus is just as happy to invade tomatoes as the smokers' foul weed. Smokers who grow tomatoes should dip their fingers in milk, preferably "raw" milk, before handling the plants.

The greenhouse white fly, a member of the genus aphis, can be a problem. There are now predatory wasps available that are specific feeders on white fly. Sticky traps of yellow card coated in gum can be purchased or made. The flies are attracted to the colour yellow and are trapped on the sticky gum. Pyrethrum is the last resort of the organic tomato grower.

The remnants of the tomato crop can be ripened indoors. Placing them on a warm, sunny window sill is not as good as putting them in a drawer, individually wrapped in brown paper. The ripening process can be accelerated by putting them in a paper bag with a ripe apple or banana. Ethylene gas, given off by all ripening fruit, is the ripening agent, not warmth, or sunlight.

Capsicums

CULTURALLY, CAPSICUM'S REQUIREMENTS are nearly identical to that of the tomato. They do require somewhat more heat to set fruit. Capsicums are very often eaten before fully ripe, that is green, as well as when ripe, which can be red or yellow. The hotter capsicums, often called peppers, need a lot of heat to grow well. Fully ripened peppers can be threaded on strings and dried in an airy shed. This is more successful with the thinner-walled varieties than those whose walls are fleshy. A larger crop will be harvested when fruit is removed regularly before ripening. Plant them in rows 45–60 cm (18–24") apart with 40 cm (16") between plants.

I think that places, like people, ought to have boundaries. Who ever said that gardening was a public activity, anyway? Gardening, like making love, feels a lot better than it looks. Nobody buys tickets to gardening competitions. There's no such thing as the Gardening Olympics. There is no gold medal in Speed Weeding or Double Digging. Maybe there should be, but I wouldn't compete in a gardening Olympiad for all the compost in China. I go through ungainly contortions when I garden. I squat. I crawl around on my hands and knees. Most of the time I bend over, upended. That angle may be flattering to a Dallas Cowboy cheerleader, but it is not flattering to me.
— Cassandra Danz

Tomato Varieties
Bush

Burnley Gem	Smooth, round. Resistant to *Fusarium* wilt.
Earliest of All	Prolific cropper. Small to medium size fruit.
KY1	Early, excellent flavour. Prolific.
Roma VF	Pear shaped for bottling. Resistant to *Fusarium* and *Verticillium* wilts.
Rouge de Marmande	Large bush (needs staking and pruning), excellent flavour. Sets in cool weather.
Tiny Tim	Miniature bush, tiny fruit. Good for containers.
Pixie Hybrid	Indoor/outdoor type. Quickest maturing.

Staking

Apollo	Resistant *Verticillium* wilt. Prune to 5 leaders.
Better Boy Hybrid	Resistant to *Fusarium* and *Verticillium* wilts and nematodes. Needs hot conditions.
Burnley Surecrop	Early. Needs staking but no pruning. Earlier than Grosse Lisse. Resistant to *Verticillium* wilt.
College Challenger	Similar to Grosse Lisse but earlier.
Grosse Lisse	Large fruit. Mid to late season. Probably Australia's favourite tomato.
Superbeefsteak VFN	Huge fruit. Resistant *Verticillium*, *Fusarium* and nematodes.
Kelstar	Production continues into the cooler autumn weather.
Long Keeper	Excellent keeper, poor flavour.
Oxheart	Large fruit. Best in temperate areas.
Sweet 100	Massive clusters of small, sweet fruit. Skin is tender, unlike many miniature tomatoes.
Vivian VFN	Medium size fruit. Suits glasshouse or outdoors.

Yellow Types

Golden Sunrise	Very sweet. Resistant to target spot. Stake and prune to 2 leaders.
Jubilee	Tall bush. Few seeds. Stake.
Yellow plum	Similar to Roma but needs staking.
Yellow Baby	Tiny pear-shaped fruit. Prolific.

Capsicum Varieties

California Wonder	Reliable older cultivar. Green fleshy fruit.
Sweet Banana	Early. Long yellow fruit. Suits cooler districts.
Habanero	Very hot chilli. Prolific. Warmer climates only.
Jalapeno	Tastier than most chillies and only moderately hot. My favourite. Fleshy, so difficult to dry.
Birdseye	Fiery. Essential for Thai cuisine.

Vine Crops
Pumpkins, Marrows, Cucumbers and Melons

PUMPKINS, MARROWS, MELONS, squash, zucchini, cucumbers, and chokoes are all members of the cucurbit family. They are vines, even the sort that have been bred to grow only into bushes. They are all killed by frost and need lots of warm weather to produce. They are also gross feeders, so the more compost in the soil the better. Apart from the bush varieties, they also need lots of room to grow. The small-scale gardener often trains them against a fence, putting the larger fruits into slings to support them while growing. The gardener with lots of space will put a rock or tin can under the maturing fruit, to prevent rotting of the part that would otherwise be in contact with the ground. The members of this family are all very competitive with weeds and fast growing, so little in the way of weeding is needed after the first few weeks.

Since they like heat, it is a good idea in cooler areas to delay mulching until the ground has thoroughly warmed up. Some growers

---

I'm struck by the insidious, computer-driven tendency to take things out of the domain of muscular activity and put them into the domain of mental activity. The transfer is not paying off. Sure, muscles are unreliable, but they represent several million years of accumulated finesse.

—Brian Eno

overcome this by using large rocks as a mulch. The rocks absorb heat during the day and release it at night, ameliorating the climate around the plants.

The cucurbits rely on insect pollination to set fruit. When pollinating insects are in short supply, the gardener needs to step in. The female flower has a swelling at the base which is the immature fruit. The male flower has no swelling. (See page 184) A male flower is stripped of its petals and the protuberance bearing the pollen brushed against the female counterpart. One male flower is good for fertilising four or five females. The flowers must be absolutely fresh. By hand pollinating you can ensure nearly every female flower will set fruit. The growing tips of the vines can be pinched off later in the season when any further fruits that set are unlikely to ripen. The main leader will produce more side branches, which are more fruitful, when the end is pinched off at a length of about one metre (3').

Like tomatoes, cucurbits hate wet leaves. Water them in the morning underneath the leaf canopy if possible. Water regularly and deeply; yield is severely restricted when water supply is uneven.

Pumpkins and Winter Squash

THERE IS AN AMAZING VARIETY of pumpkins, both in appearance and in flavour. There are actually two sorts, winter squash and true pumpkins, but there is no cultural difference as far as the gardener is concerned. Their main characteristic is the setting of sweet fruit that has a hard skin, many of them keeping very well because of it. The size of the fruit varies from the size of a grapefruit in the case of the bush variety *Golden Nugget* to the 50 kg (110 lb) of the large vined *Big Max*. In between there are a multitude of colours, shapes and sizes, pink, red, yellow, green, banana, spherical, ribbed, acorn and turban. Try a sowing of each until you know the sorts you like and do well in your district. Some have moist flesh, some dry and some more or less sweet. The keeping quality appeals in some and the exquisite flavour in others. One of our favourites is *Green Warty Hubbard*, a winter squash.[3] The skin is so tough it has to be broken into with an axe! It keeps well though, we like the taste and the famous keeper, *Queensland Blue*, does not ripen in our cool climate.

Pumpkins are best picked fully mature. For storage, they should be ripened in the sun, turning regularly to expose all sides. If a frost seems likely, cover them or carry them indoors overnight. Well-ripened pumpkins of some varieties will keep for two years or more.

---

3 Another used to be *Golden Delicious*, an early poor-keeping variety of winter squash. It had delightful flavour and it's a cause for some regret we didn't realise it was going to become impossible to purchase seed.

Make sure you leave the stalk on though and do not use it for a carrying handle. Damage at the junction of the stalk and fruit allows rots in. Store them in an airy, dry place, spaced away from each other to prevent rots spreading.

Summer Squash

MARROWS, ZUCCHINIS (COURGETTES), and summer squash are all variations on cucurbits that keep poorly and have little flavour. They are all prolific and whole cookery books have been devoted to zucchinis alone. Treat them much as you would pumpkins except that you pick them immature. Marrows are a giant zucchini, but this does not mean that a zucchini allowed to grow to the size of a marrow will necessarily taste the same. Zucchinis are generally harvested about 10–15 cm (4–6") in length. Patty pan squash are harvested before the flower falls off, more often than not. *Golden Crookneck* is somewhere in size between zucchinis and marrows. The more you harvest of this group, the more they produce. Do not grow too many. You have been warned.

One stand-out in this group is *Manchurian* squash. More recently it has been renamed *Vegetable Spaghetti*. The whole fruit is cooked, cut in halves, the seeds discarded and the pulp pulled out with a fork. It is in strings, much like spaghetti and is treated as such. That is, a tasty sauce is used to supply flavour.

Cucumbers

GOOD, FRESH CUCUMBERS are hard to beat in salads or sandwiches. To grow them well requires a trellis. For some reason they like a trellis angled at about 45 degrees to the ground. The foliage scrambles over the trellis and the fruit hangs below. For people who suffer from gas when eating them, there are so-called *burpless* varieties available. The cultural requirements are the same as the rest of this group except they need slightly more heat to do well. The bush varieties do better in cooler climates than the trailing sort and need no trellising. They do not produce so well, though. Ignore peculiar overseas advice that tells you to remove the male flowers to prevent pollination. They say it makes the fruit bitter. My response is what fruit? If my cucumbers go unfertilised, they do not make cucumbers; the immature, incipient fruit turns yellow and drops off the vine. There is a female flower only variety, *Pepinex*. It is hard to grow. One might presume because

---

When all is said and done, is there any more wonderful sight, any moment when man's reason is nearer to some sort of contact with the nature of the world than the sowing of seeds, the planting of cuttings, the transplanting of shrubs or the grafting of slips.
   —St. Augustine

hybrid seeds are reputed to have insufficient life force to germinate reliably. I suspect that this rumour among organicists is due to the use of stale seed. Commercial growers mainly purchase hybrid seeds and poor germination is something they will not tolerate under any circumstances. *Pepinex* also cost an arm and a leg for a packet of five seeds. If you demand the absolutely maximum yield per plant and do not care about the provenance of what goes in your mouth, then give it a try.

Cucumbers should be picked before they're fully mature, that is before they start to turn yellow, for best flavour.

Melons

THERE ARE THREE SORTS OF MELONS. Watermelons require the most heat, and rock melons/musk melons require slightly less. Both require more than pumpkins, squash and cucumbers. Culturally, their requirements are the same as the rest of this group. Watermelons are picked when they sound hollow upon tapping with the knuckles. The other sorts are ripe when slight pressure on the stalk disengages the fruit. If picked before fully ripe, they will not ripen any further off the vine.

Varieties
Pumpkins and Winter Squash
Bush types

Bush Table Queen	Sweet, dry flesh. Good for baking whole.
Golden Nugget	Grapefruit size. Good keeper.
Butterbush	Butternut type and flavour.

Medium Vines

Baby Blue	Small fruit, very dry and sweet. Good keeper.
Buttercup	Dry flesh.
Hercules Butternut	Large butternut. Keeps well. Stands adverse weather.

Large Vines

Big Max	Good for largest pumpkin competitions and feeding to pigs.
Blue Banana	Fruit up to 1 metre in length, tasty.
Crown Prince	Excellent keeper.
Golden Delicious	Fast maturing, very tasty, poor keeper. Wish I could still get seed!
Henderson Late Grey	Good keeper.
Jarrahdale	Good keeper.

Queensland Blue	Good keeper.
Red Hubbard	Medium size fruit, firm flesh. Our favourite for flavour!
Green Warted Hubbard	Large, tasty, tough skin, good keeper. Need an axe to get to the flesh!
Triamble	Good keeper.
Windsor Black	Early maturing.
Tripletreat	Hull-less seeds, good keeper.

Cucumbers
Bush Types

Bush Champion	Full size fruit on compact bush. Heavy bearer.
Spacemaster	Suits containers. Fruit 20 cm long.

Burpless types

Muncher Burpless	Fruit pale green, paper thin skin.

Long Green Types

Marketmore 70	Vigorous, prolific, holds well. Uniform size fruit.
Poinsett, or Green Gem	Resistant to downy and powdery mildew.
Armenian	Long ribbed fruit. Requires no peeling.

Apple Types

Crystal Apple	Round, cream skinned, tasty, heavy cropper.
S.A. Large Apple	Larger than Crystal Apple. Excellent quality and flavour.

Pickling Type

Super Pickle	Grown exclusively for gherkins. Heavy crops over long period.

...there's never a garden in all the parish but what there's endless waste in it for want o' somebody as could use everything up. It's what I think to myself sometimes, as there need nobody run short o' victuals if the land was made the most on, and there was never a morsel but what could find its way to a mouth.
  — George Eliot

Watermelons

Sugarbush	Small bush. 80 days to maturity.
Candy Red	Resists *Anthracnose* and *Fusarium* wilt.
Charleston Grey	Resists sunburn, *Anthracnose* and *Fusarium* wilt.
Kleckleys Improved	Wilt resistant. Bright red flesh.
Sugar Baby	Ripens in cooler districts. Small fruit.
Warpaint	Underside of fruit changes to creamy yellow when ripe. Wilt resistant.

Potatoes

IT SOMETIMES SEEMS THAT only Tasmanians truly appreciate their potatoes. They grow *Up-to-Date*, a variety dating from the 1830s or earlier, for baking. The Southern Tasmanian *Pink Eye* is the only potato that can be successfully frozen fresh. Unfortunately, it cannot be *consistently* frozen. It is a waxy, yellow fleshed variety that only seems to do really well where it was bred. Its flavour is incomparable and remains popular despite its relatively meagre yield.

Potatoes and milk, it is said, provide an almost complete diet. Indeed, the Irish under British rule were allowed precious little else for many years. The Irish have become synonymous with potatoes, not just because they died in their millions during the potato famines, but because of a unique method of growing them: lazy-bed gardening.

The seed tubers were laid on the turf within an area some 1.2–1.5 metres (4–5') across and as long as required. The surrounding turf was excavated and placed in layers on top, interspersed with cow manure. The turfs were laid grass side down. Since the climate in Ireland provides copious rainfall that was all there was to it until harvest. It is very similar to the approach used by the modern day organic gardener, except the turf is replaced by straw or hay. If hay is used, it should be shaken on loosely, to allow the weed seeds to fall to the ground, before being compacted, by walking on it. The weeds growing where the potatoes are to be grown should be trampled rather than cut, as cutting stimulates them. Truly remarkable yields are possible using this approach providing sufficient water can be provided to the crop. The spacing between tubers is generally about 300 mm (12") each way. *Bandicooting*, or premature stealing of potatoes from the growing plant, is easier when the tubers are growing

---

Gardening is the only unquestionably useful job.
 —George Bernard Shaw

under mulch. Just lift the mulch, take what you fancy and replace the mulch. Keep your eyes open though. If bandicoots prowl your garden, you might just seize a wriggling, furry creature rather than a cool firm spud. Take it from one who knows — it does make your heart leap. I don't think the bandicoot was too impressed either.

Potatoes are more often grown in rows 75 cm (30") apart. Early potatoes are sown shallowly and 30 cm (12") apart, late varieties 10 cm (4") deep and somewhat further apart (40 cm or 15"). As the potatoes grow, the soil from between the rows is drawn up into a ridge. This protects the tubers from exposure to light, which makes them green and poisonous. It also affords some protection from the potato moth. The ridging process also destroys the weeds that arise, so potatoes are known as a cleaning crop, leaving relatively weed-free soil for subsequent crops.

Potatoes are very hungry, the more compost the better, though they are more tolerant of straight animal manure than any other crop. They crave copious quantities of potash, which can be supplied with

This bucket of Pink-eye potatoes came from one plant.

well-wilted comfrey in the trenches. If the comfrey is not killed by wilting, you will create a new permanent patch of comfrey that is almost impossible to eradicate without herbicides. Young bracken fronds are also a good source of potash though somewhat tedious to harvest.

Potatoes cannot abide fresh lime. It makes their skins scabby. Wood ashes, otherwise a good source of potash should not be used. They do need copious quantities of water, preferably from flood irrigation. The major disease of potatoes is blight, and this is encouraged by humid conditions. If blight has appeared in your district, wet the leaves of the plants thoroughly with Bordeaux mixture (copper sulphate and lime). Do not use this as a preventive, the copper is toxic to earthworms and the fungicidal property of the spray is just as effective against beneficial soil fungi as it is against the dreaded blight. Should blight catch you out, remove the dead tops, then leave the ridges alone and undisturbed for some time. The tubers are only affected if the spores from the leaves come into contact with them.

Early potatoes are lifted somewhat before maturity, while the skins are still tender and easily rubbed off. Late potatoes are allowed to die off before the tubers are lifted and allowed to dry and harden for a few hours before storage. Do not expose them to the light for too long, or they will green. Do not attempt to store tubers damaged by digging — they will rot. Store them in a dark, cool shed, away from light and all danger of frost. Rats love to eat spuds so make sure you take precautions to prevent them gaining access.

You will read that you should only grow your potatoes from certified seed. This advice is good as far as it goes. Under average conditions, aphids transmit virus disease to potatoes that are passed on via the tubers. As the viral organisms build up in numbers, they reduce each subsequent crop by about 20% on average. Of course, organic gardeners are not average and will have been giving their crop a fortnightly spray of liquid seaweed, an aphis repellent and all-round tonic. The ground will have been manured with good, rich compost, so the plants will resist invasion by the viruses. You can save quite a bit of money by growing your own seed from a planting of certified. The time taken for subsequent home-saved seed to run out could be five years or more. I know of one organic grower (Ray Mason) whose seed was just as good after more than twenty years, as the mother seed used to grow certified.

There can be no other occupation like gardening in which, if you were to creep up behind someone at their work, you would find them smiling.
   —Mirabel Osler

Using home-saved seed is the only way you are going to grow some of the older, almost extinct varieties. The turning of food into a commodity has led to the creation of general purpose vegetables that are not particularly good for any one thing. The *Up-to-Dates* mentioned are far and away the best for baking, but they turn to water when boiled. The *Pink Eye* makes "interesting" chips, but is unsurpassed boiled or steamed. The *King Edward* in the right soil can rival the *Pink Eye* for flavour, but requires double digging to give of its best. A row of *Pink Eyes* in my garden was blasted by the blight while an adjacent row of *Tasmans* remained untouched. You must experiment to discover the best for your district and palate. The rewards are greater than you probably realise.

Potatoes have an undeserved reputation as being bland and fattening. I am not normally inclined to hatred, but the originator of these filthy rumours should be shot if he/she is still alive. Potatoes are mostly water and the balance is mostly minerals and high quality protein. There are less calories in French fry chips than the same weight of *unbuttered* bread, and most of the calories come from the cooking oil. To maintain body weight requires about 3.5 kg (8lb) of potatoes per day for the average person, a mammoth feat of eating for anyone.

Sow your early potatoes shortly before the last expected frost. Early potatoes should be chitted, that is left in a light airy place to sprout. The sprouts must not get too long and lanky, or they are too easily knocked off. Large seed tubers can be cut to one eye on each piece. Some growers dust the cut surfaces with cement, but this is not necessary if they are planted immediately after cutting. Each piece should be about 50 gm (2 oz). Main-crop spuds are sown later, after all danger of frost is past and the soil has warmed. Frost on the tops will kill them. There is no need to chit main-crop potatoes.

Varieties	Comments
Brownell	Subject to hollow heart. Main-crop.
Bintje	Dutch version of Kennebec.
Bismark	Good "new" potato. Knobbly. Early.
Coliban	All purpose main-crop.
Dutch Cream	All-purpose. Main-crop.
Kennebec	Early or main-crop. Sets tubers high on stem. Some hollow heart. Normally doesn't make flowers. They are said to be a sign the seed has "run out" (become infested with virus).
King Edward	Red skin. All purpose, good flavour. Main-crop.

Varieties	Comments
Pinkeye	Yellow waxy flesh. Best "new" potato. Early.
Pontiac	Red skin, deep eyes. Main crop.
Russet Burbank	Long tuber. High water requirement. Main-crop. Used by MacDonalds for their chips.
Sebago	All purpose. Used by processors. Main-crop.
Tasman	Good all round variety. Pink skin, crisp white flesh. Main-crop.
Up-to-Date	The best baking potato. Steam, don't boil. Main-crop.

Some Useful Perennials
Rhubarb, asparagus and globe artichokes

RHUBARB, ASPARAGUS AND GLOBE ARTICHOKES are all perennial vegetables needing a permanent location in the garden. Before planting them out, it is necessary to ensure that the soil is free of perennial weeds. Permanent mulching will enable the beds to be kept weed free.

Rhubarb is useful to the organic gardener, not just for its culinary and wine-making attributes. The leaves are extremely toxic to livestock, people and some insects. This latter enables the gardener to make a cheap and useful insecticide.

Recipe:

Boil 400 gm (14 oz) leaves in 1 litre (1 quart) of water for half an hour. Strain and add a little soft soap (potassium soap, *Safers*). Dilute one part of solution to one part water. This spray is safe to bees and lethal to aphids.

Rhubarb crowns are available in winter from most nurseries and are planted out with the eye, or incipient bud, just showing above the ground. Feed and mulch the ground heavily. Make only a light picking the first spring. Remove flower stalks when they arise as they weaken the plant. Allow 1 metre between rows and 60–80 cm (24–32") between plants.

Alternatively, rhubarb seed can be sown in the spring and the plants sorted for colour and vigour. The seed is sown in shallow

---

The many great gardens of the world, of literature and poetry, of painting and music, of religion and architecture, all make the point as clear as possible: The soul cannot thrive in the absence of a garden. If you don't want paradise, you are not human; and if you are not human, you don't have a soul.

— Sir Thomas More

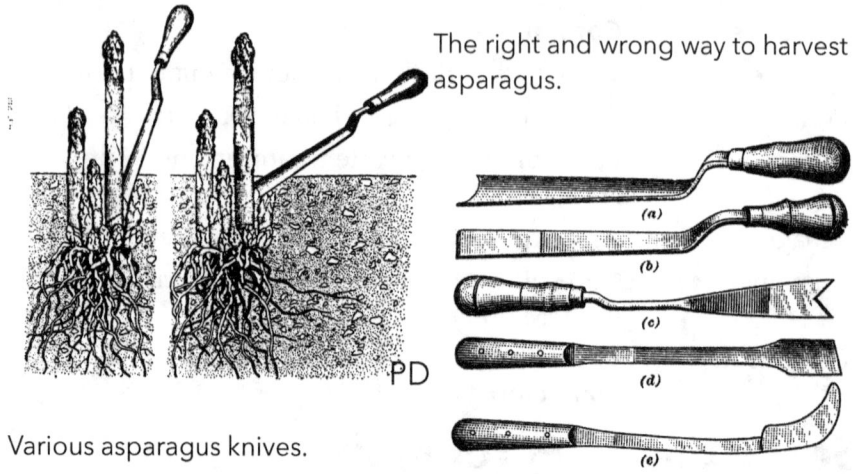

The right and wrong way to harvest asparagus.

Various asparagus knives.

drills in a seed bed and any that are poorly coloured are removed during the growing season. The following winter they are planted out in their final position.

Once every four or five years the plants should be lifted and the crown broken into pieces with a sharp spade, leaving one eye per piece. This is then replanted in the same or new ground to grow on.

Asparagus needs to be off to one side of the garden as its tall feathery foliage will shade nearby plants. It can be grown from seed in early spring. The seed is usually soaked overnight in water to speed germination[4] and sown about 7.5 cm (3") apart in drills. In the second season after sowing, the female plants will flower and these should be removed. The male plants produce more vigorously and the spears are thicker. Alternatively, crowns can be purchased in winter. Unfortunately when we purchased crowns for our third planting the female plants had not been culled. There's another reason for growing only male asparagus plants: the females set seed that the birds distribute hither and yon, especially where you don't want them to germinate.

Asparagus needs perfect drainage to do well, which means raised beds in heavy soils. Mix as much compost or rotted animal manure as possible with the soil before planting. This vegetable also has a very high calcium requirement and liming to a pH of 6.5 to 7.0 is essential. Each winter, the foliage should be cut off and composted.

Many gardeners burn the foliage on the grounds that asparagus is susceptible to a rust and the spores might survive the composting process. We have had no problem with the rust and prefer as far as possible to avoid burning perfectly good organic matter.

---

4 I haven't tested this. Unlike peas, one doesn't sow asparagus seed frequently.

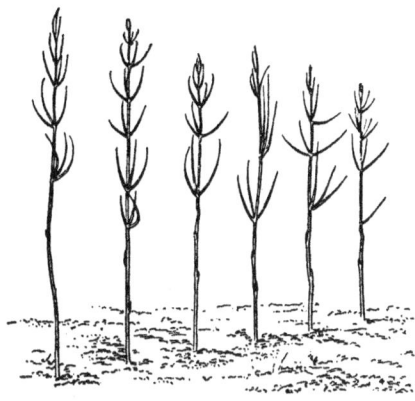 

Asparagus seedlings (L) and harvesting the crop (R).

The mulch should be renewed and compost applied as heavily as possible. A well cared for asparagus bed will produce for two decades or more, so it is worthwhile to install underground drainage in poorly drained sites.

When planting out two year old crowns, place them 15 cm (6") deep in rows 90 cm (36") apart with 30–40 cm (12–16") between plants. Take only a light picking the first season in order to give the plants time to build up their reserves. Cut the spears carefully to avoid damaging nearby juvenile spears. Cut below the surface of the mulch. When the plants are in full bearing, they can be harvested until the first peas are picked and then they should be allowed to grow on to store nutrients for the following season. We have also left a portion of the bed until early autumn. We then cut the foliage off early and had a late autumn harvest.

As this plant originated near the sea, salt is sometimes used as a weedicide around asparagus beds. If you do this, be sure that the drainage from the bed does not go near plants sensitive to salt.

Globe artichokes are tall, attractive, vigorous thistle-like plants and can make an excellent summer windbreak. The plant is grown for its immature flower buds which are a delicious spring treat. They should be eaten before the buds start to open. They are either grown from sets in a way similar to rhubarb division, or from seed. The seed is sown in spring 2.5 cm (1") deep in rows 30 cm (12") apart and 10 cm (4") between plants. The following year they are transplanted to their

---

Always leave enough time in your life to do something that makes you happy, satisfied, or even joyous. That has more of an effect on economic well-being than any other single factor.
—Paul Hawken

final position in rows 2 m (6') apart with 1 m (3') between plants. They should be composted and mulched heavily. Suckers arising from the base of the plants should be removed. These are used to renew the planting every two or three years. Under optimum growing conditions artichoke plants will produce for five years. Cardoons are a less vigorous type of artichoke and can be treated in a similar fashion.

Celery and Celeriac

CELERY AND ITS TURNIP-ROOTED relative, celeriac, are not easy plants to grow. Their shallow root system, high water requirement and the necessity for heavy applications of compost are the reason for this. Keeping the seed-raising mix moist enough for germination and simultaneously avoiding damping-off[5] of the seedlings is difficult. The tiny seed is sown shallowly in a seed bed and the seedlings transplanted into rows 35 cm (14") apart with 25 cm (10") between plants. Early sowings should be under glass. The rows are commonly interspersed with cabbages as the celery repels the cabbage white butterfly. As well as needing copious quantities of well-rotted animal manure or compost, celery has a high calcium requirement, so lime must be applied to the preceding crop.

---

5 A sprinkling of wood-ashes or finely sifted lime on the seed-raising mix will help to avoid this.

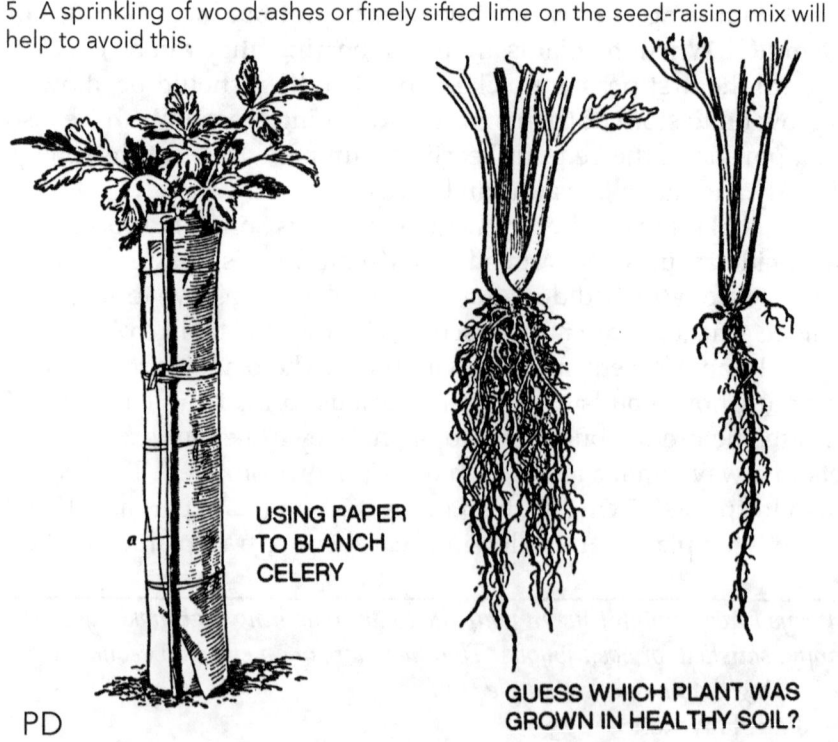

USING PAPER TO BLANCH CELERY

GUESS WHICH PLANT WAS GROWN IN HEALTHY SOIL?

PD

During the growing season, the soil must never be allowed to dry out. In hot weather, this may mean daily or twice daily watering. The water should preferably be applied to the soil surface, rather than by overhead irrigation, as celery is susceptible to several fungal diseases on its leaves.

In Australia, most celery is blanched. That is, the stems of the plant are wrapped in paper to exclude sunlight for two weeks prior to harvest. So-called self-blanching celery will have green outer stems unless this is done. Celery for cooking needs no blanching. Blanching reduces the nutritional value of the plant, so you may wish to follow the American practice of not bothering.

Celery should be mulched, both to conserve moisture and to avoid cultivating around the plants and damaging its shallow root system.

Celeriac is also known as turnip-rooted celery. It is grown in a similar way to celery, but needs no blanching. The soil is drawn up around the bulb as it develops, or mulched. Celeriac seed needs even more moisture than celery in order to germinate, so keep the soil in the seed bed extremely moist. Failure to do this is a common cause of failure to germinate celeriac seed. Celeriac is more hardy and disease resistant than celery. The bulb is used for flavouring soups and stews and is delightfully tasty. I'm not a fan of celery stalks, raw or cooked, but I do love celeriac. You can take a few leaves off the plants for flavouring your braised lamb shanks, but don't steal too many.

Golden Self Blanching	Early maturing.
Stringless American	Up to 60 cm (24") tall. Normally used unblanched.
Giant Red	Deep red stems. Best when blanched.
Giant Pink	As above, but pink.
Utah Tall	Green variety up to 75 cm (30") tall.
SA Giant White	Will grow to 1 metre (3') or more in height.

Sweet Corn

Sweet corn needs plenty of heat and compost to grow well. The seed is sown in spring 2.5–5 cm (1–2") deep, in rows 1 m (3') apart with 30 cm between plants. Pollination is better if they are sown in blocks rather than long rows. Pollination is also improved by shaking the plants when the pollen has formed on the male spike at the top. Poor pollination leads to gaps in the rows of seed on the mature cob. Some varieties of corn that are extra sweet will lose that extra sweetness if they are pollinated by another variety. Sow corn at frequent intervals during the sowing season for your area, to avoid a glut. Sweet corn rapidly deteriorates in flavour after picking and ideally should be cooked within minutes of harvest. If you have never tasted truly fresh sweet corn, you are in for a pleasant surprise.

Sweet corn can be mulched heavily or the soil in the rows cultivated and gradually hilled up around the plants for support. As the sweet corn nears maturity, the tassels on the cobs begin to dry off. To test the readiness of the cob for picking, expose the kernels and prick one. If it exudes a milky juice, it is ready. Over mature kernels will feel tough and no juice will flow. Immature cobs will exude a clear juice. Harvest the cobs by pulling them in a downward and twisting motion.

Sweet corn is susceptible to infestation by grubs in the top of the cobs. This can be overcome by the application of a couple of drops of mineral oil to the tassels. Some books advise the removal of the small suckers that arise from the base of the plant. Unless you are an obsessively tidy person, there is nothing useful to be achieved by this.

Companion planting of corn, beans and squash (Three Sisters) was a common practice of several North American Indian tribes. The beans climb the corn and the squash acted as living mulch over the ground.

Rosella	93 days to maturity. Processing variety.
Miracle	75 days. Earliest maturing. Performs well under poor early season conditions.
Honeysweet	86 days. Short plants. Excellent flavour. Stores better than most.
Silvan O.P.	Tall, late maturing. Not as sweet as hybrids.
Silver Gem	105 days. Tasty, white seeded.
Golden Cross Bantam	Excellent flavour. Smaller seeds than most.
Honey and Cream	100 days. Very sweet. Two colour seeds.
Sweet Miracle	80 days. Higher sugar content than most.
Golden Champion	100 days. Tall, rust resistant. High yields.

Our most important job as vegetable gardeners is to feed and sustain soil life, often called the soil food web, beginning with the microbes. If we do this, our plants will thrive, we'll grow nutritious, healthy food, and our soil conditions will get better each year. This is what is meant by the adage "Feed the soil not the plants."
— Jane Shellenberger

Scorzonera and Salsify

SALSIFY IS KNOWN AS the oyster plant because its flavour is vaguely reminiscent of oysters. Scorzonera is also known as black salsify, since its skin is black rather than white. Both are sown in spring in deeply worked soil manured as for carrots, or parsnips. The long and slim seeds are sown 7.5–10 cm (3–4") apart in rows 30 cm (12") apart in early spring. The roots are used through winter and early spring. The roots are scraped and boiled or the skins may be slipped off after boiling. The addition of a little lemon juice or vinegar to the water prevents the roots darkening.

Salsify varieties include *Sandwich Island Mammoth* and *Improved Mammoth*. Scorzonera comes as only one named variety, *Omega*.

Okra

OKRA, OR GUMBO, NEEDS at least four months of frost free growing to produce. The seed is sown into warm soil in the spring in rows 1 m (3') apart with 30 cm (12") between plants. The pods must be picked regularly to keep the plants from producing. The pods must not be allowed to mature. They are picked four to six days after the flowers open, when they are 7.5–10 cm (3–4") long. The pods are used for thickening soups and stews and are at the heart of the southern US Creole cookery. The slimy nature of the pods' contents will put the squeamish off, but it is a gourmet's delight.

The pods can be used green, dried, frozen or pickled in brine. *Clemson's Spineless* is the usual variety grown in Australia.

Rosella

ROSELLA REQUIRES SIX frost free growing months, so is not suited to cooler districts. It is popular for jams and preserves. Sow seed 1 cm deep in boxes after all danger of frost is past. Transplant into rows 1.5 m (60") apart with 1.5 m (60") between plants. Copious quantities of compost should be used.

Mustard and Cress

THESE ARE GROWN FOR USE as green salad and are eaten raw at the seedling stage. When grown together, mustard is sown three to seven days later than the cress. Keep the soil moist with a sheet of plastic, until the seeds germinate. It takes about four weeks to reach harvest. The seed is generally sown in boxes of humus rich soil, by scattering

---

If these are the achievements of man, give me the achievements of geraniums.
 — Beverley Nichols

the seed on the surface and covering with a thin layer of similar soil. The crop is harvested by cutting off the seedlings at ground level with a pair of scissors. Take care to keep the seedlings from falling on the soil, so that they do not become gritty. We've never needed to grow cress as it's growing wild in the semi-permanent stream between our property and the neighbour's.

Jerusalem Artichokes

THERE ARE TWO SORTS OF ARTICHOKES. Globe artichokes are a perennial thistle and described elsewhere. Jerusalem artichokes are a relative of the sunflower and are grown from the underground tubers, the edible portion. Artichokes, or fartichokes as a nearby neighbour calls them (they cause flatulence), are very tolerant of soil conditions, and little in the way of soil preparation is needed. They grow very well under a mulch of rotted hay or straw. Once they have started growing, they compete very successfully with weeds. Select tubers about 2.5–3.5 cm (1–1½") in diameter. Larger tubers should be cut up into similar sized pieces with two eyes, or buds per set. Too many buds results in a multitude of stems per plant and a large number of small tubers that are difficult to prepare.

Sow the tubers in mid-winter about 10 cm (4") below the soil allowing 45 cm (18") between plants. As they grow to a height of 2 metres (6') or more, they can form a useful summer windbreak. Flowering affects both tuber size and quality, so cut off the flower buds. The tubers are mature enough to use about a month following the formation of the flower buds, but are more generally eaten during the winter months. The tubers will store well in sand providing they are kept cool. They are worth growing for artichoke soup alone. Make sure you remove the skins after boiling in water for thirty minutes. The addition of a little vinegar or lemon juice prevents them discolouring.

Fennel

FLORENCE FENNEL, ALSO KNOWN AS *Sweet Fennel* or *Finnochio*, is a variety of the common fennel found growing in railway yards and other unused patches of waste ground everywhere. Florence fennel is distinguished by a much thickened base caused by the base of the

---

As my grandmother discovered long ago, the Japanese excel in cultivating nature. Their gardens come in numerous styles, including paradise gardens, dry-landscape gardens, stroll gardens, and tea gardens. Although each type has its own goal, tray all share the same principle: nature is manipulated to create a miniature symbolic landscape.

— Victoria Abbott Riccardi

thickened leaf stalks. It is this mass, just above ground level that is the edible portion. The seed is sown in early summer in deep, well-drained soil. Fennel cannot stand water-logging. The edible bulb is harvested from autumn until mid-spring.

Fennel is an unsociable plant that inhibits the growth of other plants in the vicinity. As a consequence, it is best grown away from the main part of the garden if possible. It is grown in rows 30 cm (12") apart with 15 cm (6") between plants. They are generally sown direct, but transplanting is possible. A dense planting needs no blanching, but where stands are thin draw the soil up to cover the bulb.

Hamburg Parsley

HAMBURG, OR TURNIP-ROOTED parsley is grown for its swollen root, which is used for flavouring soups and stews. The seed is sown in rows 30 cm (12") apart with 15 cm (6") between plants. The seed must be kept moist for the month it takes to germinate. It is sown from spring until mid-summer. The leaves are usable as conventional parsley, but do not rob individual plants too much, or the size of the root will suffer.

Gobo

GOBO, OR BURDOCK is a very popular Japanese vegetable. It is sown in spring or autumn in rows 30 cm (12") apart with 30 cm (12") between plants. It produces edible roots similar in appearance to parsnips, so work the soil deeply before sowing. The roots are mature three months after the seedling emerges. Keep the soil well-watered. When I was a child growing up in the UK we used to have a soft drink made with dandelion and burdock. They can become a terrible weed so cut the flowers off before they set seed.

Strawberries

THERE ARE TWO SORTS OF STRAWBERRIES. The most popular have large, succulent fruit and come in various shades of red. Almost invariably, they are propagated vegetatively, by planting runners. The plants make shoots which terminate in a miniature plant that, given the opportunity, will form roots and grow into a full size strawberry plant. The other sort is generally grown from seed. These are variously known as *Alpine*, or *Ever-bearing*. The fruits are much smaller and the crops are lighter. The berries of some strains of this species are white, or cream, as well as various shades of red. Many have a more intense flavour than the common strawberries, but the yield is very low. To make up for this, they set fruit over a much longer period.

Strawberries are very easy to grow, provided their requirement for copious quantities of food and good drainage are met. As they can have a long and productive life (two to five years) it is important to plant them in weed-free soil. Mulching is generally used to keep the beds that way. The most common mulch is black plastic, but this material, apart from being an ecological disaster, removes the benefit of rainfall. Irrigation used is the trickle sort underneath. Also, the plastic reduces gas exchange between soil and the air, to the detriment of root health. Organic mulches are definitely to be preferred. The most common is pine needles, as strawberries are said to like the acid conditions this creates. Certainly, strawberries *tolerate* acid conditions well. Straw, seed-free hay and compost also make excellent mulches.

When a lot of strawberries are grown, they are planted in raised beds 15–20 cm (6–8") high and 1.2 m (4') wide with 45 cm (18") wide footpaths. The strawberries are planted 30 cm (12") apart in a double row. With 132 plants per 10 m (33') of bed space, 1,000 square metres (a quarter of an acre) will accommodate about 6,600 plants. These could yield 7 tonnes, or more, of fruit.

In cool and mild climates, planting is mostly from late autumn to mid-winter; in warmer climes, earlier planting ensures a good winter crop. Summer planting of cool-stored plants is often practised. These plants crop within a couple of months and the following spring, out-produce those planted in autumn. Planting in summer requires trimming the leaves, to reduce the stress of transpiration, and they must be kept well-watered.

Strawberries must be protected from birds with netting.

Water requirement is estimated to be 4.5 litres (1.2 US gal) per plant per week at an evapotranspiration rate of 25 mm (1") per week. This would double in hot weather. Trickle systems are the most commonly used to deliver the water needs of strawberries, but overhead irrigation is probably better in hotter conditions as the water helps cool the plants.

Runners must be removed throughout the growing season to keep the plants' energy for fruiting. Runners used for propagation are generally taken from young, non-fruiting plants. Plants for reproduction are grown where there is no danger of infestation by the strawberry aphid, which carries a number of virus diseases. It is build-up of these diseases that necessitate the introduction of new, virus-free plants every two years or so. Under organic conditions, the build-up of virus appears to be much slower than where conventional methods are used.

Removing the leaves immediately after the summer crop can stimulate the plants to grow a second crop in the autumn. Some growers remove the first flowers in the second year of fruiting in order to encourage more vigorous growth and a higher, though later, yield.

The fruit is picked by severing the stalk between finger and thumb. The fruit is easily bruised and should be handled as little as possible. The time to pick is as soon as the fruit is fully coloured. In hot weather, daily picking will be necessary.

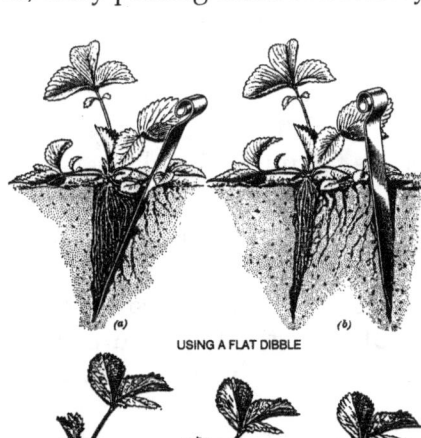

USING A FLAT DIBBLE

PLANTING: (B) IS THE CORRECT DEPTH

Varieties

THERE ARE DIFFERENT VARIETIES of strawberries for different climatic regions. Plants can be obtained from your local nursery, or purchased by mail order.

Cambridge Vigour is an early variety and very difficult to obtain these days. The fruit has wonderful flavour and the plants can be forced to grow an autumn crop. It crops too lightly to be considered commercially viable these days. This variety suits cool districts.

Red Gauntlet is the main commercial variety because of its high yields and extended fruiting season. However, it has very little flavour and on that count is probably not worth growing.

Rabunda is said to produce a light coloured, soft fruit with a flavour resembling wild strawberries. Unfortunately, I cannot comment on this, as here in Southern Tasmania, my plants failed to flower or set fruit. Perhaps they do better in warmer conditions.

Shasta is a warm climate, mid-season variety and is reputed to have good flavour.

Tioga has an extended fruiting season and the berries are the best tasting of the commercial varieties. The fruit is large and the colour excellent.

Totem has a small, dark red berry and is said to have a very aromatic flavour. Its yield is low.

Sweetheart is grown from seed, crops well though it has nothing startling to recommend it above Tioga. The seed needs cool conditions to germinate satisfactorily.

The *Alpine*, or *Ever-bearing* strawberries are all grown from seed. The seed is sown in autumn or spring in cool, damp soil. The seedlings are pricked out and planted where they are to grow. Generally, they are grown as annuals, though they are perennial. They are grown somewhat closer than conventional strawberries, about 20 cm (8") apart. They bear earlier than their cousins and crop continually through until autumn. The yields are too low to consider them as a commercial venture, unless a restaurant can be found willing to compensate the grower satisfactorily.

Strawberry aphids are the main insect pests of strawberries and are found under the leaves, that become distorted, and they transmit a variety of viral diseases. Reflective foil under the plants is said to repel them, and soft soap solution, or pyrethrum will kill them. Compost-fed plants are less attractive to them than those grown with water soluble fertilisers. The most serious pests of strawberries are snails and birds. Netting keeps the birds at bay and regular removal of snails will keep them under control. Nets must be secure at the edges where they touch the ground; the determination of birds to eat the fruit is very great.

There are several fungal diseases of strawberries. Grey mould (Botrytis) is the most common and destructive. It rots the blossoms and fruit in humid weather. It is probably worth trying regular sprays of 3% waterglass (sodium silicate) solution in these conditions. Verticillium, fusarium and nematodes are all soil borne organisms that should not be a problem if strawberries are not grown in the same ground for too long.

Leaf Crops
Lettuce, Endive and Corn Salad

LETTUCES COME IN an amazing number of varieties and in many areas a year round supply is possible. There are the small, tasty butter-head types called mignonettes (red and green), the upright types that you tear leaves off as you need them and the more common cabbage-head types. The heading varieties all have one thing in common. That is they have a very short harvest life (about two weeks). As a consequence, they are best sown in small amounts frequently. Alternatively, you can grow only the loose-leaf sorts and take what you need, leaving the plants to grow on.

Lettuces have the undeserved reputation of being difficult to grow. Providing you understand their requirements, you can grow lettuces with great success. They are shallow rooted. Cultivate shallowly, if at all. Since they also have a high water requirement, regular and frequent watering is needed. Mulching helps, but regular checking of the moisture content of the soil is advisable. A temporary water shortage makes the lettuce very bitter and/or run to seed. Lettuces are also prone to mildews that are exacerbated by moist leaves, so flood irrigation is preferred where possible. Failing that, water in the morning, before sunrise, to allow the leaves to dry out before the water droplets can focus the sunlight and burn the leaves.

Lettuces are a hungry crop, so feed them copious quantities of well-rotted compost before sowing direct or transplanting. Lime is needed to bring the soil up to a pH of about 6.5. Some growers give side feeds of nitrogenous liquid manure throughout the growing period, to increase their size. This is unwise for several reasons. First, increased levels of nitrate in the soil are translated into nitrosamine in the plant. This is a toxic substance that causes *blue baby syndrome*

Nearly all human cultures plant gardens, and the garden itself has ancient religious connections. For a long time, I've been interested in pre-Christian European beliefs, and the pagan devotions to sacred groves of trees and sacred springs. My German translator gave me a fascinating book on the archaeology of Old Europe, and in it I discovered ancient artefacts that showed that the Old European cultures once revered snakes, just as we Pueblo Indian people still do. So I decided to take all these elements — orchids, gladiolus, ancient gardens, Victorian gardens, Native American gardens, Old European figures of Snake-bird Goddesses — and write a novel about two young sisters at the turn of the century.
— Leslie Marmon Silko

in infants. Second, the elevated nitrate levels in the plant are an attraction to pests and diseases. Third, the plant's increased size is a result of the extra water the plant takes up in response to the elevated nitrate levels. In other words, you are diluting the nutrient value and flavour of the lettuce. Since they have precious little flavour in the first place, gourmets will resist the temptation to engage in the foolish pursuit of size at any cost.

Lettuce seed needs to be chilled before sowing during the warm summer months. Put the seed in the fridge for seventy two hours before sowing. The seeds should be sown shallowly in punnets, pots, flats, or direct where they are to grow. The plants should be spaced 25–30 cm (10–12") apart. Transplanting increases time to harvest by about two to three weeks. Some growers sow at a close spacing and transplant the extra seedlings to spread out the harvest.

In hot areas, it is advantageous to sow lettuces where they will receive a little shade from neighbouring plants during the heat of the day. Sweet corn, sunflowers, and climbing beans all make suitable companions for this purpose. Transplanting during the hotter months may require temporary shade, such as boards placed across the bed supported on bricks.

Different varieties have different seasonal requirements and, to a degree, different times to maturity. Sowing a hot weather lettuce in the autumn or an *Imperial* strain in summer will give poor results. You should experiment to find the varieties that do best in your locality at

Young lettuce transplants.

different times of the year. Cos lettuce, lamb's lettuce (corn salad) and endive (a sort of chicory) all grow during the cooler months of the year. Endive, also known as curly lettuce, should be blanched to remove the bitter taste. Blanching can be achieved by tying the leaves together at the top, or by covering with a box for a week before harvest.

The major pests of lettuces are snails and slugs. Snails are creatures of habit that live away from their feeding area, so barriers are effective against them. Slugs live in the lettuce and require more stringent control. The section on snails and slugs contains several strategies for dealing with these slimy creatures.

Silver Beet and Spinach

SILVER BEET IS CALLED spinach in some parts of Australia, but they are really two different vegetables. Silver beet will produce all year round from two or three sowings. Spinach though, is a cool climate crop and will bolt, or run to seed in hot weather. Other leafy vegetables are also eaten as "spinach", and these include New Zealand spinach, orach, stinging nettles, fat hen, and amaranth. They are all heavy feeders, requiring copious quantities of compost in the soil. The warning given regarding supplementary feeding of lettuce applies equally to these leafy vegetables.

Silver beet and spinach have been bred into a multitude of garden varieties and in the process have lost a lot of vigour compared to the wilder members of this group. Another consequence of this breeding has been a reduction in the amount of minerals taken up. Not only are the so-called weeds in this group richer in minerals, they are stronger and many think better flavoured. Nettles make a particularly flavoursome and nutritious soup. They should be gathered with gloved hands and wilted. A five minute simmer totally eliminates the sting.

Spinaches have been both highly praised for their nutritional qualities and condemned because many contain oxalic acid.[6] While an excess of oxalic acid is certainly not good for you, spinaches fulfil an important role during the *hungry gap*. The period in spring when you are waiting for the early carrots, broad beans and peas, and you are totally sick of winter brassicas, is filled with a wonderful variety of leafy greens.

While silver beet and spinach are high in oxalic acid, some cultivars are much lower in this substance. The silver beet called *Lucullus*, known as *Snaebeet* by the Dutch, has a better flavour on this account. It is less vigorous and a paler green than the *Fordhook* type, and on this account less favoured commercially. The conventional silver

---

6 Oxalic acid is what sets your teeth on edge.

beet varieties do less well over the winter in the district where I live, so Lucullus is held in higher regard both for its hardiness and superior flavour.

All of this group should be sown direct where they are to grow. While transplanting is possible, they do establish better when sown direct. Since they are mostly cut-and-come-again, the more vigorous they are, the longer they will last before running to seed.

Lettuce

Variety	Sow
Green Velvet	Late Winter to Early Autumn
Harvest Pride	Early Spring. Late Summer to Early Autumn
Winterlake	Autumn
Imperial Triumph	Autumn
Black Velvet	Late Summer to Early Winter
Great Lakes	Spring
Sunnylake	Late Winter and Spring
Calmar	Spring and Summer
Greendale	Spring and Summer
Yarralake	Spring and Summer
Silvio	Late Winter and Spring
Yatesdale	Spring and Summer
Acefield	Spring and Summer
Yarra Prince	Spring and Summer
Marion	Late Spring through mid-Summer
Great Lakes	Spring and Summer
Westlake	Spring and Summer
Wannero	Spring and Summer
Imperial 847	Spring and Summer
Felicity	Spring and Summer
Kirralee	Spring and Summer
Cabrillo	Late Spring through early Summer
Penlake	Spring and early Summer
Green Mignonette	Summer through early Winter
Red Mignonette	Summer through early Winter

Variety	Sow
Prizehead Red	Summer through early Winter
Cos Verdi	Late Summer through early Winter
Narromar	Late Winter through Spring. Late Summer to early Autumn
El Toro	Late Winter through Spring. Late Summer to early Autumn
Summergold	Late Summer

Endive

Green Curled	Spring and Summer
Batavian Green	Spring and Summer
Salad King	Spring and Summer

Silver Beet

Yarralong Giant	Spring to Autumn
Fordhook Giant	Spring to Autumn
Yarralong King	Spring to Autumn
Lucullus	Spring to Autumn
Rainbow Chard	Spring to Autumn
Perpetual Beet	Spring to Autumn

Spinach

Winter Bloomsdale	All year round in cool areas
New Zealand	Spring
Hybrid 102	All year round
Summertime	Spring
Wintergreen	Autumn
Spring Slowbolt	Winter

Corn Salad

Verte de Cambrai	Spring and Autumn

Who doesn't enjoy a little gardening? As we plant the seeds and remove the weeds we reap a wonderful harvest of blessings. What are the weeds? Anyone or anything that sucks the nutrients from the seeds we have planted. The seeds are our goals, desires, good thoughts and feelings, good works and deeds, anything that uplifts us. If we don't keep up on our weeding then our garden will die.
— Lindsey Rietzsch

Roots
Carrots, Parsnips and Beetroot

CARROTS, PARSNIPS AND BEETROOT are all root vegetables. That is, they store food in a swollen root ready for making seed in the following season. They like rich soil, but cannot abide fresh manures due to their low nitrogen requirement. Excess nitrogen produces leaf at the expense of root, makes them fork and reduces their flavour, which can be exquisite. When conventionally grown produce is compared to organically grown, the superior flavour of organic carrots and beetroot frequently rates a mention. If they are grown after a heavily manured crop, they will rarely need supplementary feeding.

They should all be sown in spring and summer, allowing plenty of time for them to mature before the onset of cooler weather stops growth. Baby carrots require 8–9 weeks, conventional types 10–15. Beetroot needs 9–12 and parsnip 18–25. Parsnip will continue to grow in colder weather than the rest.

All require copious quantities of moisture to give of their best and the water must be applied deeply. The onset of watering is held off for as long as possible to allow the roots to dive deep and create long, shapely roots.

You will often read that carrots and parsnips prefer sandy soil. This is sheer nonsense. While *gardeners* may prefer growing them in sand (it makes for easier harvest) the best *flavoured* roots grow in heavier soils. Heavy soils pose germination difficulties for carrots. Their seeds are small needing shallow sowing. To keep the soil moist for the rather long period until germination, cover the drills with old

Carrot seedlings two weeks after emergence and ready for thinning.

carpet, sacks, boards or whatever. Inspect daily after a week or so and remove the temporary cover as soon as germination is evident. While heavier soil holds moisture well, it does tend to crust and the carrot seedlings have difficulty breaking through. Lighter soils dry out quickly near the surface inhibiting germination of the carrot seed.

Baby carrots should be thinned to about 2–3 cm (¾–1¼") apart, parsnips and larger carrots about 5–7 cm (2–2¾"). Beetroot needs 6–10 cm (2¼–4"), depending on the size you require at harvest time. The larger beetroot and carrots can be left in the ground over the winter for eating as required, provided the drainage is good. Growing these crops in raised beds is often all that is required to ensure this. If the plants are sown in a swathe across the raised bed, they rapidly grow to shade the bed, creating living mulch.

Beetroot seeds are actually tiny fruits containing a number of seeds. As a consequence, they always require thinning to single plants if they are to grow to any size. There are several sorts of beetroot. Apart from the common red varieties, there are white and golden varieties. If the staining caused by red beetroot juice concerns you, the golden is almost as finely flavoured and bleeding is not a problem. There are two sorts of red beetroot, the common globe shape and a long cylindrical type. The cylindrical varieties have a much higher yield per unit area and are excellent for slicing. The leaves of beetroot can be eaten as spinach. Take only a few leaves from each plant though, or you will starve the root and reduce the yield.

Parsnips are rather starchy until the onset of cold weather and many growers wait until a hard frost before harvesting them. The cold converts the starch to sugar and parsnips are higher in sugar than any other garden vegetable.

Varieties
Carrot
Baby Types

Amsterdam Forcing	Will grow to medium size if allowed to. Crisp.
Round French	Spherical rooted; ideal for containers and shallow soils.

Medium Types

Sunshine	Shorter Western Red type
Chantenay Long	Very good flavour and red colour
Midwest	Slow to bolt
Redland	Very quick growing
Tiptop	Far and away the best for flavour we have grown.

Long Types

Topweight	Virus tolerant.
All Seasons	Virus tolerant.
Western Red	Up to 45 cm (18") long.
Western Queen	Holds better than Western Red.

Parsnips

Champion Hollow Crown	The most widely grown variety.
Melbourne Whiteskin	Better for late sowings.
Smith's Strong	The best winter grower.

Beetroot

Cylindrica	Long cylindrical roots. High yields.
Detroit Dark Red	Best flavour.
Early Market	Slow to bolt from early sowings.
Golden Beet	Yellow variety, non-bleeding.
Rapid Red	Quick maturing.
Melbourne Early	Slow bolting type.
Choggia	Alternating white and red rings through flesh that disappear when cooked. Usually sliced and eaten raw in salads.

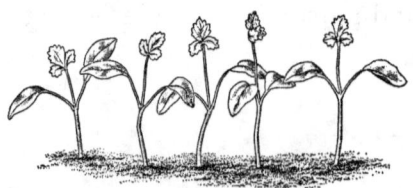

Above: Parsnip seedlings.
Below: Carrot seedlings.
Right: Various types of carrot.

CARROT SEEDLINGS

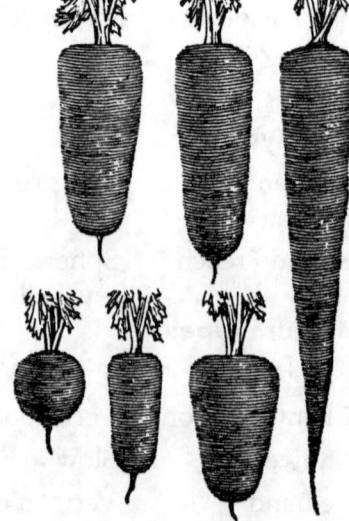

PD

Culinary Herbs

HERBS ARE THE LEAST DEVELOPED of our food plants. They have suffered far less than most vegetables from the ill-effects of the plant breeders. As a consequence, they are far less bothered by pests and diseases. This property makes many of them useful as companion plants to repel pests when they are planted throughout the vegetable garden.

Many books seem to imply that herbs grow best in poorer soils. Nothing could be further from the truth in my experience and that of many other organic growers. In general, the richer the soil is in humus the better the crop.

Most herbs are prolific and a small space will produce all of a family's needs. Many are readily dried for winter use. This is done by gathering the herbs as soon as the dew is gone and hanging them in bunches under cover. They should not be dried in sunlight as this destroys much of the delicate flavour and aroma. They are best stored in air-tight glass jars when they are thoroughly dry. Store the dried leaves whole if possible and pulverise them only immediately before use to reduce the amount of oxidation of the leaf contents.

Some herbs are suited to freezing. Basil leaves for example can be put into ice cube trays and the ice cubes stored in a Ziploc bag. When some basil is called for in a soup or sauce, the requisite number of ice cubes can be added.

Another method of storing herbs is to use them to flavour vinegar or vegetable oil. The herbs are steeped for a period before being strained out and discarded.

The germination of herbs seeds is often erratic like weeds. Soaking the seeds in dilute liquid seaweed overnight before sowing can improve germination. Parsley should be covered with a sheet of newspaper after sowing. Pour boiling water over the newspaper and remove after it has cooled.

Basil (Ocimum basilicum) annual

BASIL IS THE KING OF HERBS and goes particularly well with tomatoes both in the kitchen and as a companion in the garden. It needs plenty of heat, shelter from the wind and prefers light, well-drained soil. It needs plenty of water to keep the leaves succulent. Basil takes longer to dry than other herbs because of this and bruises easily. Handle as little as possible. Plant out indoor raised seedlings 20 cm (8") apart as soon as the weather is suitable for tomatoes. In hot climates it is perennial.

There are several varieties with many being more decorative than flavoursome. That's fine in a salad, but in most dishes we use sweet basil. The larger leaf strain is slightly less tasty than the smaller.

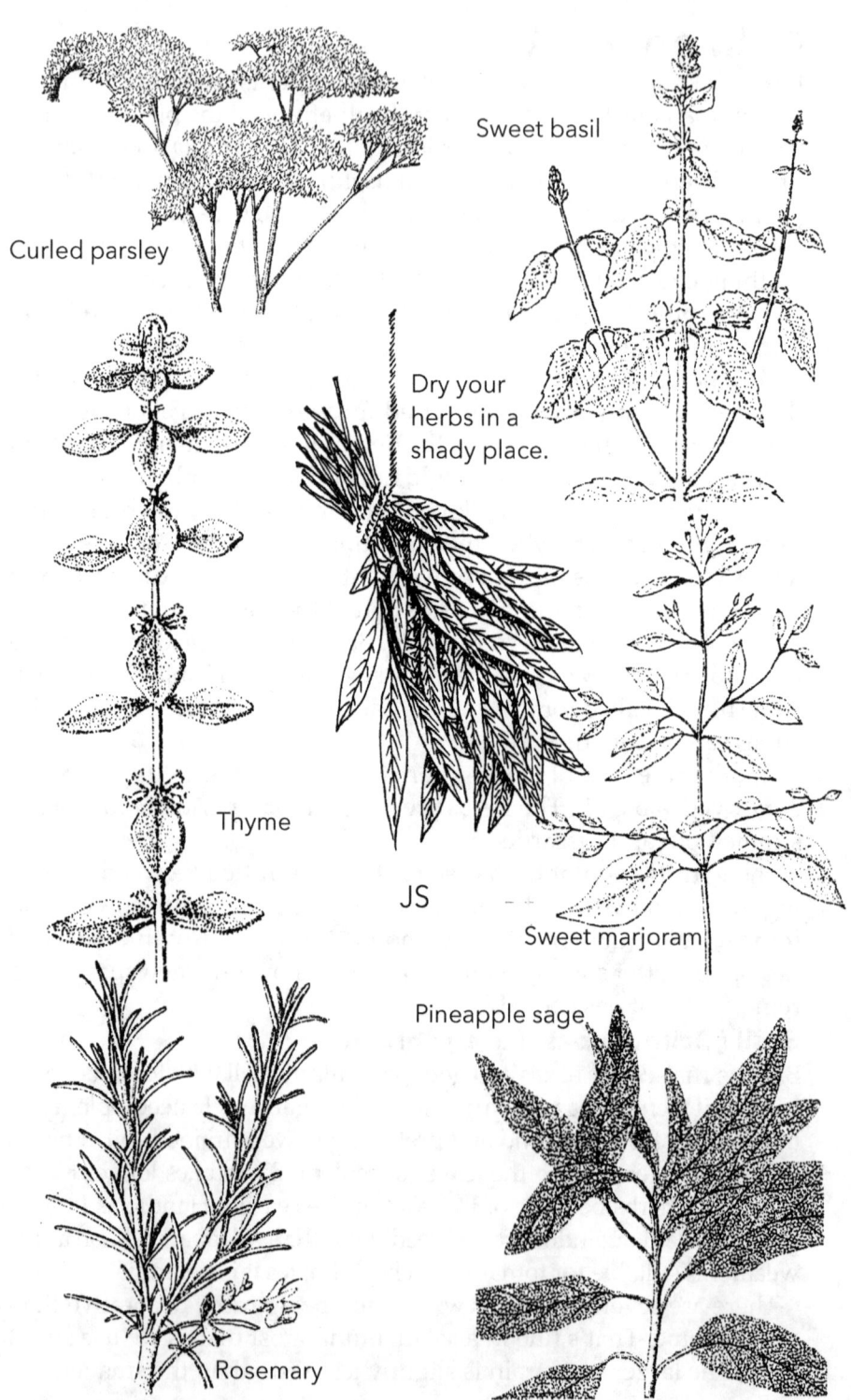

Borage (Borago officinalis) annual
To stimulate your mind and fortify the spirit, add a sprig to your wine. The brilliant blue flowers and leaves are used in salads to impart a cucumber taste. Borage needs a sunny spot that is well drained. It self-seeds prolifically, so once you have it, you have it forever. Sow direct about 90 cm (36") apart.

Burnet (Poterium sanquisorba) perennial
The young and tender leaves of burnet give a cucumber flavour to salads and iced drinks. They go particularly well with cottage cheese. It likes dry, light, well-limed soil. Sow from seed in early spring about 30 cm (12") apart. It can also be grown from cuttings. It self-sows readily. Full sun is essential.

Chamomile (Matricaria chamomilla) annual
This herb is chiefly grown for medicinal purposes. The tea made from its flowers is an aid to digestion, a mild soporific, and is mildly fungicidal. Thin the plants grown from seed sown in early spring to 20 cm (8") apart. The flowers are picked on sunny days when the oil content is highest. There are several chamomiles. You can tell the medicinal one by cutting a flower head in half. The one we want is hollow inside, the others are not.

Chives (Allium schoenoprasum) perennial
Chives are used chopped green to impart an onion flavour. They are used in salads, on baked Idaho potatoes, in omelettes, and soups. Sow from seed in early spring or from a divided clump. They will grow into a mass that needs dividing once every couple of years. Plant divisions about 10 cm (4") apart. Harvest by cutting them with scissors close to the ground. They like a warm, shady spot and plenty of water.

Marjoram, Pot (Origanum onites) perennial
This perennial marjoram has less flavour than the sweet annual. It prefers light, dry soil in full sun. Sow in spring and transplant to 30 cm (12") apart.

Marjoram, Sweet (Origanum majorana) annual
The spicy flavour of this herb is an excellent adjunct to soups, stews and poultry stuffing. It likes plenty of compost and a warm sheltered spot. Sow under glass in early spring and transplant in early summer to 30 cm (12") apart.

For me, food quality isn't a question of organic versus conventional, or no-till versus digging-in, or heirloom versus hybrid. It's a question of what I want to grow, and what I should do to help each seed or plant become the best vegetable it can possibly be."
— Matt Mattus

Marjoram, Wild (Origanum vulgare) perennial
THIS PERENNIAL IS ALSO KNOWN as *Oregano* and has the strongest flavour, so use it in spicy dishes. It needs warmth and well-drained soil. Sow in early spring and thin to a distance of 20–30 cm (8–12"). It can also be grown from cuttings.

Mint (Mentha sp) perennial
THOUGH THERE ARE MANY SORTS of mint, they are all cultivated in the same way. They need rich, moist soil and should be confined by some sort of barrier in the soil to prevent them taking over. Their roots are very invasive and will travel quite long distances. Plant out roots or runners in autumn or spring. It needs full sun for the best flavour. Frequent cutting keeps the plant growing well, but do not cut in rainy weather.

Nasturtium (Tropaeolum major or minus) annual
THE ROUND PEPPERY LEAVES are a delicious addition to salads, as are the flowers. The young seeds can be pickled and used as a substitute for capers. They grow almost anywhere, but like well-drained soil, rich in compost. Sow in late spring near plants that are troubled by pest attacks. Spacing depends on the variety as some are dwarf and others runners.

Parsley (Carum petroselinum) biennial
THERE ARE TWO MAIN SORTS OF PARSLEY, curled and plain leaf. If it's flavour you want, go for the plain leaf. If you want appearance the curled stuff doesn't taste too bad I suppose. We only grow the Italian plain leaf. The seed takes a long time to germinate, so sow it into weed-free soil. It needs lots of compost. Sow two or three times between early spring and autumn for a year round supply. Thin to 20 cm (8") apart. Remove the leaves where they are attached to the stalk by pulling downwards and sideways.

Rosemary (Rosmarinus officinalis) perennial
THE GREEKS USED THIS SHRUB to stimulate the mind. We use it to stimulate meat (particularly mutton and lamb), fish and potatoes. Some varieties will grow up to 1.5 m (5') tall, albeit very slowly. There are also prostrate sorts. All like a dry, sheltered position and lots of lime. Plant cuttings about 15 cm (6") apart for a season of growth. Plant out in the final position about 90 cm (3') apart. Leaves can be picked from the second year on.

Any garden demands as much of its maker as he has to give. But I do not need to tell you, if you are a gardener, that not other undertaking will give as great a return for the amount of effort put into it.
  —Elizabeth Lawrence

We like to roast lamb slowly under the barbecue hood. Shortly before it has finished cooking, we put a big bunch of rosemary twigs on the char-griller and smoke the joint.

Sage (Salvia officinalis) perennial

SAGE IS BEST KNOWN FOR ITS USE in stuffing for meats, but is an excellent medicinal herb. A tea made from the fresh leaves will quickly cure a tickly, unproductive cough. It grows to around 60 cm (24") tall and needs about 60 cm (24") between plants. Second year plants are best for flavour. Narrow leaf is grown from seed sown in spring, broad leaf from cuttings taken in spring. Keep the plants pruned to stimulate fresh growth.

Savory, Summer (Satureja hortensia) annual

SUMMER SAVORY IS THE BEAN HERB and is used to enhance the flavour of all bean dishes. Sow seeds in late spring and thin seedlings to 15 cm (6"). The plants grow to 30 cm (12") in height. There are two cuts for drying, one in midsummer and the last in autumn.

Savory, Winter (Satureja montana) perennial

WINTER SAVORY'S STRONG FLAVOUR goes well with fish, lamb and sausages. It makes a good hedge in well-drained soil with plenty of lime. Propagate by cuttings in spring about 60 cm (24") apart. Use shoots and tips from early summer in the second year and onwards. The flavour is best before flowering starts.

Tarragon (Artemesia dracunculus) perennial

SHELLFISH, CHICKEN AND OMELETTES benefit greatly from tarragon; the right sort, that is. French tarragon is a sterile perennial that does not set seed. Russian tarragon, which does set seed, would taste terrible by comparison if it had any flavour. It needs plenty of space, about 60 cm (24") apart and it grows more than a metre (3') in height and likes full sun. Pull underground runners in late spring, or take cuttings in spring or autumn to propagate.

Thyme (Thymus vulgaris) perennial

THERE ARE LOTS OF DIFFERENT SORTS of thyme, but they are all used the same way. It is very strongly flavoured, so use sparingly to complement rich food as an aid to digestion. The oil in thyme is antiseptic, so it can be used on cuts and for sore throats when made into a tisane. Sow seed in spring or take cuttings. The plants should be 30 cm (12"), or a little less, apart. Some are prostrate and make good ground covers. Some are more upright. Trim the plants after flowering to stop them becoming too "leggy".

The man who makes no mistakes does not usually make anything.
—Edward Phelps

Seeds and Sowing Times

FAILURE IN THE BEGINNER's vegetable garden is often due to attempting to grow crops at the wrong time. Sowing tables that are averages for your district are an approximate guide only. Some years the growing season is cool and late, other years it is warm and early. Gardeners in the nearby village of Franklin can sow French beans a good two weeks before us due to the elevation of our property.

While it is possible to grow extra early or late crops, this is more difficult than growing at the ideal time. The especially early or slow bolting varieties have been bred for that characteristic alone and often lack the full flavour of less tolerant varieties. Altering the growing environment to extend the season with cloches and greenhouses is covered in the section: Extending the Growing Season.

Carrots and beetroot, for instance, sown into ground that is too cool will germinate, but will be prone to viral disease and never give of their best. Seeds sown three or four weeks later will often rapidly overtake those sown earlier. Again using carrots and beetroot as an example, there must also be sufficient time for them to reach maturity before the onset of cooler weather.

The following tables give the optimum growing temperature ranges and soil temperature conditions for vegetable seed germination. Most seasons, using a thermometer and this table will be a much more accurate guide to sowing times than the usual tables for cool, temperate or tropical conditions.

Planting Distances

ONE THING PLANTS REMAIN blissfully unaware of is our concept of distances. Seeds scattered in the wild fall on the surface of the soil, not 10 mm (¼") below. The germination rate is considerably more erratic than we are prepared tolerate, however. In general, sow seeds shallower in cool, wet conditions and deeper in hot, dry conditions. A reasonable rule-of-thumb is to sow seeds at a depth three times the small diameter of the seed.

Spacing between rows is determined to allow free passage of the gardener through most, if not all of the growing season. If you are growing in raised beds with permanent, or semi-permanent footpaths between, as so many of us do these days, just ignore the between row spacing.

Spacing between plants can be closer in many cases if the soil is heavier and/or above average in fertility, further apart if the reverse obtains. In general, closer spacing results in smaller plants, but higher yields per unit area. In a very humid climate, close spacing can be an invitation to fungal disease. Different varieties require adjustment and only your preference and experience over a number of years will enable you to optimise these distances. Gardeners in the district where you live can be an invaluable source of information, both in regards to varieties and sowing times. They are also useful for finding suitable fertiliser materials.

Season	Temp Range	Optimum Temp	Crop
Cool Season Crops	0°C+	Not known	Asparagus, rhubarb
	7–29°C	13–24°C	Chicory, chive, garlic, leek, onion, salsify, shallot.
	4–24°C	15–18°C	Beetroot, broad bean, broccoli, Brussels sprouts, cabbage, collard, horse radish, kale, kohlrabi, parsnip, radish, silver beet, sorrel, spinach, swede, turnip.
	7–24°C	15–18°C	Artichoke, carrot, cauliflower, celeriac, celery, chicory, Chinese cabbage, endive, fennel, lettuce, mustard, parsley, pea, potato.
Warm Season Crops	10–26°C	15–21°C	French bean.
	10–35°C	15–24°C	Sweet corn, New Zealand spinach.
	10–32°C	18–24°C	Pumpkin, squash.
	15–32°C	18–24°C	Cucumber, cantaloupe.
Hot Season Crops	18–26°C	21–24°C	Sweet capsicum, tomato.
	18–35°C	21–29°C	Eggplant, hot capsicum, okra, sweet potato, watermelon.

Seed Raising Mix

When sowing seeds in punnets, pots or flats, ordinary garden soil will not do. The best seed raising medium is generally made up of three equal parts of sharp sand, good garden soil and peat moss[1] or other moisture retaining medium. Turf-loam can substitute for garden soil. Make this by stacking cut grass turf in heaps and cover. Leave for twelve months. Compost can be substituted for peat moss as can coconut coir or leaf-mould. A tight handful each of dolomite, blood 'n' bone and seaweed meal per bucketful are beneficial. Be careful not to overdo the seaweed meal. The mixture needs to be both water-retentive and free-draining. Water from below by preference in order to avoid soil compaction and washing. Light seeds can easily float to the surface so when dunking seed-raising containers keep the water level to a smidgeon below the surface of the mix.

Covering the containers with a sheet of plastic or cardboard until the seeds germinate is a good practise, as it prevents the soil from drying out. The cover must be removed *immediately* the seeds germinate, though. While the seedlings are growing, they must receive adequate light, or they will be weak and spindly.

Damping-off is a fungal disease that particularly afflicts brassicas and lettuce. It attacks the stem at soil level, and makes the plants keel over. Covering the seeds in the punnet with sand rather than seed raising mix can help here, as can watering with dilute chamomile tea. Sphagnum moss also has mild fungicidal properties. A light dusting of the soil surface with sifted wood ashes is effective as it increases the pH, a condition fungal spores dislike intensely.

Many crops are seeded directly where they are to grow. Transplanting seedlings of many crops confers no benefit, or is downright impossible. Examples of the first include radishes that grow so quickly and suffering transplant shock would delay maturity. An example of the second would be carrots that are reputed to be impossible to transplant.

One organic grower of our acquaintance, a rather famous one at that, once claimed otherwise. When Allan Moult introduced him to a meeting of The Living Soil Society on the Tasman Peninsula many years ago, he referred to him as "the man who transplants carrots". This occasioned considerable embarrassment for the speaker as it eventuated he'd never actually tried it; he'd merely "read it somewhere". Ever so many things I've "read somewhere" have turned out not to be true.

---

1 See https://www.sgaonline.org.au/should-i-use-sphagnum-or-peat-moss/

My friend Tim Marshall has successfully transplanted carrots, though not by the dubious method just mentioned. He fills empty toilet roll tubes with seed raising mix and transplants the whole thing to avoid transplant shock. The depth is slightly deeper than a standard seed-raising punnet. You'd need to be sure to plant them out before the growing tip of the carrots reached the bottom or you would end up with one very short, fat carrot!

One exampleof the "impossible" was that apple cuttings could not be successfully struck. Indeed, when I tried it the cuttings survived for a couple of years, but never made any roots, or top growth. Then one year a neighbouring orchardist struck a few dozen cuttings he took from our stool bed of M9 dwarfing apple rootstock. In the very same year a friend on the North West coast of Tasmania successfully struck several hundred apple cuttings. The neighbour used ordinary rooting hormone powder that's used for rose cuttings. The acquaintance in the north used a "tea" made by steeping macerated willow twigs in water for a few days as a soil drench. Willows produce such an abundance of rooting hormones that a limb falling from a willow tree will often take root.

Buying Seed

THE PACKETS OF SEED YOU SEE for sale in the nursery, gardening section of the hardware store etc with pretty pictures on them are generally not the sort to buy. They tend to have a less than superb germination rate when they're packed, never mind after they have been on display for an unknown amount of time under less than ideal conditions.

SEED BOX AND MULTIPLE DIBBER TO MARK SEED STATIONS

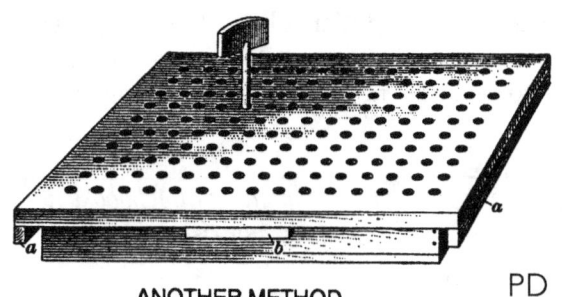

ANOTHER METHOD ...   PD

The very best seed that has a close to 100% germination rate is sold to market gardeners and in far larger quantities than a backyard gardener is likely to use. These seeds are not cheap. The worst seed I have purchased has come from "organic" sources claiming to sell open-pollinated heirloom varieties. I believe that these claims may well have been true. It was hard to tell though when the germination rate was zero percent. When you suspect the viability of the seed you have, it's easy enough to conduct a germination test. Count out a number of seeds, a dozen or two if they are large seeds, perhaps 50 if they are tiny seeds. Put them on a piece of paper kitchen towel in a plastic bag and place that in a warm place to germinate. I use the airing cupboard where the hot water cylinder is located. You will find the optimum temperature to germinate the seeds of different plants elsewhere in this book.

After a few days (for most varieties) you will be able to see the root and seed leaves emerging from the seed. Make sure that the plastic bag isn't completely sealed so that some air exchange can occur. Germinating seeds breathe too, not just plants and animals. The plastic bag is to ensure that the kitchen towel doesn't dry out; the seeds need to be kept moist, but not so wet that they begin to rot.

If you count the number of germinated seeds, divide that by the total number of seeds and multiply the result by 100 you will discover the percentage that germinated. Anything less than 95% is going to produce a disappointing result in many if not most cases.

At the end of the book I give the contact details for New Gippsland Seeds, a family owned seed company who sell only reliable seed in my experience of dealing with them for nearly 40 years. They conduct regular germination tests on their seed stock. On one occasion I had trouble germinating some strawberry seed and wrote to Norm de Vaus about it. He replied with a printed instruction sheet how to germinate strawberry seed successfully along with a replacement packet of seed.

In my first couple of years gardening I purchased a variety of seeds from different places wanting to discover which varieties performed best in my garden. One supplier substituted every French bean variety with Coles Dwarf broad bean, and almost every herb with curled parsley. Needless to say, they never received another order from me since.

Reading books about gardens is a potent pastime; books nourish a gardener's mind in the same way as manure nourishes plants.
— Mirabel Osler

Soaking Seed

You will be advised to soak seeds (particularly large ones) in dilute seaweed solution, compost tea, or even water overnight to "speed germination". I did this to my peas and broad beans for many years until I miscounted one year. I decided to fill in the missing rows of peas with dry seeds. Much to my surprise, they broke the soil surface a good five days ahead of the soaked seeds. A replication of this occurred with subsequent sowings. My friend Ruth Young discovered the same phenomenon for herself. The five day head start for the unsoaked seed she observed was the same for her peas as well as mine.

Sowing for Transplant

There are many benefits to transplanting rather than direct sowing. First and foremost you can more easily control the environment of a tray of seedlings than you can the open garden. Tomatoes, capsicums, egg plants, cucumbers and other heat loving plants can be started indoors on a window sill, in a cold frame or in a greenhouse before being planted out. Such pampered plants need to be gradually acclimatised to their new environment before transplanting, a process called hardening off. When they are taken directly from benign to harsher conditions they suffer what is called transplant shock. Some plants, especially tomatoes, can go into a permanent sulk and never reach their full potential.

Another consideration is that it's more convenient to treat seedlings concentrated in a small area than when they are isolated individuals in the open garden. Brassicas are prone to cabbage white butterflies laying their eggs that hatch into greedy green caterpillars for example. Cauliflowers and to a lesser extent broccoli have an elevated need for molybdenum to enable the formation of a critical enzyme. This needs to be supplied during the first two weeks following germination. In 1983 I purchased a small bottle of sodium molybdate powder from New Gippsland Seeds and dilute a smidgeon (enough to cover the tip of a pocket knife blade) in a 250 ml (one cup) sprayer. Even after treating thousands of cauli and broccoli seedlings, I still have some remaining in the bottle.

While the seedlings are awaiting their turn in the open garden, the open garden can either be prepared for their arrival by being easily weeded with the garden rake, or even still be producing a crop of some sort.

When admiring other people's gardens, don't forget to tend to your own flowers.
— Sanober Khan

Seed Raising Containers
Flats
THE TRADITIONAL WAY TO SOW for transplanting is into shallow boxes made of wood filled with seed-raising mix. Seed-raising mix is a mixture of roughly equal amounts of good garden soil,[2] granulated peat moss, or similar water-holding substance and sand. If you use peat moss, it's usual to include a tight handful of blood 'n' bone and the same of garden lime per bucketful. If you use sieved compost instead, these additives aren't necessary.

The disadvantage of flats is that removing the seedlings for transplant unavoidably damages their roots. A number of systems have been developed to overcome this root disturbance.

Cell Systems
PLASTIC TRAYS WITH RECTANGULAR depressions to hold the seed raising mix are very popular. Some have cubic depressions and some inverted pyramid-shaped cells. These latter enable ejection of the seedling with the least amount of root disturbance as it's possible to obtain from a cell system.

Soil Blocks
MANY YEARS AGO WORLD-RENOWNED market gardener Eliot Coleman led a seminar for vegetable gardeners at my friends Ian and Caryl Cairns' market garden in northern Tasmania. He demonstrated a device that you fill with wet seed raising mix and by pressing on a plunger to create cubic blocks of soil complete with a small depression to take the seed. This is far and away the best system I have come across if you can justify the expense of the soil-blocking machine. Root disturbance of transplants is minimal.

There are small and large blocking machines. Very slow-growing plants like cauliflower can be sown into small blocks that are later transplanted into a much larger soil block. Eliot said that when using such a system, you also gradually increase the available nutrient levels at each stage.

Open Seedbeds
ONIONS AND LEEKS BOTH BENEFIT from being sown initially in a seedbed in the open garden. They are very slow-growing and weed control is

---

2   This is best pasteurised by raising the temperature to 60°C (140°F) for half an hour. You don't want to sterilise the soil as that entails killing beneficial organisms as well as pathogens. You can do this in the domestic oven (while the wife is out) or make a solar device with greenhouse polythene. Temperature control may be difficult when using the latter approach.

Above: Soil-block machines.
Below: Milk cartons.

There are two kinds of people, those who do the work and those who take the credit. Try to be in the first group; there is less competition there.
—Indira Gandhi

essential — much easier when the seedlings are small and concentrated in a small area. I have tried growing them in flats, but this reduced the growth rate and the vigour of the plants at transplant time. Leeks and onions send their roots to a surprising depth. Both crops are in the ground for such a long time that delay due to transplant shock is quite negligible.

Milk and Egg Cartons

I'M NOT SURE WHY MILK CARTONS are so popular for raising seedlings. They have a thin film of plastic on the outside that doesn't disintegrate. If you do use them, they need drainage holes made in the bottom; snip a small part of the bottom four corners off. Completely remove the bottom at transplanting time so the seedling roots don't all need to squeeze through the drainage holes when you plant them out. The paper portion will eventually break down allowing the plastic film to blow where it will.

Egg cartons work much better since they don't need to be waterproofed with plastic. Fill them with seed raising mix and plant out the individual cells in the garden. The paper will eventually disintegrate completely. Since they're made of cellulose, they become the plant foods water and carbon dioxide.

Peat Pellets

PEAT PELLETS COME AS COMPRESSED, flattened disks that swell when thoroughly wetted. The seeds are then put in the central hole and some of the peat scraped over the top with a finger. The whole thing is planted out later when the seedling is mature enough and the peat becomes incorporated in the soil except for its thin plastic wrapper.

PVC Pipe Offcuts

WHEN WE WERE MARKET GARDENING, we used short lengths of PVC pipe as open-bottomed pots. They sat in mesh-bottomed trays and were filled with seed-raising mix. At planting out time, a short length of wooden dowel was used both to make the planting hole and to shove upwards into the pipe to release the seedling. When making the planting hole a quick jiggle ensured it was slightly wider than the plug of seed raising mix.

Transplanting

THE DOWNSIDE TO TRANSPLANTING seedlings is the extra labour involved and the likelihood of transplant shock that delays the maturity of the crop. To minimise this, seedlings should be watered beforehand to ensure the leaves are fully turgid and that the roots of the seedling are as little disturbed as possible. Immediately following planting out it's a good idea to water a little around the transplant with a little dilute seaweed and/or fish emulsion. Watering-in helps to eliminate air pockets that stress the transplants' roots. In very hot weather, they may also need or appreciate some temporary shading from the midday sun

When transplanting most seedlings, plant them a little below the level they were at in the punnet. Tomatoes benefit from being planted much deeper. The roots are then well into the zone of moisture, and further adventitious roots will arise from the stem at the junction of the leaf axil and stem. Lower leaves should have been removed.

Crops that do not mind being transplanted include: asparagus, cabbage, capsicum, cauliflower, celery, silver beet, eggplant, leek, lettuce, onion, tomato. The rest are all best sown where they are to grow to maturity. If the truth be known, it is best to sow all crops direct. There are several reasons for transplanting, however.

Eliot Coleman explains the virtues of soil-blocks for seed-raising—not the least being the fun of making mud-pies!

The first reason for transplanting is that where the growing season is short, crops like tomatoes, egg plants and capsicums are best sown indoors, long before the weather is warm enough to plant them outside. If you waited until the weather was warm enough to sow the seeds outside, the crop would not have a sufficient time to mature. The second reason for transplanting is that it gives you a longer period to reduce the weed-seed population in the growing bed, using the rake. Alternatively, you can be growing a crop and transplant into the bed immediately it has finished. Seedlings do not require the large amounts of space that the mature plants do. This is an advantage when controlling cabbage moth caterpillars in your brassicas. Less of the expensive *Dipel* spray or hand picking is needed.

When transferring plants sown indoors to their final outside positions, a period of acclimatisation is necessary. This is referred to as *hardening off*. If your seedlings came from a nursery, it is good practise to harden them off as well, since they are generally much pampered before coming to you. Failure to observe this procedure will at worst kill the plants and at best, they will sulk and never give of their best. Hardening off consists of exposing the plants to gradually increasing periods outdoors for one or two weeks, until they can be safely left out overnight.

When transplanting seedlings into their final position, firm the soil around their roots to eliminate any air pockets and water them in with a dilute seaweed tea. Watering in greatly increases the success of transplanting. If the weather is windy and/or warm, remove some of the leaves on top, to reduce the amount of water loss by the plants. This is particularly necessary where significant root disturbance (damage) has taken place. In extreme conditions, a shading device for the first few days will help reduce losses.

Moon Planting

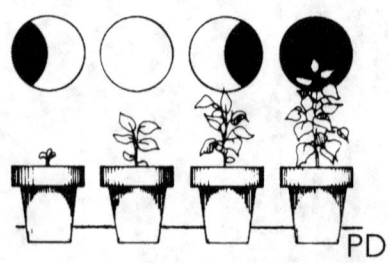

MANY GARDENERS SOW their seeds and transplant according to the phases of the moon. Given the dramatic influence the moon has on terrestrial conditions, the tides and so forth, this seems a perfectly reasonable thing to do. The slightly shorter than a month period between full moons is an almost ideal interval between the sowing of successional crops, such as lettuce and peas. Unfortunately, there is not just one system of moon planting. Biodynamic growers sow seeds just before the full moon and transplant just before the new moon. Bio-intensive gardeners sow their seeds just before the new moon and transplant at the full moon. Since both schools of thought, and doubtless there are others too, all obtain acceptable results, I believe that the weather has the greater influence on the outcome of gardening activity.

Sowing seeds, transplanting and cultivation according to the phase of the moon is one of the more controversial aspects of organic growing. Biodynamic growers take things one step further by also taking into account the sign of the zodiac the moon is in when farming or gardening. The practise is based on the belief that the moon influences the behaviour of water, both in the soil and in plant tissue. Practitioners claim that plants are more turgid (watery) at the full moon and less turgid at the new moon. Hence, traditionally, woodcutters cut down trees and haymakers cut hay at the new moon in order to reduce the amount of drying required.

In Biodynamics, followers of the Koliskos work sow seeds two days before full moon, and transplant around the new moon. Followers of Maria Thun sow seeds according to the constellation the moon is standing in and the portion of the plant to be used. Roots are sown in Taurus, Virgo and Capricorn, flowers in Gemini, Libra and Aquarius, leaf crops in Pisces, Scorpio and Cancer, fruits in Aries, Sagittarius and Leo. These two systems are not necessarily mutually contradictory. The Koliskos and Thun spent decades sowing seeds and meticulously recording the results.

In Alan Chadwick's bio-intensive system, short and extra-long germinating seeds are sown two days before the new moon; long-germinating seeds are sown at the full moon. Transplanting takes place at the full moon.

Yet another system, popularised by the astrologer Louise Riotte,[3] is summarised below.

Beans, second quarter, Cancer, Scorpio, Pisces, Libra, or Taurus.
Beetroot, third quarter, Cancer, Scorpio, Pisces, Libra, or Capricorn.
Broccoli and *Brussels Sprouts*, first quarter, Cancer, Scorpio, or Pisces.
Cabbage, first quarter, Cancer, Scorpio, Pisces, Taurus, or Libra.
Chinese Cabbage, first quarter, Cancer, Scorpio, or Pisces.
Capsicum, second quarter, Scorpio, or Sagittarius.
Carrots, third quarter, Cancer, Scorpio, Pisces, or Libra.
Cauliflower, first quarter, Cancer, Scorpio, Pisces, or Libra.
Celeriac, third quarter, Cancer, Scorpio, Pisces, Taurus, or Libra.
Celery, first quarter, Cancer, Scorpio, or Pisces.
Chicory, second, or third quarter, Cancer, Scorpio, Pisces, or Sagittarius.

---

3 "Carrots Love Tomatoes", by Louise Riotte, Storey Books 1976.

Cucumber, first quarter, Cancer, Scorpio, or Pisces.
Egg Plant, second quarter, Cancer, Scorpio, Pisces, or Libra.
Endive, first quarter, Cancer, Scorpio, Pisces, Libra, Virgo, Gemini, or Sagittarius.
Garlic, first, or second quarter, Scorpio, or Sagittarius.
Kohlrabi, first quarter, Cancer, Scorpio, Pisces, or Libra.
Leeks, second, or third quarter, Sagittarius.
Lettuce, first quarter, Cancer, Scorpio, or Pisces. Libra, or Taurus in late spring.
Okra, first quarter, Cancer, Scorpio, Pisces, or Libra.
Onions, third, or fourth quarter, Libra, Taurus, or Pisces.
Parsley, first quarter, Cancer, Scorpio, Pisces, or Libra.
Hamburg Parsley, third quarter, Cancer, Scorpio, Pisces, or Libra.
Parsnips, third quarter, Cancer, Scorpio, Pisces, or Libra.
Peas, second quarter, Cancer, Scorpio, Pisces, or Libra.
Potatoes, third quarter, Cancer, Scorpio, Taurus, Libra, Capricorn, or Sagittarius.
Pumpkins, second quarter, Libra, Cancer, Scorpio, or Pisces.
Radishes, third quarter, Libra, Taurus, Pisces, Sagittarius, or Capricorn.
Rhubarb, third quarter, moist signs.
Salsify, first or second quarters, Cancer, Scorpio, or Pisces. Taurus for late plantings.
Silver Beet, first, or second quarter, Cancer, Scorpio, Pisces, or Libra.
Spinach, first quarter, Cancer, Scorpio, or Pisces.
Sweet Corn, first quarter, Cancer, Scorpio, or Pisces.
Sweet Potatoes, third, or fourth quarter, Taurus.
Tomatoes, second quarter, Cancer, Scorpio, or Pisces.
Turnips and Swedes, third quarter, Cancer, Scorpio, Pisces, Taurus, Capricorn, or Libra.
Zucchini, second quarter, Cancer, Scorpio, Pisces, or Libra.

All advocates of moon planting point out that their particular system is an ideal to be strived for, rather than a system to be slavishly followed. Weather conditions will necessitate compromise. They also claim that the effects are not noticeable in soil that is under the influence of chemical fertilisers and pesticides. Only rich, organically active soil will respond to the cosmic influence.

Some people have beautiful gardens inside their hearts, some have graveyards.
  — Nitya Prakash

While I cannot recommend one system over another, the Biodynamic does have a literature of experimental results to support it. The writings of the Koliskos and Thun, if nothing else, impress me with the fanatical devotion to repeating the same activity (sowing seeds), day after day, year after year, and recording the results. In the same way, the foremost writer on Chadwick's system, John Jeavons, has published extensive tables of yields from his experimental gardens.

My gardening activity has been directed towards producing an abundance of high quality food, both for my own consumption and for sale. One visitor from the United States commented on the better flavour of my parsley as compared to Jeavons' in California. Her husband said that it was great being able to pull a piece off and just eat it, without it having to be weighed and included in a research project. They both considered my garden to be a friendlier and more comfortable place, and I suspect that were I to obsessively conduct extensive trials to test moon planting, it no longer would be.

Maintaining Records

WHAT DOES MAKE MORE SENSE is to observe the seasonal activity of perennial plants in relation to the results you get from transplanting and seeding. For instance, my apple trees began blossoming a full three weeks later this year than they usually do. Since they are responding to the actual growing conditions, they are an indicator that planting and sowing of spring crops should be three weeks later than average. Carefully maintained records of your observations in the garden are of far more use to you as a gardener than any amount of dogma, or theory. Your garden is unique, in its micro-climate, insect, fungus, bacteria and weed populations. By careful observation and gentle guidance, you will be able to insinuate your influence into the constantly changing relationships between all these organisms. Try to dominate them and you will lose the battle, as conventional growers so often do. Instead of having Nature's support, you will reap a harvest of a bewildering variety of new pests and diseases, decreasing soil fertility and self-loathing at your lack of ability to achieve your goal: domination. When you adopt the organic approach, you will see the various organisms in your garden as unique and important for the roles they have to play and that yours is but one among many. Feed the soil and its micro-organisms and not the plant. Discourage the weeds and undesirable insects, rather than trying to eliminate them. If this means donating 5% of your crop to Nature, so be it. Your garden will reward you with a bounty of produce and peace of mind.

Temperatures for Germinating Seeds[4]

Crop	Seeds/gm	Min Temp (°C)	Temp Range (°C)	Opt Temp (°C)	Max Temp (°C)
Asparagus	50	10	16–30	24	35
Beetroot	60	5	10–30	30	35
Broad bean	1	*	*	*	*
Broccoli	300	†	†	†	†
Brussels sprouts	300	†	†	†	†
Cabbage	300	5	7–35	30	38
Cantaloupe	40	16	24–35	32	38
Capsicum	150	16	18–35	30	35
Carrot	1000	5	7–30	27	35
Cauliflower	300	5	7–30	27	38
Celery	3000	5	16–21	21	30
Chicory	500	‡	‡	‡	‡
Cucumber	40	16	16–35	35	10
Egg plant	250	16	24–32	30	35
French bean	4	16	16–30	27	35
Kale	300	†	†	†	†
Kohlrabi	300	†	†	†	†
Leek	300	#	#	#	#
Lettuce	800	4	5–27	24	30
Onion	200	4	10–35	24	35
Parsley	800	5	10–30	24	32
Parsnip	300	4	10–21	18	30
Pea	5	5	5–24	24	30
Pumpkin	5	16	21–32	35	38
Radish	100	5	7–32	30	35
Silverbeet	60	5	10–30	30	35
Spinach	100	4	7–24	21	30
Squash	5–10	16	21–35	35	38
Swede	300	†	†	†	†

[4] Tabular data largely based on "Handbook for Vegetable Growers" by James Edward Knott, John Wiley & Sons, New York, 1957.

Crop	Seeds/gm	Min Temp (°C)	Temp Range (°C)	Opt Temp (°C)	Max Temp (°C)
Sweet corn	5	10	16–35	35	40
Tomato	300	10	16–30	30	35
Turnip	300	5	16–40	30	40
Watermelon	10	5	21–35	35	40

* Not known, similar to pea. ‡ Not known, similar to lettuce.
\# Not known, similar to onion. † Not known, similar to turnip.

Every kind of work can be a pleasure. Even simple household tasks can be an opportunity to exercise and expand our caring, our effectiveness, our responsiveness. As we respond with caring and vision to all work, we develop our capacity to respond fully to all of life. Every action generates positive energy which can be shared with others. These qualities of caring and responsiveness are the greatest gift we can offer.
—Tarthang Tulku

Seed Saving

THERE ARE TWO SORTS OF SEED available, open pollinated and hybrid. Hybrid seed is created by cross-pollinating two or more varieties to create a more vigorous plant. These plants are, more often than not, sterile, which means that seed saved from them can't be relied on to be true to type. Sometimes the seed is viable, but very weak. The purported advantages of hybrid seed include greater uniformity of size and maturation, resistance to certain diseases, improved response to artificial fertilisers and resistance to certain herbicides. While uniformity is a desirable attribute for the commercial grower, the home gardener may prefer the longer harvest period of the more traditional open-pollinated varieties.

Open-pollinated plants from home-saved seed often have better germination rates, superior flavour and higher resistance to pests. A big attraction is that you can save their seeds without the prospect of unpleasant surprises. Also, as the multi-national chemical companies have been buying up seed merchants, there are fewer and fewer open-pollinated varieties available. Unless you save your own favourites, they may become unavailable in the future. A big advantage to saving seeds is the opportunity it gives to develop strains that are particularly suited to your locality, or taste. Into the bargain comes a significant cost saving. Fresh home-saved seed usually exhibits maximum germination rates, particularly noticeable with pea and bean seeds.

Saving seeds from different types of plants requires a variety of approaches. Some are self-fertile, both male and female organs residing in the one flower. Accidental cross-pollination is infrequent with these sorts of plants. Some plants require the presence of several plants cross-pollinating each other to set viable seed. If these plants are in the open, you must be sure that the cross-pollinating insects are not visiting undesirable plants in the vicinity. Commercial seedsmen often ensure distances of several kilometres to prevent

VEGETABLE SEEDS

tomato   pepper   cabbage   carrot   beet

AS

unwanted crosses, but the home gardener can eliminate the odd undesirable plant from the breeding program. Another alternative is caging the plants with insect-proof gauze and propagating a few insects in there, such as house flies, in the cage.

Fortunately, many garden plants are very easy to save seed from. Lettuces, tomatoes, peas, beans, capsicums, and egg plants are all very reluctant to cross. These are all good plants for the beginner to save seed from. The pumpkin family can easily be pollinated by hand.

It is important to know the genetic relationship of different vegetables to avoid unwanted crosses.

The grass family, *Gramineae*, is represented by sweet corn in the garden. It will cross with popcorn and field corn.

The lily family, *Liliaceae*, is represented by asparagus, onions, garlic, chives and leeks. Leeks will cross with pearl onions, but not the ordinary sort. Chives and asparagus will not cross with the rest of the family. Garlic is propagated by bulb division and most varieties do not set true seed.

The goosefoot family, *Chenopodiaceae*, includes beetroot, silver beet (chard) and spinach.

The cabbage family, *Crucifera*, includes many common garden vegetables and unfortunately many weeds. Broccoli, Brussels sprouts, cabbage, cauliflower, kale, and kohlrabi will all cross if any are flowering at the same time. Chinese cabbage will not cross with the latter, but will cross with turnips, radishes, swedes and mustard.

The pea family, *Leguminosae*, includes peas, French beans, broad beans, scarlet runner beans, lima beans, soybeans and cow peas. None of these groups will cross with members of the others. Note that climbing French beans are often called runner beans. Scarlet runners are a short lived perennial, and despite their name, there is a white flowered variety, though it is rare in Australia. Climbing French beans are mostly white flowered, though there is a variety called Molly's, that has pinkish flowers.

The parsley family, *Umbelliferae*, includes carrots, parsnips, parsley, celery, celeriac, and several culinary herbs. Apart from celery and celeriac crossing, the only problem in this group is carrots crossing with Queen Anne's Lace, a weed that some gardeners grow for the pretty flowers.

The nightshade family, *Solanaceae*, includes potato, tomato, eggplant, capsicum, chillies, tobacco and several weeds. None of these will cross and crossing those that will cross takes some effort. Even a distance of two metres reduces the chances of cross pollination to negligible proportions.

The cucumber family, *Cucurbitaceae*, includes cucumbers, winter squash, summer squash, pumpkins, zucchini, watermelons and melons. Despite some gardeners' claims, cucumbers will not cross with melons or pumpkins. There is limited crossing between some members of winter squash and pumpkin groups.

The daisy family, *Compositae*, includes lettuce, Jerusalem artichoke and salsify. Lettuces will reluctantly cross with each other, but not the others.

Vegetable	**Life cycle**	**Viability**	**Pollinated**	**Minimum Isolation**
Asparagus	perennial	3 yrs	insect	400 m *
Beetroot	biennial	4 yrs	wind	400 m
Broad bean	annual	3 yrs	self	50 m
Broccoli	annual	5 yrs	insect	100 m
Brussels sprouts	biennial	5 yrs	insect	100 m
Cabbage	biennial	5 yrs	insect	100 m
Capsicum	annual	4 yrs	self	2 m
Carrots	biennial	4 yrs	insect	400 m
Cauliflower	biennial	5 yrs	insect	100 m
Celeriac	biennial	5 yrs	insect	400 m *
Celery	biennial	5 yrs	insect	400 m
Chinese cabbage	annual	5 yrs	insect	100 m
Chive	perennial	2 yrs	insect	400 m *
Cucumber	annual	5 yrs	insect	150 m #
Eggplant	annual	5 yrs	self	2 m
French bean	annual	3 yrs	self	50 m
Kale	biennial	5 yrs	insect	100 m
Kohl rabi	biennial	5 yrs	insect	100 m
Leek	biennial	3 yrs	insect	400 m
Lettuce	annual	5 yrs	self	5 m
Melon	annual	5 yrs	insect	150 m #
Okra	annual	2 yrs	self	2 m
Onion	biennial	2 yrs	insect	400 m
Parsley	biennial	2 yrs	insect	400 m

Vegetable	Life cycle	Viability	Pollinated	Minimum Isolation
Parsnip	biennial	1 yr	insect	400 m
Pea	annual	3 yrs	self	5 m
Pumpkin	annual	5 yrs	insect	150 m
Radish	annual	5 yrs	insect	400 m
Salsify	biennial	2 yrs	self	2 m #
Soybean	annual	3 yrs	self	50 m
Spinach	annual	5 yrs	wind	400 m
Squash	annual	5 yrs	insect	150 m
Swede	biennial	5 yrs	insect	400 m
Sweet corn	annual	2 yrs	wind	100 m
Tomato	annual	4 yrs	self	2 m
Turnip	annual	5 yrs	insect	400 m

The recommended isolation distance is the minimum. Some crossing can be expected at the minimum distances. Those vegetables marked #, are easily kept pure following the directions below. Those marked * are vegetables of which there are so few varieties grown that crossing is not likely to be a problem.

The cucumber family are easily pollinated by hand. The plants set two sorts of flowers. The female is easily distinguished by a swelling at the base; this is the incipient fruit. This will become the fruit. The male flower has no swelling. Learn to identify which flowers are going to open the following day. Tie some up with cotton or rubber bands to prevent the insects beating you to it. The following day, remove a male flower and strip its petals. Open a female flower and rub the male part against the female. One male flower will pollinate several females. The cucumber family do not mind if the flowers all are from the one plant. Place a paper bag over the female flower for three or four days, so the insects do not intrude. Mark the specially pollinated fruit by placing a ribbon around the stem.

The seeds of the cucumber family and the nightshade family all benefit from being fermented in some lukewarm water for several days. This frees the seeds from the pulp and destroys several virus diseases into the bargain. Dry them thoroughly afterward on absorbent paper.

All seeds should be dead ripe at harvest. Wait until the seeds start to fall off, or out of the pods. This is called shattering. Because it is dead ripe, home saved seed often germinates much better than commercially grown seed that was artificially dried before it was completely ripe. The best storage containers are brown paper bags. Clearly label them with the name of the variety and the year of collection. Store them in a cool, dark place. A ten Celsius degree lower temperature will double the storage life of many varieties.

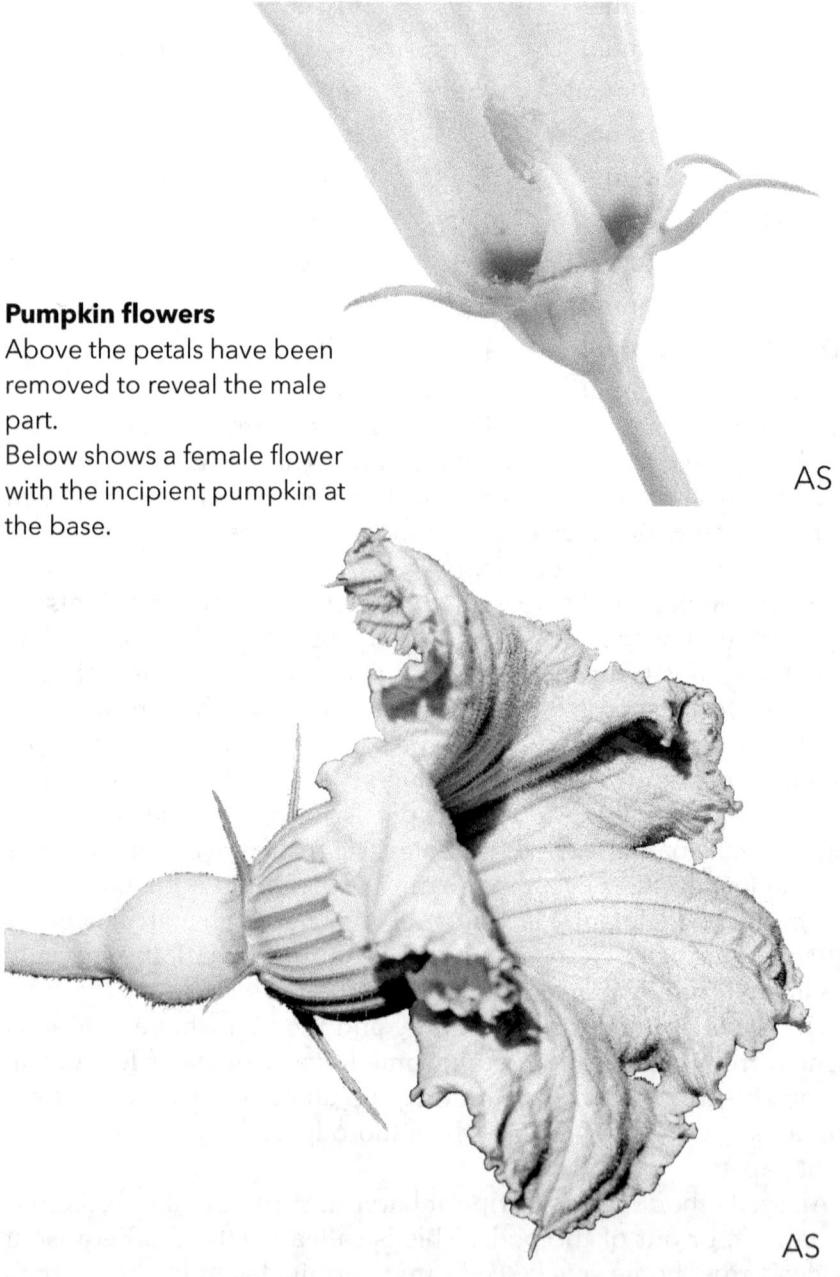

Pumpkin flowers
Above the petals have been removed to reveal the male part.
Below shows a female flower with the incipient pumpkin at the base.

AS

AS

Storage of Vegetables

ONE OF THE GREAT DELIGHTS of gardening is the improved flavour and texture of fresh vegetables. One of the main reasons store-bought produce is so lacklustre is the fact that the fruit and vegetables have been stored, and poorly at that. Fruit is picked before it is fully ripe because it is tougher then and withstands the rigours of transport better. The same varieties allowed to ripen on the tree or vine taste much better. Nevertheless, there are gaps in production and there is ample reason for storing produce to carry us through. As well, some produce is grown specifically for storage.

The most economical place to store produce is in the ground where it is growing. Where the soil is well drained, hard frosts do not occur, and the winters are reasonably cool, roots are best kept in the garden. The overseas practice of using root cellars and earth covered mounds (clamps) is totally unnecessary in South Eastern Australia. The brief gap between them running to seed in the spring and the harvest of the earliest from the new plantings gives the palate time to relearn how to relish them.

Peas and beans are particularly suited to drying. Allowed to ripen on the vine and shelled out, they will keep for a couple of years. There is no great need to grow the special varieties developed for this. We prefer broad beans to limas, which we could not grow in Southern Tasmania anyway. Home-dried peas and beans seem to cook quicker than the shop-bought sorts. Another product worth drying is the mushroom. When there is a glut of field mushrooms, we dry and crumble them for thickening and flavouring winter soups made with the relatively bland dried peas and beans.

Garlic and onions ripen fully in the summer and autumn, and must be dried for storage. Hung in a cool, well ventilated place, they will keep for several months.

Tomatoes can be stewed until they thicken to make a kitchen ingredient partway between passata and tomato paste. This sauce ingredient is infinitely superior to any factory product I've tried. Do not believe the commercials that tell you only the best produce is used to make this and other processed products. The price received by the grower from the processor is much less than the price for fresh. Only the malformed, over-ripe, inferior stuff is sold to the factory. In the

---

This is the real secret of life — to be completely engaged with what you are doing in the here and now. And instead of calling it work, realise it is play.
—Alan Watts

home kitchen, the home cook can be far more discerning than the commercial manufacturer.

Conditions for long storage of vegetables

Vegetable	Temp	Relative humidity	Approximate storage life
Artichoke, globe	0°C	Very high	3–6 weeks
Asparagus	0°C	Very high	2–4 weeks
Bean	7°C	High	2–4 weeks
Beetroot (topped)	0°C	High	12–20 weeks
Broccoli	0°C	High	1–2 weeks
Brussels sprouts	0°C	Very high	2–4 weeks
Cabbage	0°C	Very high	1–3 months
Capsicum	7°C	High	2–3 weeks
Carrot	0°C	Very high	1–5 months
Cauliflower	0°C	Very high	2–4 weeks
Celery	0°C	High	6–10 weeks
Cucumber	7°C	High	2–3 weeks
Eggplant	7°C	High	10 days
Endive	0°C	High	2–3 weeks
Garlic	0°C	Dry	6–7 months
Leafy greens	0°C	Very high	1–2 weeks
Leeks	0°C	High	1–3 months
Lettuce	0°C	High	1–3 weeks
Marrow (hard)	10°C	Dry	6–12 weeks
Melon	5°C	Medium	2–3 weeks
Mushroom	0°C	High	1 week
Okra	7°C	High	2 weeks
Onion	0°C	Dry	1–8 months
Parsley	0°C	Very high	1 month
Parsnip	0°C	Very high	6 months
Pea	0°C	High	1–3 weeks
Potato	7°C	Medium	4–6 months
Pumpkin	10°C	Dry	2–4 months *
Rhubarb	0°C	Very high	2–3 weeks

Vegetable	Temp	Relative humidity	Approximate storage life
Shallot	0°C	Very high	1–2 weeks
Silver Beet	0°C	Very high	1–2 weeks
Spinach	0°C	Very high	1–2 weeks
Squash (summer)	7°C	Very high	1–3 weeks
Squash (winter)	10°C	Dry	2–4 months *
Sweet Corn	0°C	High	4–8 days
Sweet Potato	13°C	Medium	4–6 months
Tomato (ripe)	7°C	Medium	4 days
Tomato (unripe)	13°C	Medium	2–4 weeks
Turnip	0°C	High	4–5 months
Water Melon	7°C	Medium	2–3 months
Zucchini	7°C	High	2 weeks

* Some varieties will keep up to 24 months, though the flavour deteriorates slowly.

Root vegetables must be topped as the leaves continue to transpire moisture. Leaving them on will shrivel the roots.

Ethylene gas is given off by ripening fruit. We use this property when we put unripe tomatoes in an unventilated paper bag with a banana or apple. The tomatoes ripen quicker because the apple or banana increases the level of ethylene. Some vegetables are very sensitive to ethylene and will deteriorate rapidly when stored alongside fruit giving off the gas. This is most noticeable with broccoli and other members of the cabbage tribe.

Produces Ethylene	Sensitive to Ethylene	
Apple	Asparagus	Potato
Apricot	Bean	Rhubarb
Avocado	Broccoli	Shallot
Banana	Brussels sprouts	Silver Beet
Fig	Cabbage	Squash
Kiwi Fruit	Carrot	Sweet Corn
Mango	Cauliflower	Sweet Potato
Nectarine	Celery	Zucchini
Papaw	Cucumber	

Produces Ethylene	Sensitive to Ethylene
Passion Fruit	Endive
Peach	Gooseberry
Pear	Leafy Greens
Plum	Lettuce
Rock Melon	Okra
Tomato	Parsley

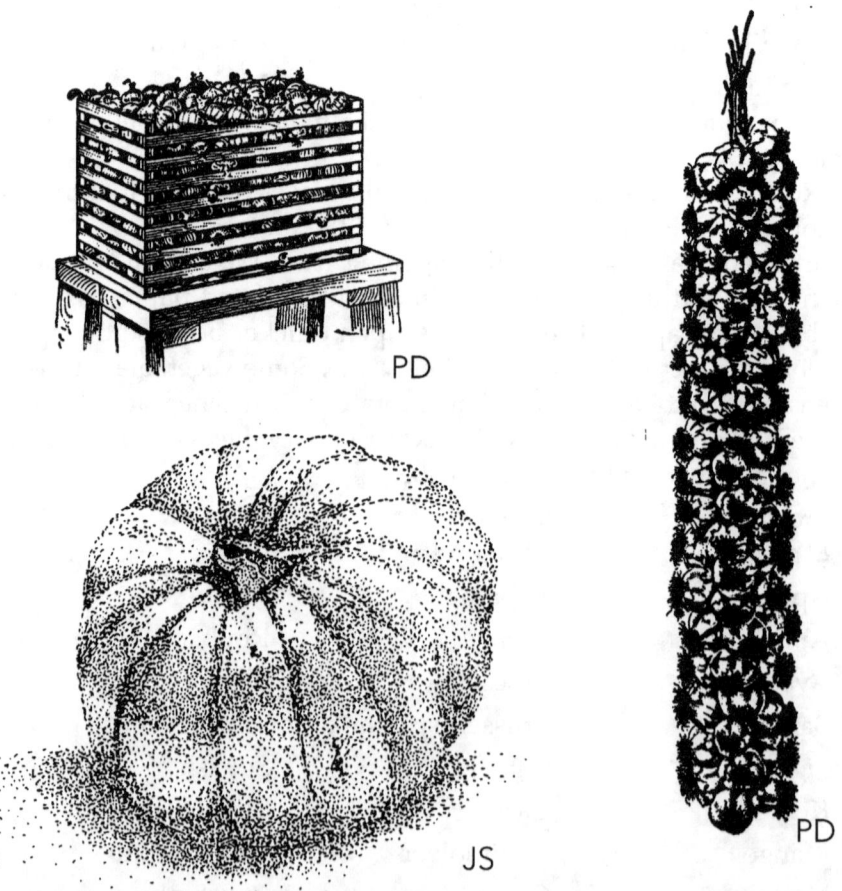

Excellent air circulation is required for storing onions, garlic and pumpkins.

The Rival Growing Systems

THERE IS A SPECTRUM between anti-chemical organic extremism at one end and pro-chemical lunacy at the other. The following list of the various camps, while comprehensive, is not exhaustive. As with such systems in religion and politics, the followers of any one camp believe they have an exclusive truth and that any who disagree are foolish people who must be converted. The writer fervently hopes that there will come a day when we talk about good or bad farming, not which camp we belong to.

Albrecht

IN THE UNITED STATES, Dr William Albrecht took an approach midway between his conventional counterparts and the extremism of the US organic movement led by Robert Rodale. He was head of the Missouri Agricultural Research Station for several decades and he published an enormous number of papers about his ideas of plant nutrition and animal health. He took considerable pains to distance his work from that of organic and Biodynamic researchers.

The basic precept behind Albrecht's work was that there should be an explanation for why stock health was observably superb in some regions and poor in others. He conducted extensive soil testing in various parts of the United States and found a correlation between the ratios of certain elements in the soil and protein content of the plants growing in them. When the mineral balance in a poor soil was adjusted to equate with that of a known good soil, protein content of crops increased and animal health improved. He further discovered that water-soluble fertilisers were inferior to simple crushed rocks containing the required minerals.

Albrecht was also keenly interested in the effects of farming on human health. Having discovered that the prairies of the Midwest produced the healthiest livestock, he postulated that human health in this region should, in turn, be better. Since good health was a prerequisite for acceptance into military service, he perused the army intake records for the various regions of the United States and indeed confirmed his suspicion. The rejection rate for army service

---

There is a set of religious, or rather moral, writings which teach that virtue is the certain road to happiness, and vice to misery in this world. A very wholesome and comfortable doctrine, and to which we have but one objection, namely, that it is not true.
   —Henry Fielding

was lowest where soil fertility was highest and highest where soil fertility was lowest.

Biodynamic

IN GERMANY, RUDOLF STEINER founded a school of philosophy, Anthroposophy. Some of his followers were farmers and they brought their agricultural problems to Steiner for his advice. In response, he eventually gave them a series of lectures published in his book, *Agriculture*. This farming system he named Biodynamic and it bears more than a passing resemblance to Howard's organic farming with a similar emphasis on humus. It differs however in taking account of cosmic and spiritual forces, as well as the influence of soil. The association with spiritual beliefs and astrology has limited the appeal of Biodynamics for scientists trained to ignore what it reflexively calls pseudo-science.

"One should be careful to separate the phenomenon from the explanation. That is, a mystical explanation is not sufficient grounds for denying that the phenomenon does not exist. Planting by the phases of the moon has long been practised by some and ridiculed by others. The following can be noted however:

1. Slight flexure of the earth's crust occurs when the moon passes overhead (similar to the tidal effect in the oceans).

2. Crustal flexure prior to earthquakes releases gases from deep within the continental crust.

3. The unusual behaviour of animals prior to earthquakes is attributed to these gases.

So here is a mechanism that links the position of the moon with animal behaviour. Is our knowledge of the influence of soil atmosphere on germination so complete that we can unequivocally deny the possibility that the slight crustal flexure caused by the moon's passage has no effect on the soil atmosphere, or on seed germination?"[1]

Conventional

WHAT IS NOW CALLED CONVENTIONAL agriculture was called scientific agriculture when it arose in the late nineteenth century. Arguably its greatest promoter (though not its originator) was the great German chemist, Justus von Liebig, who applied his considerable intellect to understanding plant nutrition. He discovered through many pot trials that plants depended on a handful of elements in the soil, most notably nitrogen, phosphorus and potassium. Furthermore, he discovered

---

1 From the University of New England (Orange Agricultural College) Graduate Diploma Program in Sustainable Agriculture.

that he could feed these substances to plants in water-soluble form and achieve yields much higher than when they weren't present.

Liebig postulated that the element in shortest supply was the limiting factor in crop yield and that all of the elements removed with the crop must be replaced. These simple, common-sense concepts have been taught in agricultural and horticultural institutions ever since. Shortly before he died, Liebig wrote about his later discovery, his theory did not quite work out in practise. Unfortunately this work has never, to the best of my knowledge, been translated into English.

The barrel shows Liebig's theory diagrammatically. If the potential yield of the soil is represented by a full barrel of water and the individual staves the quantity of individual fertility elements in the soil, then the barrel can only be filled to the height of the shortest stave.

Following the publication of Liebig's ideas on crop fertilisation, John Lawes invented what he called superphosphate. He discovered that turning animal bones into fertiliser with sulphuric acid was much less expensive than grinding them up, since sulphuric acid was a cheap by-product of the Industrial Revolution's chemical industry. This acidified phosphate could be demonstrated to give crop

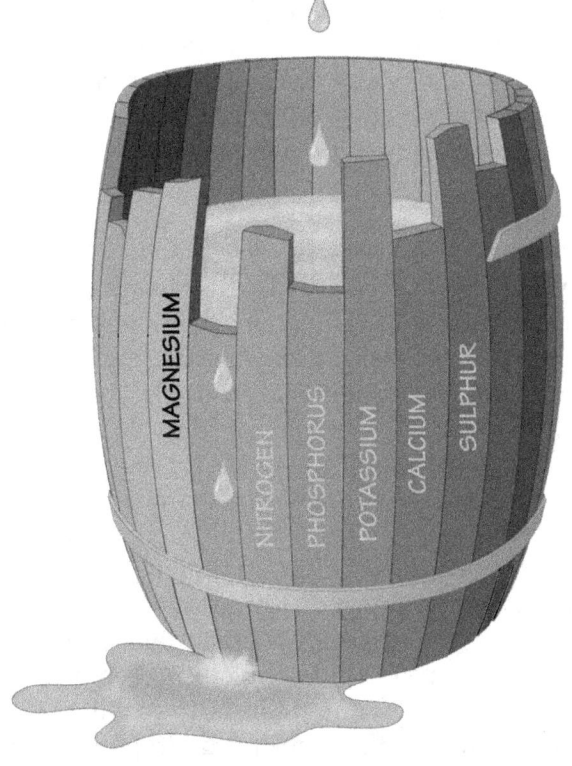

yield increases for little financial outlay. When the supply of bones became insufficient, rock phosphate, the petrified residues of bird excreta, was an even cheaper substitute. Interestingly, Lawes' original directions for using superphosphate recommended reverting it with lime to neutralise its acidity.

The second major impact of modern industry on agriculture came after the First World War. The conflict gave rise to a huge demand for explosives based on nitrogen. Large factories were built to convert atmospheric nitrogen into ammonia and nitrates. When the battle ceased, there was an understandable reluctance to cease production. Although it was "the war to end all wars", the potential for future conflict meant that it was politically expedient for the factories to remain productive. The factories were converted to nitrogenous fertiliser manufacture which made the shareholders happy and governments feel more secure.

The two decades between the First and Second World Wars is when the revolt against scientific agriculture began in earnest. Scientific agriculture was seen by more perceptive farmers to have lost something in the pursuit of increased production. Animal health was in decline with new diseases and crop health also was suffering from new pests and diseases. Lucerne fields that had previously yielded well for decades needed to be ploughed up and resown after less than ten years. To some farmers and scientists this was a clear indication of the failure of modern, intensive methods of production. To others, it was a marketing opportunity to sell "cures" for these problems.

Hydroponics

HYDROPONICS IS THE "SCIENTIFIC" system taken to its extreme. The soil is replaced by an inert medium, or dispensed with entirely in the Nutrient Film Technique. Maintaining the balance of nutrients in hydroponic solutions requires considerable expertise and the fertilisers used are more expensive than conventional artificials. While there is always a concerted effort to push hydroponics as the solution to all our problems, it has remained economically viable for only a very small range of high-value crops such as tomatoes and marijuana. Continual inputs of pesticides and fungicides are required, as the crops' self-defence mechanisms are largely nullified by the growing system.

We are often asked how to grow organically using hydroponics. The simple answer is you can't grow organically without soil and its associated organisms. You may very well succeed in growing crops with organic fertilisers and without soil, but you will likely experience many and perhaps most of the problems hydroponic growers face.

Natural Farming

Masonabu Fukuoka's stimulating book, *One Straw Revolution*, caused a world-wide sensation. He expanded on his ideas in a further volume, entitled *Natural Farming*. His ideas have had a major influence on David Holmgren and Bill Mollison's *Permaculture*. Basically, Fukuoka practises a no fertiliser, no cultivation, no pruning farming system based on mulch and legumes. As in any universal solution to our agricultural problems, it fails. Like many systems, it works well in its home environment, but there are many different environments on planet Earth. I thoroughly commend Fukuoka's works as a source of ideas that may very well work in your locality. They certainly failed in mine.

For example, Fukuoka recommends that rather than thinning fruit that the tree be allowed to decide how much to shed. Apparently this worked well with oranges, the fruit that he was growing. Apples, a typical fruit in our much cooler environment, do not respond at all well to this approach. The apple's goal is to produce as much seed as possible so unthinned apples remain tiny and the proportion of core to flesh reflects this. We consume the flesh, not the core or its toxic seeds and leaving the fruit to self-thin greatly reduces the amount of desired product.

Worse, the health of the apple tree instead of being enhanced is diminished. The tree responds by becoming unable to set fruit in the following season, or such fruit that does form is of much inferior quality. In order to reduce this alternate-bearing as the condition is called, you need to reduce the number of fruit by as much as 95% in some varieties. There is an exception here. The Granny Smith self-thins satisfactorily, but I can't think of any other variety that does so.

As well I have always thinned my apples to singles in order to be able to more easily control the Light Brown Apple Moth. The larvae are tenting caterpillars and they will hide between apples that are touching where the small birds that eat them find it difficult to reach.

Organic

In India, Sir Albert Howard was studying the role of certain fungi and humus (compost) in plant health. This work gave rise to a concept called *organic farming*. This wasn't simply a return to the conventional farming of the past, which we might call unconsciously organic, but built on new concepts of plant nutrition and the relationships between crops and livestock. "Progressive" farmers in Europe, the USA and Australasia were simplifying their farms after the fashion of factories; artificial fertiliser inputs at one end and produce and "waste" coming out the other. Howard believed there was more benefit to be gained from using animal manures and crop residues to build soil fertility. The concept of the organic farm included that of mixed farming, where the by-products of one part of the farm were the inputs for another. Rather than burning straw, it was used as animal bedding. The mixture of dung and urine-soaked straw was then composted with crop residues to become fertiliser for crops.

Howard had found that some plants he was studying relied on a symbiotic root fungus (mycorrhiza) for their phosphorus needs. In return for supplying the plant with phosphorus, the fungus took its carbohydrates from the plant. These fungi needed particular soil conditions for their survival and the plants with which they were associated failed to thrive in their absence. The soil conditions they favoured were high in humus and biological activity. The source of humus was decomposed crop residues and animal manures, the very materials that factory farming was assiduously burning or dumping, often in the belief that they were eliminating a source of disease.

Howard further discovered in his experiments with humus manufacture and use (composting), that its presence in the soil conferred many benefits. Perhaps the most important from the point of view of the farmer beset by pests and diseases, was the relative absence of these problems in compost-grown plants. Tomatoes grown with compost were more resistant to Tobacco Mosaic Virus. Plants infected with TMV were placed among the plants in Howard's trials to increase the chance of infection. Even tomatoes grown using compost made from plants infected with the disease were shown to be resistant.[2]

When Howard was eventually allowed to experiment with feeding compost-grown crops to cattle, he found that they became resistant to infection by foot and mouth disease, even where infected cattle were allowed to rub noses with those in his feeding trial. It must be pointed out that the strain of FMD was much less virulent than that which caused so many problems to British farmers in the 1960s.

Howard returned to England and began publishing his ideas. They gave rise to the Soil Association which he co-founded with Lady Eve Balfour. The Soil Association was formed to scientifically investigate the differences between scientific and organic agriculture. This work was published in Balfour's book, *The Haughley Experiment* which

---

2 Steiner singled out a peculiarity of tomatoes. They preferred he said to be grown more or less continually in the same ground rather than as part of a rotation. Tomatoes are actually perennial even though we treat them as if they're annuals. Also Steiner said they preferred a compost made largely from tomato plants.

these days is printed as a single volume with her earlier book, *The Living Soil*.

The work at Haughley clearly showed marked differences between systems that used chemical fertilisers, with or without crop and animal manure residues. Although chemical fertilisers increased grass yield, the output of milk per cow was reduced. Crop yield increases were shown to be insufficient to pay the cost of the artificial fertiliser used. One anomaly that showed up was egg production appeared to be dependent on amount fed, rather than quality of feed.

Permaculture

IN THE EARLY NINETEEN SEVENTIES, David Holmgren and Bill Mollison started to develop their ideas on a design system for permanent agriculture, hence Permaculture. Since their ideas didn't seem to work particularly well in Tasmania, they decamped for more tropical climes where I am led to believe it worked much better. Permaculture borrows heavily from a number of sources and synthesises them in several fascinating and very readable books. As well, it has spawned an international movement and Permaculture Design Consultants charge comfortable fees for their work.

In the *Permaculture International Journal*, Leigh Davison wrote a letter lamenting his difficulties getting Permaculture to work on what was intended to be a commercially profitable farm. I found some irony in this and that for a decade local Permaculture classes came to my farm to experience its possibilities. Permaculture ideas have played no great role in my thinking. Albrecht, Biodynamic and French-intensive gardening have been far greater influences than my few conversations in the 1970s with Bill Mollison. Unlike Leigh I never attempted to implement a commercial Permaculture system and from the several conversations I had with him never would. That is not to say that I don't think it's workable at a subsistence level where making a profit is not an issue.

This comment should not be taken to mean I am at all opposed to Permaculture. It just seems odd to me that since I have never claimed to be a Permaculturist that my farm was considered for a decade to be the best exemplar of that system in its place of origin. I would have thought that someone trained and presumably certified as a Permaculturist would have already created a better example. I'm equally certain that had I claimed to be a Permaculturist I would be taken to task since I have not undertaken any training/certification in that discipline.

Thoughts on Commercial Production

You will read that organic fertilisers cost much more than artificial. When I first commenced market gardening, I went shopping. The most expensive nutrient is nitrogen. While you can obtain it "for free" from the use of legumes, this will only provide for a fraction of the needs of an intensive organic garden, unless you have a separate legume pasture for hay production. For example a one hectare paddock of white clover will produce about 100kg of N per annum, sufficient for a 0.4 Ha cabbage crop. When I looked at purchasing off-farm nitrogenous fertilisers, blood 'n' bone was far and away the most expensive. The cheapest was chicken deep-litter (poultry manure mixed with sawdust) trucked from 70 km away. It must be pointed out that this was much bulkier than urea, a popular artificial nitrogenous fertiliser. On the other hand, chicken deep-litter contains phosphorus, potassium and the essential precursors of humus: cellulose and lignin. It also has an abundance of trace elements.

My friends Ian and Caryl Cairns have a neighbour with a dairy farm down the road where they obtain cow manure. In almost any farming district, you will come across crop residues that are available for minimal cost that are a valuable source of major nutrients and humus. On one occasion I removed the cow manure from a disused jam-factory that had been converted into a hay-shed *cum* feeding area. On another occasion, I emptied a friend's goat shed. Both of these sheds were full of manure that had been aging for many years and was used direct on the soil. Most importantly, it was free apart from my labour and transport. We have also in the past taken a trailer to a beach and collected copious quantities of seaweed that is in abundance following storms. Until my farming neighbours woke up to the fact that they could be doing the same as us, we were given spoiled hay, either for nothing, or the cost of baling.

It is important for the economics of organic market gardening that you locate accessible, inexpensive sources for your compost. Other materials we have come across at little or no cost, have been hop mark, pyrethrum mark, cocoa bean shells, pea straw, cereal straw, pig slurry, spoiled fish meal, lawn clippings, sawdust, spent barley malt, spoiled vegetables and trimmings from shops, barber shop hair, sheep manure from underneath shearing sheds, poppy straw and seed meal, and apple pomace.

Even an organic fertiliser that looks expensive on the surface may be better value when looked at more closely. A friend who compared the effect of superphosphate to blood 'n' bone on pasture, noted that while the effect of super was confined to the season of use, the blood 'n' bone treated section was well ahead in the year following its application. This prolonged and cumulative effect is noticeable with all organic fertiliser programs. In the writer's garden, after a decade soil testing showed the equivalent of an additional one tonne per hectare of super, above the phosphorus applied and ignoring what was exported in crops. This phosphorus had previously been locked up by the chemistry of conventionally managed soil.

Crop Rotation, Green manures and Cover Crops

A GREEN MANURE IS A CROP grown specifically for fertility enhancement. Quite often, green manure is confused with cover cropping. The latter is specifically grown for weed suppression and prevention of soil erosion when the ground would otherwise remain bare for a period of three months, or more. Of course, a crop can be grown for both purposes, but the type of crop grown is determined by the most important purpose.

European organic farmers have brought green manuring to a state approaching perfection. They almost invariably sow a mixture of a legume, a cereal and a crucifer. The legume fixes nitrogen. The cereal straw produces soil binding materials when it decomposes, called mucins. They bind the soil in the crumb structure that is essential for good drainage, aeration and ease of tillage. The sulphur compounds in the crucifers are believed to enhance the health of the soil.

Typical legumes include lupins, tick beans, field peas and tares (vetch). Typical cereals include oats, rye and barley. Typical crucifers include oilseed radish, rape and mustard.

The optimum time to plough a green manure under is when the flowers are just starting to form. At this point, the protein content is at a peak. Afterward, the fibre content increases, necessitating the application of additional protein, or a longer wait for complete decomposition. The effectiveness of a green manure is enhanced when the carbon to nitrogen ratio is between 25 and 35 to 1. That is, the protein content complements the fibre. Looked at from the point of view of using pelletised poultry manure, its effects too are greatly enhanced when used in conjunction with a fibrous green manure due to the low fibre content of the poultry manure. The remarks above applying to ploughing in pasture also apply to green manures. Wilting the green manure by rolling or mowing prior to turning under promotes an increase in decomposition rate.

Cover cropping requirements are rapid establishment to get ahead of the weeds, and for plenty of fibrous roots that will hold the soil together. Usually this is a cereal, or annual ryegrass. One suspects that a mixture of species would perform better from the point of view of the soil biology preferring a mixed diet, but this may not be as economic as using a single species.

Crop	**Area per kg**	**Comments**
Lupins	70 sq metres	Sow late summer, or early autumn. Grows O.K. in acid soils.
Ryecorn	100 sq metres	Slow to decompose. Grows very tall (up to 2 metres). Germinates in cold soil. Sow autumn to spring.
Barley	100 sq metres	Needs warmish soil to germinate. Prone to fungal disease in very wet winters. Sow autumn or spring.
Oats	100 sq metres	Does not mind cold, wet conditions. Algerian is the most common variety used for green manure. Sow autumn.
Tick Beans	60 sq metres	Also called Fava beans, or horse beans. Prefers neutral soil and need plenty of potassium to remain disease free. Sow autumn.
Field Peas	100 sq metres	Grow better in cold weather than tick beans. Tick beans are preferred where amount of nitrogen required is high. Sow autumn.
Buckwheat	130 sq metres	Very rapid growth. Matures in less than two months. Needs warm soil to germinate.
Vetch	60 sq metres	Called tares in British books. This is a legume. Grows over winter. Sow autumn.

Crop	Area per kg	Comments
Red Clover	450 sq metres	Sow autumn. Good nitrogen fixer, but hard to sow accurately due to fineness of seed.
Weeds	n.a.	If your weeds are predominantly annuals, such as chickweed, or fat hen (lamb's quarters), they are the cheapest of green manures. Do not allow them to seed as they are erratic germinators.

Crop Rotation

CROP ROTATION IS THE SUCCESSION of crops grown over time and space. If plants from the same family are grown too frequently in the same soil, there is a build-up of soil borne disease. Also, some plants leave residues in the soil that affect the following crop. Peas and beans, for instance, do not grow well following the onion tribe. Reversing the order creates above average results. The shortest period between closely related crops should be three years.

Brassicas are prone to the disease club root, also known as finger and toe in turnips and swedes. The brassica family includes cauliflower, broccoli, Brussels sprouts, cabbage, kale, and many of the newly introduced Asian leaf vegetables, senposai, mizuna and bok choi for instance. Even though radish is a member of the tribe, it is in the ground for too short a time to develop the disease.

The Solanums include tomatoes, potatoes capsicums and eggplant (aubergine). Tomatoes are said to benefit from being grown in the same ground for up to five years. I would not risk it myself.

The legumes are peas and beans. They all have the property of fixing atmospheric nitrogen in a form plants can use via bacteria in nodules on their roots. If these nodules are absent on your mature plants, you can purchase the bacterial inoculant, or cadge some garden soil from a friend that does not have your problem, but do make sure that you are not importing one of your friend's problems, such as white root rot of onions.

The umbellifers include parsley, parsnips and carrots;
The Chenopodiceae include silver beet, spinach and beetroot;
The cucurbits include pumpkins, squash, cucumbers and melons;
The alliums include onions, garlic, chives and leeks;
The Compositae include lettuce, Jerusalem artichoke and salsify;
Sweet corn is on its own in the grass family.

In the average garden it is not too difficult to arrange a rotation that prevents relatives being grown too close together in time. A fairly typical rotation is potato tribe followed by brassicas followed by peas and beans followed by everything else and then back to the potatoes again. This takes account of brassicas and potatoes being two great staples in our diet. The brassicas are generally transplanted as seedlings, a necessity in most areas if they are to closely follow potatoes. Most rotations published in books from overseas are based on the assumption that nothing is grown in the winter, which is far from the case here in Tasmania. My own rotation was peas and beans followed by onion tribe followed by brassicas followed by everything else and then back to peas and beans, taking three years to complete. This is because I grew rather a lot of garlic and leeks, which I sold.

If you plan your garden well, you can have something growing to eat all year round. There will be gaps between crops from time to time. If the period is to exceed a couple of months, grow a green manure crop to protect and "rest" the soil.

Some rotations are based on the feeding needs of the plants. Peas and beans generally use few nutrients from the soil and do not mind fresh lime. Leaf vegetables need lots of compost and are heavy

A Willing Worker washes and trims vegetables for sale in Ian and Caryl Cairns' market garden at Liffey in Northern Tasmania.

feeders, as are the fruiting vegetables and potatoes. The roots, carrots, onions (not really roots, but gardeners call them roots), salsify, swedes, turnips, and beetroot are light feeders, and like the peas and beans, require no manure, or compost if the application for the heavy feeders was great enough.

To make your rotation workable, divide your garden into as many sections as there are groups in your rotation. This can still create monoculture-type pest problems in a garden if you're not careful. You need physical space between crops, not just space in time. Eel worms (nematodes) are quite capable of travelling from where they infested a crop of potatoes to next year's crop if there's only the width of a footpath to traverse. If you grow on narrow raised beds in the French-intensive system, as many gardeners do these days, rotation is more easily accomplished.

Some gardeners do away with rotations by so thoroughly mixing up their plants that disease has no chance of being encouraged. This has the snag of making it difficult to plan how closely yield is going to match consumption needs. Where the garden is supplemented by purchased vegetables this is not so much of a worry. One of the problems of organic growing is finding quality produce that equals the quality of your own to purchase, so this may not be such an attractive option.

Where garden space is limited, crops can be chosen under four different sets of criteria, demand, flavour, cost saving and yield per unit area. You cannot buy asparagus or sweet corn that tastes as good as you can grow because they deteriorate so rapidly following harvest. Unfortunately, both yield very poorly for the area they take up. Organically grown carrots have astonishingly better flavour than conventionally grown and also yield well, but are a very low-cost item. Organic potatoes taste better, but take up a lot of room and are bought so cheaply, there is little *financial* incentive to grow one's own. Commercial tomatoes are so totally lacking in flavour that tomatoes are the single most common garden vegetable grown in Australia. They also yield well. The following table will act as a guide. Value is problematic as cost varies considerably according to seasonal availability. Lettuces can cost between 30 cents and two dollars or more, for instance. The asterisk (*) means do not know.

Believe in yourself, your neighbors, your work, your ultimate attainment of more complete happiness. It is only the farmer who faithfully plants seeds in the Spring, who reaps a harvest in Autumn.
 —BC Forbes

Crop	Yield	Value	Flavour Difference
Artichoke, Jerusalem	high	medium	marked
Artichoke, globe	low	high	*
Asparagus	low	high	marked
Beans, broad	high	low	some
Beans, French	low	medium	little
Beetroot	medium	high	little
Broccoli	medium	high	marked
Brussels sprouts	high	high	some
Cabbage	high	low	marked
Carrots	high	low	marked
Cauliflower	medium	medium	marked
Capsicums	low	medium	little
Celery	high	medium	marked
Cucumbers	high	medium	some
Eggplant	medium	medium	little
Garlic	medium	high	little
Kale	medium	low	little
Kohl rabi	medium	low	some
Leeks	high	high	little
Lettuce	medium–high	low	some
Melons	medium	medium	little
Onions	high	low	little
Parsnips	high	low	marked
Peas	low	low	marked
Potatoes	high	low	marked
Pumpkin	medium	low	some
Silver beet	high	medium	little
Swede	high	low	marked
Sweet corn	low	low	marked
Tomatoes	high	low	marked
Turnips	high	low	some

Financial Considerations

THE PRIMARY PURPOSE OF market gardening is to make a profit. Profit-making relies on thorough knowledge of what your finances are doing. First of all, there is the depreciation on any equipment you have purchased. This is simply worked out by estimating its useful life and this is divided into its cost to work out its cost per week, month or year. Other costs include rates, phone, electricity, seeds, fertilisers, labour, containers etc. All of this data is then put into a table, called a spreadsheet.

Tabulating the data like this and keeping it up to date will enable you to have a snapshot of your business's health both today and for each week in the past, so you can assess progress. It will also show you where you need to improve in order to make more profit. The easiest and least expensive way to keep these records is in a ledger, which is a book designed for the purpose. The best way is to do it electronically on a computer. Your business needs a reasonable turnover to justify the expense if you do not already possess one, but when it comes to forecasting the financial effect of changes (what ifs), the computer makes light work of number-crunching.

Some of the factors influencing profit are:
- Business planning
- Labour efficiency
- Labour cost
- Weather
- Cost of fertiliser
- Market demand
- Prices received
- Business Planning

You cannot expect to run a successful business without planning. While budgetary considerations are at the core, they merely tell you the possible results of planning. Planning is attempting to forecast what those results will be. The more effort that is put into planning, the greater the likelihood you will succeed. For instance, making a profit from fresh herbs for the Tasmanian market in the 1980s was much harder than from fresh vegetables. A little research showed that Tasmanians purchased only $2 per capita per annum of fresh herbs, a tiny fraction of what they spent on fresh vegetables. Producing fresh vegetables is by no means an assurance that you will make a profit either. In my early days, I came across a man who told me he had just made $20,000. Seeing early spring lettuces for $2.00 each in the shops, he had planted out 20,000 lettuces. By the time they were ready to harvest, the price had dropped to 10¢ each. At this price, it was not profitable to harvest them, so he ploughed them in as green manure.

This illustrates a number of important points to consider. The first is market research. You must know what your potential customers are likely to want, when they want it and what price they are prepared to pay when you deliver. You should also be aware of your harvest costs so that you do not make a loss merely in order to have cash flow. All of your information should be completely up-to-date due to the volatility of prices, unless you can step outside the system with some creative thinking.

Taking the lettuce and herbs example to heart, my friends Ian and Caryl Cairns came up with an innovative approach. They dismembered their lettuces, which were a bewildering variety of leaf shape, colour and texture. They mixed the washed leaves with various herbs, bagged them and received consistently high prices throughout the growing season. Even though mesclun salad mix has since become a popular and widespread product, the Cairns maintained a good profit by staying ahead. Their mesclun was improved by the suggestion of the addition of fresh edible flowers and other salad leaves, such as chicory. They also worked hard on improving efficiency of production and processing, so as the retail price declined due to competition, their profits were maintained.

Your business plan should take account first of who you are going to sell to, what they are likely to want and when, and how much they are prepared to pay you. Only then can you realistically decide what to grow. Nearly all growers I have met have reversed this process. They decide to grow something and then try to work out how to sell it. Occasionally this is successful, but more often it is not, or competition keeps profits lower than they could have been.

Many people comment on the conservative nature of farmers and their slowness to take on new ideas. There is a reason for this. Conservative farmers stay in business. Farmers with radical ideas often fail. The ideal is to strike a happy medium. You should strive to continually try out new ideas while maintaining a firm and large enough base of the tried and true. The reason for failure with radical ideas, more often than not, is putting too many eggs in the same basket. Just as biological diversity in the garden makes life easier, spreading

---

The one small garden of a free gardener was all his need and due, not a garden swollen to a realm; his own hands to use, not the hands of others to command.
—J R R Tolkien

the risk factor over a number of products or enterprises means you are protected from disaster if one product or enterprise is an abysmal failure. Nearly always a "failure" is actually a step toward success if you can ascertain what that entails. There's no substitute for human ingenuity and imagination. "We didn't leave the stone age because of a shortage of rocks" as the saying goes.

Labour Efficiency and Cost

YOUR OWN LABOUR AND THAT of your family is nearly always the most efficient and least costly. If, as in the case of Ian and Caryl Cairns, it's a business partnership, business income and costs are halved. A warning here, unless you are absolutely certain that your proposed business partner is someone you can work with harmoniously, you are better off going it alone. Many partnerships fail under the stresses of day to day business.

A reasonable rule of thumb is that hired labour will cost at least twice as much as your own. Hired labour brings with it the added costs of taxation, workers' compensation insurance, training, supervision and usually lower efficiency. You cannot expect the average worker to take the close personal interest in your business health as you, or your family do. If you find someone who does, you should

Ian Cairns in his market garden at Liffey in Northern Tasmania.

plan on losing them when they leave to start their own business, or work out some profit share arrangement that will provide sufficient incentive to delay the inevitable.

Managing hired labour is a skill in itself, mastered by very few. Here are some guidelines. Tell people what you want done and why. If you tell people *how* to do something, you risk stifling their creativity, which reduces their satisfaction and consequently their efficiency. The former approach also gives you the opportunity to discover through them new and better methods. This does not mean you must let them continue to do a job in a less efficient manner than

Eliot Coleman discusses the use of the oscillating stirrup hoe.

the one you have developed. If their method *is* less efficient, tell them so, keeping any note of criticism from your voice. Praise work well done — often. And don't forget to thank them.

Eliot Coleman developed his unique hoe as a result of observing which tools his apprentices chose and how they used them.

Weather

IT MAY COME AS A SURPRISE, but there are things you can do about the weather. Not just by having a greenhouse, either. You can plan in the knowledge that seasons are often too wet, too cold, or too windy. By growing a range of crops, you can insulate yourself from excessive fluctuation of income. Being psychologically prepared for when disaster strikes, you are less likely to come apart at the seams. If you don't believe you can cope with disaster, then market gardening and farming are most definitely not your cup of tea.

Percentages of Nitrogen (N), Phosphorus (P) and Potassium (K) in Common Organic Materials

Material	N	P	K
Cow	0.4	0.3	0.4
Horse	0.7–0.8	0.3–0.6	0.5–0.7
Pig	0.3	0.3–0.4	0.5
Sheep & goat	0.7	0.5	0.2
Chicken	1.1–1.8	1.0	0.5
Turkey	1.3	0.7	0.5
Rabbit	2.0	1.0	0.5
Blood'n'bone	5.0–7.0	4.0–7.0	nil
Fish emulsion	5.0	2.4	1.2
Fish meal	8.0–10.5	4.0–9.0	2.0–3.0
Granite dust	nil	nil	3.0–5.0
Hard rock phosphate	nil	25–33	nil
Soft rock phosphate	nil	15–20	nil
Kelp meal	0.8	0.2	1.4
Sawdust	0.2	0.1	0.2
Wood ashes	nil	1.0–2.0	4.0–10.0
Seaweed	0.5–3.3	0.1–2.0	1.0–5.0
Lucerne hay	3.0–4.0	na	na
Red clover hay	2.0–3.2	0.3–0.5	1.3–2.0
Broiler litter	2.6	2.7	2.0

A Philosophical Note

THE WORD "ORGANIC" HAS several meanings and it's important to understand what it means in the context of this book. Critics of organic production often misrepresent it by assuming that organic practitioners mean it as the chemist does: "applied to … [chemical] compounds… as in organic acid, organic base, organic compound, organic molecule, organic radical; all these contain or are derived from hydrocarbon radicals, hence organic chemistry, that branch of chemistry which deals with organic substances, is the chemistry of the hydrocarbons and their derivatives." The Oxford English Dictionary clearly differentiates this from: "Belonging to the constitution of an organized whole" where "constitution" means the natural order of things.

The original reaction against the introduction of synthetic fertilisers to agriculture were the followers of the Austrian philosopher Rudolf Steiner who coined the term Biodynamic to describe a system he introduced in a series of lectures he gave.

Consciously organic agriculture[1] began in Central Europe and India early in the twentieth century. The British agronomist Sir Albert Howard is usually referred to as the father of modern organic agriculture because he was the first to apply modern scientific knowledge and methods to traditional agriculture. He had been sent to India by the British government to teach the Indians how to farm; Howard learnt how to farm from the Indians instead and he brought their methods back to Britain.

The term organic however is due to Walter James (Lord Northbourne),[2] a student of Biodynamic Agriculture. The word is first used in his book *Look to the Land*.[3] Northbourne took Rudolf Steiner's idea of "the farm as organism" and derived from it the term "organic farming". He wrote of "the farm as a living whole" and declared that: "the farm itself must have a biological completeness; it must be a living entity, it must be a unit which has within itself a balanced organic life". A farm that relies on imported fertility could never be self-sufficient nor an organic whole. "The farm must be

---

1 As opposed to traditional or peasant agricultural methods that are described as unconsciously organic.

2 I am grateful to Tim Marshall for correcting the misunderstanding that I had when writing my first book on organic gardening where I attributed it to Sir Albert Howard. See also "Lord Northbourne, the man who invented organic farming, a biography", by John Paull (School of Land & Food, University of Tasmania, Hobart). https://orgprints.org/26547/12/26547.pdf

3 *Look to the Land*, Lord Northbourne, JM Dent 1940.

organic in more senses than one". He maintained the holistic view that: "The soil and the micro-organisms in it together with the plants growing on it form an organic whole".

This is more an ideal goal than for it to be achieved in many parts of the world. For example, my own land is deficient in molybdenum, magnesium and boron. Realistically I need to import these minerals, preferably not from some very distant part of the planet.

Just as an animal doesn't exist apart from the billions of organisms in its digestive tract, plants do not thrive in the absence of a living soil that similarly contains billions of organisms acting as a coherent whole. This is often enough referred to as "ecological balance", but I remain uncomfortable with the word "balance" here just because it implies a unique state. The proportions of organisms vary over time and space. A farm or garden is never in a constant single state which the word "balance" implies; there are changes from season to season and differences between one year and the next. A healthy functioning ecosystem is a dynamic entity, not static.

There is a saying "all flesh is grass" and is usually taken to be a reference to the transitory nature of human life. It is also literally true in that all life on the planet is dependent on plant-life and its ability to convert energy from the sun into carbohydrate, not just for the benefit of the plant where this happens, but also for the animals that consume those plants. As I learnt in secondary school:

$$6CO_2 + 6H_2O \rightarrow C_6H_{12}O_6 + 6O_2$$
(carbon dioxide plus water and energy from the sun makes sucrose and oxygen via chlorophyll)

The rate of energy capture by photosynthesis today is on the order of 130 terawatts, or about eight times the total energy consumption of humanity. There's a cartoon (from NASA) on the next page showing what's called the Carbon Cycle. The numbers in brackets are the size of what are called carbon sinks or reservoirs. Half a billion years ago the amount of carbon in the atmosphere was nearly twenty times as great as today. The slightly increased carbon dioxide level in the atmosphere during the 20th century has had a profound effect on Earth's biosphere: an increase of 15% in Net Primary Productivity (NPP) or total biomass.

Animals consume plant carbohydrates (or animals that do so) and convert them back into carbon dioxide and water, extracting their stored solar energy in the process. The carbon dioxide they respire feeds the plants in an apparently never-ending cycle. Usually this cycle is *assumed* to be closed, but the existence of a sink (coal) that has

The Carbon Cycle from https://earthobservatory.nasa.gov/features/CarbonCycle

grown enormously over the last 500 million years or so shows this not to be so. Rather than worry about an excess of CO_2 I believe we need to worry about the 90% decrease over the last 150 million years.[4] It might be slow, but eventually must fall to the 150 ppm that is the lower limit for most plants. If those plants disappear, so does almost all multi-cellular life on Earth.

Carbon dioxide is not the "toxic pollutant" as it is so often described by the mass media, but an essential part of terrestrial life. At the geological time-scale, current carbon dioxide levels are very near the lower limit. If the levels recorded in the ice cores taken in Antarctica are a true indication, the level of carbon dioxide in the atmosphere dropped perilously close to the point where some plant species were near the lower limit for their survival during the last glacial episode a few thousand years ago. Plants evolved in an atmosphere with several times the amount of carbon dioxide than today.[5]

Just as the rise in carbon dioxide in the 20th century increased the planet's biomass, a decrease reduces it. On the page opposite is the standard chart of CO_2 and temperature over the last few hundred million years. Clearly the planet has a small number of preferred temperature states and flips between them. These states are also clearly unrelated to atmospheric carbon dioxide levels at the time and are currently the lowest for 250 million years. Atmospheric CO_2 levels do affect temperature, but not by very much.

In contrast the following graph shows the strong correlation between sea surface temperature and cosmic ray flux. Correlation does not mean the relationship is causal. There's a similar correlation between marriage and deaths in the general population for example. However, a *lack* of correlation definitely means there's *no* noticeable causal relationship.

In the case of Nir Shaviv's discovery of the major changes in Earth's climate, a reason for the correlation needs to be shown. This was provided by Henrick Svensmark's demonstration that low cloud cover is modulated by cosmic rays. Low clouds as you may have noticed have a cooling effect during the day and a warming effect at night. Climatologists have known for some considerable time that a 5% change in low cloud cover or less is sufficient to explain all of the 20th century climatic warming.

This does not of course mean that it did. Just that we now have two explanations for the one phenomenon. Quite how CO_2 fluctuation

---

4   This is a position I share with Greenpeace co-founder Patrick Moore.

5   See: Plant responses to low [CO2] of the past, *New Phytologist* (2010) 188: 674–695 doi: 10.1111/j.1469-8137.2010.03441.x

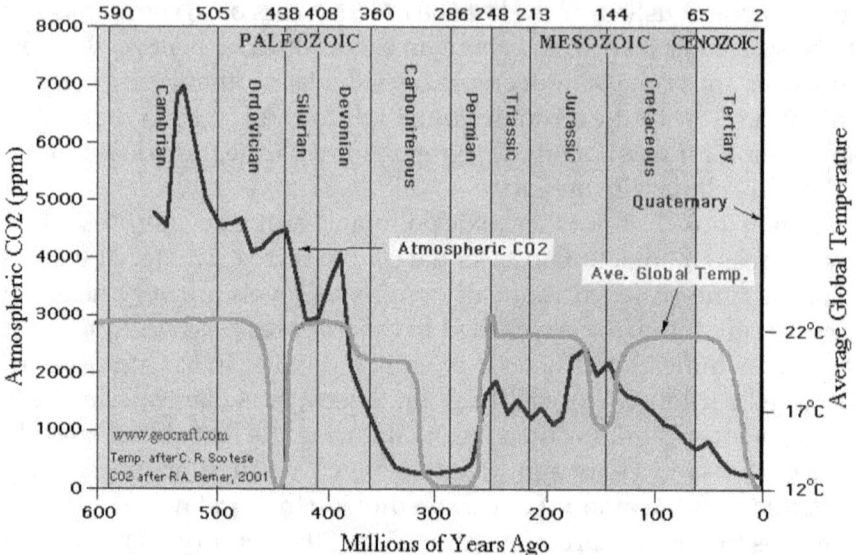

The graph above shows CO2 versus temperature with CO2 the black line and temperature in grey. From Sivaramanan, Sivakumaran. (2015). Global Warming and Climate change, causes, impacts and mitigation. 10.13140/RG.2.1.4889.7128.

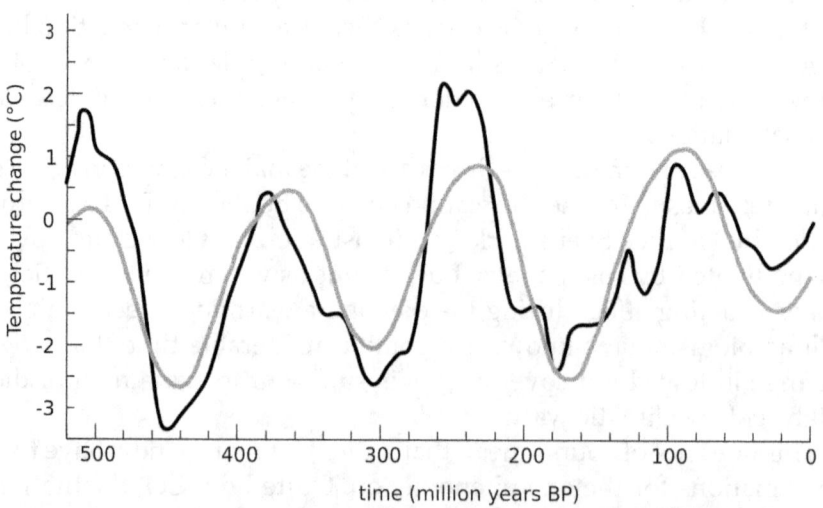

In Nir Shaviv's graph above sea surface temperature is black and cosmic ray flux is grey. From Nir J. Shaviv, NJ, Veizer, J, "Celestial driver of Phanerozoic climate?", pp4-10, GSA Today, vol 7, Issue 7 (July 2003).

explains recent observations, but not those in the past is beyond me.

The organic approach to farming and gardening is one that places emphasis on harmony. This requires us to see ourselves as embedded in the ecosphere, not something separate from it. Without humans and the Industrial Revolution it seems clear that plant-life would be facing extreme deprivation if not actual extinctions during the next glacial episode. We are making withdrawals from a bank account established half a billion years ago and we need to acknowledge it for what it is while ensuring that we do not overdraw the account.

The Earth's fossil fuels are not the only bank account established by Nature. The sea contains ever so many nutrients washed there by aeons of rainfall and consequent soil erosion. Earthworms have also played a prominent role in this as Charles Darwin pointed out in his excellent monograph *The formation of vegetable mould through the action of worms, with observations on their habits* in 1881. I see it as our role to judiciously reverse that trend by using seaweed, fish and carbonate rocks from the oceans to return some of those nutrients to their origin. I believe we can "save the planet", not by destroying industry, but by nurturing the life-forms we share with the planet, including our fellow human beings.[6]

While climate activists are apparently vigorously opposed to climate research of the sort conducted by Nir Shaviv and Henrik Svensmark, and the improvement of the standard of living of those who live in what used to be called the Third World, as an egalitarian I am not. It pleases me greatly that far more women now can wash their clothes in a washing machine than hitherto.[7] I also note that the increased prosperity of my dusky skinned cousins has brought the world's population growth down from 6 children per woman to 2.5, well on the way to zero population growth. I hope that more folks in the privileged white minority to which I belong begin to think of the aspirations of those living outside of Australasia, Europe, and North America.

But there's another book needed here. Effective climate control that benefits the majority might very well be feasible. Watch this space...

https://ashwoodbooks.com

---

6 See "Gaia: A New Look at Life on Earth", James Lovelock, OUP 2000

7 See Hans Rosling:
The Magic Washing Machine (https://www.youtube.com/watch?v=-4Hzc0owz5k)

About the Author

BACK IN THE 1970s MY FRIENDS and I mostly had very long hair and often, while doing what people with very long hair did in those days, we talked about moving back to the land as an ideal way of life.[1] I remember that one summer several did. And all returned early in the ensuing winter. Well, almost all.

The end of the decade found me broke and contemplating the good life. I had always more or less carefully tailored my income to maximise my leisure-time. Leisure to me was eating at gourmet restaurants (where my long hair was not always appreciated), buying and reading good books, conversation with people who could think rather than merely air their prejudices, and fornication.

My source of income at the time was painting landscape pictures to compete with the sterile prints sold in department stores. My long-haired friends went from door-to-door selling the paintings and gaining an occasional commission for a painting from a favourite photograph. They also sold prints of my pen and ink drawings. The sales staff paid me for what they sold, keeping the balance in their pockets.

The sales staff kept approximately 30-35% of the money taken and each week I paid bonuses to whoever sold the most. And that person often made more than I did due to my considerable manufacturing costs. That didn't bother me in the least. I was making several times per hour what I had as a clerk and above all I was contented. We were all working less hours than the ordinary Joes, approximately 20 per week giving me plenty of time for reading and my other pursuits. I was particularly happy with the business model: everyone was in control of their own income.

Occasionally, sales would be beyond my capacity to provide, so I would pay wages to someone to help make the canvases: reject linen table cloths from a laundry glued to plywood and gessoed. The prints were mounted on acid-free mat boards. I also commissioned other artists to make drawings for me and had those printed off as well. My drawings were of historic buildings, Karen Young's were of cuddly animals such as possums, wallabies and koalas.

Not everyone was happy, however. Some people were incapable of understanding how to sell the paintings. The sales staff were in essence entertainers competing with television. If the evening's TV shows were popular, like Starsky and Hutch for example, sales were down. If there was shite on TV, the reverse was true. Invariably,

1 This was largely due to the popularity of Stuart Brand's *Whole Earth Catalogue*, a profound influence on many of us.

when records were broken, it was a Tuesday night! When given instruction, the people who couldn't sell very many would say: "I couldn't say/do that! I'd feel silly." The instruction wasn't in the form of scripts; just general approaches that one had to weave into a personal approach. The best sales staff were very creative people, often talented artists or musicians. Most went on to much bigger and better things. The best now co-owns a chain of pharmacies.

Some of the discontent was in the "poor starving artist" community. While they waited forlornly for the world to beat a path to their door, I beat a path to the door of my clients, many of whom became repeat customers. (I would have given my eye teeth for a computerised system to replace the card-file I used to track customers, and the paper spreadsheets to keep track of my costs!) The poor starving artists and people who couldn't sell, or be bothered selling, became increasingly vocal in their opposition to my business. They declared that I was ripping off the public and the sales staff.

Regarding the former, I introduced a cooling off period before it was made law for door-to-door sales. The advantage to this is well illustrated by the following. I had accepted a commission to paint a picture of the Arthur River from a photograph. A week or so after the sale was consummated, Terry, who was particularly adept at procuring commissions, phoned me: "The client's decided he doesn't like your painting, but it's a commission".

"Give him his money back and double the price," I said. The painting had taken twice as long as I anticipated. Such things happen when you're having fun! Terry was delighted with the result! Fifteen minutes later, he sold the painting to the customer's next door neighbour who was far from annoyed when he discovered what had happened.

I was losing my talented sales people to bigger and better things and finding it hard to recruit replacements. Hobart was a small community of only a couple of hundred thousand. Then disaster struck. My top three sales staff had taken my advice about drink-driving and caught a cab after their Friday night celebration. The incompetent taxi driver rolled the cab, killing Kahm, breaking Andreas's femur and Robert went into a 20 year depression as a result of Kahm dying in his arms.

Kahm was the most truly happy person we had ever met. His sister phoned me and asked, "Was he laughing when he died?" Indeed he was; Kahm taught me one of the most important lessons of my life: *Carpe diem!* (seize the day).

My office/home/studio was attacked by an arsonist. The end of the decade found me wondering how I'd been suckered into "selling" $A40,000 worth of my work to a company that immediately declared bankruptcy. I couldn't pay my bills, so I had to declare bankruptcy.

The business that cost me $A300 to start and made $A300 profit in its first five days was defunct. My partner had left me having trousered the last three months' rent and I sold my books for less than the four most expensive had cost me. My stamp collection returned rather more, and I managed to break even. I contemplated suicide.

I still had one asset left and I decided to do something about it before the now ex-wife remembered it. We had a rather nice collection of vintage wine and I commenced to drink it. A somewhat blurry few weeks later found me invited to a garden party by my long-time friend, Jane. As we walked along the street to the party, I asked about the $50 bill tucked between her breasts. "Oh, that's for whoever proposes marriage to me," she hinted. As usual, I ignored Jane's hint, preferring her friendship to a life of mutual misunderstanding.

One of my favourite drawings. I painted and drew several versions of Clifton Priory at Bothwell in Tasmania's Midlands over the years. You can download and print this and others from:
http://sturmsoft.com/ Writing/pix.htm

Also, I must have had a premonition. At the party was the most stunning woman I ever met. I don't mean in the Hollywood Movie Star sense; it was something else. Not, I hasten to add, that Marguerite is unlovely, just not boringly glamorous. Almost our first words to each other were: "Ain't never getting married again". It took four years before we eventually took that step.

Margie and I share an interest in gardening although mine was untested at that time. Curiously, I had picked up two of the earliest issues of an organic gardening magazine while passing through airports, and they just happened to be the two missing from Margie's collection and the back issues were no longer available. We decided that since I was likely to remain poor for the near future, we would be better off living in the country. Finding the right place took almost a year.

The farmlet we bought was a hovel on almost 10 acres of good, strong land. For two years I gradually renovated the cottage and developed a small market garden almost completely with hand-tools. Only the initial ground-breaking was done with power machinery borrowed from neighbours. When Margie conceived, we decided to plunge fully into "poverty" and she gave up her full-time job in the city. Our frugal life was tough, but we often reflected on how sorry we felt for the poor "rich" people as we toasted each other with home-made wine and ate a gourmet meal from food that we had produced.

When we had dinner guests they would invariably say: "That's the best lamb we ever tasted". It would amuse me to tell them (after the meal) that it wasn't lamb. It was goat!

My closest friend who hailed from America took a trip back to the States around this time. Stuart said that Thanksgiving was particularly hard to endure. His sister had proudly prepared the meal "from scratch". This entailed instant mashed potatoes, frozen vegetables and frozen turkey. My friend said all he could think about was helping me slaughter and butcher the meat, pick those peas and dig those carrots; it was all *real* food with *real* flavour rather than food-like substances.

I suspect, though this is verging perilously close to New Age BS, that food cooked with a wood fire[2] is qualitatively different from that cooked with electricity. I can readily explain the flavour difference with hard science about organic production, but not the difference that the wood fire has on the available energy from food so cooked.

---

2   Back then we had an Everhot wood-burning cook-stove. These days we have a Bosky and it's hard for me to imagine returning to cooking with anything else. We do have a gas cooktop for summertime cooking, but more than half our cooking is done with the Bosky that also provides our hot water and space-heating.

When our local publican encouraged me to expand my vegetable gardening and become commercial, I first contacted the Organic Gardening and Farming Society. The Society's President, Neil Jordan said there wasn't much he could do to help. There were no other organic market gardeners in Tasmania. Neil elicited a promise from me to share what I learnt, a promise I have kept many times over. I also contacted the Department of Agriculture who told me there was no point to market gardening; there was no demand for fresh vegetables in Tasmania.

What I did find in those early days was that despite burgeoning demand for organic produce on the mainland, locally my customers were folks in their fifties and older who remembered what vegetables used to taste like. The first bag of garlic I sold to Michael at Chung's the Hobart vegetable wholesaler he paid me double what he usually did for garlic. He told me that wasn't because it was organic, but because it was the highest quality garlic he'd ever seen and it was all destined for restaurants, not the shops.

When a specialist fresh vegetable shop opened up in nearby Huonville, I began supplying them with most of my produce. The shop-owner was a pro-organic enthusiast and the organic section proved popular. I began supplying him in the autumn and early the following summer I phoned when my French beans were due to be picked to ask how much he'd be ordering. He told me he'd made an exclusive deal with another grower so he wouldn't be taking any.

So we went searching for a new outlet for our produce and the following day Eumarrah wholefoods in Hobart agreed to become our new outlet. They were willing to pay double what we'd been receiving and that more than compensated for the extra 40 km (25 miles) distance to deliver. When the local outlet's owner telephoned a few days later asking for resupply of potatoes, cauliflowers, lettuces and so forth, I asked what had happened with his "exclusive deal". "Oh that was just for French beans," he said. My response was that perhaps he should have been more explicit and that I'd made an exclusive deal with Eumarrah. French beans alone don't justify an organic section on their own of course. Both the French bean grower and the shop had torpedoed that and the beans had to sell at the usual price, rather than for a premium.

When for several years I became a proselyte for the organic farming movement, I would talk science to the farmers and agricultural scientists. But when I talked to consumers, I talked politics:

"If you grow your own potatoes, you have done several quite important things. You have removed the necessity to earn the dollars to buy those

potatoes and if your income is subject to your control, you can then choose to pay less taxes. If, like me, you grew them organically, you have no need of the agrochemical inputs and so you have reduced the income of the agrochemical companies and in turn their taxes. You have had useful physical exercise that improves your health and so reduces the necessity to visit the doctor. You have saved transporting the potatoes from the farmer's paddock, to the warehouse, to the supermarket and home, reducing the amount of fossil fuel burned. The most profoundly political act you can make is not to vote for Tweedle Dumb or Tweedle Dumber, or protest about what you can never control, but to grow your own food and take control of your own life."

During an organic gardening field day at Ian and Caryl Cairns market garden in Lilydale, my friend Steve Kapolice asked Vermont market gardener Eliot Coleman what he thought about the certification of organic produce. Eliot said: "Get to know the first name of the person growing your food, then you won't have to worry about how it's grown." A wise man. At the time I was the Publicity Officer for the National Association for Sustainable Agriculture, Australia (NASAA) and for me that was a profound moment when I realised we were just creating another bureaucracy. Was this really the aim of the organic movement?

I was also involved with the local (state) politics of food. The NSW Department of Primary Industry had prosecuted a woman for selling organic pesticides "because they weren't registered", a requirement under NSW law. I approached the relevant person in Tasmania's Department of Agriculture who assured me that no such thing would happen locally. He explained that as a public servant he wasn't interested in making work for himself and unless someone made a formal complaint he would be turning a blind eye. Both he and the Minister for Agriculture at the time (Nick Evers) were very much on-side where organic production was concerned.

03 ❀ 80

When we took up our land and cottage in late January 1982 we were left almost penniless. Even though it cost us only $AU26,000 Marguerite had to borrow from the bank, remembering that I was still a bankrupt and therefore wasn't able to borrow. Margie also owned a small block of land that she put up for sale, though that took several years to sell. The first priority after helping the neighbours fight bush fires, was to make a garden.

At the top end of the block, over a hundred metres from the cottage, there is a dam and immediately below that is where I made my first garden. The neighbours lent us a short length of PVC irrigation pipe to siphon water to the parched ground. We had arrived in the middle of a severe drought. I knew next to nothing about gardening except what I had read in books, but we managed to be moderately successful and I began my writing career at this time. Grass Roots magazine paid me the princely sum of $AU5 per full page article and if I recall correctly I managed to persuade Organic Gardening magazine to pay me occasionally too.

While I learned the gardening business, I discovered an excellent way of reducing demand on our income: brewing my own beer. While making beer from brew-kits was economical and pleasant, I set out to invent a way to extract my own malt from malted barley. The key to doing this is very careful temperature control and the usual way to do this is with accurate thermostatically controlled electric heating. This was beyond our means. We purchased a very large stainless steel saucepan that justified its cost because of the wide variety of uses to which it would be put. At various times it has made stock from soup bones, jam, soup, ham and bacon among other things. Not just beer.

I made a giant "teapot" cosy for the saucepan using an old bedspread and worn-out woollen pullovers. By pitching the cracked barley malt into water at the upper temperature range that the enzymes will tolerate, and leaving the saucepan snuggled up in the "teapot" cosy, conversion of starch to maltose would complete overnight. Incomplete conversion leads to cloudy beer and my beer was sparkling clear.

When I conducted a time and motion study, we were saving more than double the wage paid to labourers if I costed the beer at the same price as local normal beer. In fact, whenever we had a party, we noticed that the revellers invariably drank our beer and left the commercial beer they had brought with them for us to drink. Boutique beer being double the price of normal means that in reality we were "earning" four times labourers' wages and it was tax free. I was tempted by a wealthy friend to brew for him at normal pub prices, but the illegality prevented me taking him up on his kind offer.

Most of the labour cost of production was in bottle washing. Wine doesn't need the secondary ferment to produce gas and froth that beer does, so latterly I made wine. Approximately half the wine in a fermenter gets bottled and the other half we drank from the fermenter. Wine matures more rapidly in bulk, so we usually had plenty of large food-quality plastic buckets with snap-on lids sitting quietly in the laundry. These wines were all "country" wines: blackberry, rhubarb, red currant, black currant and plum just like my grandmother used to make.

Robert Wright wrote in an article for the September 2000 issue of *Foreign Policy* magazine:

> *"The point where more wealth ceases to imply more happiness is around $10,000 per capita annually — roughly where Greece, Portugal, and South Korea are now. Above that point, additional dollars don't seem to cheer up nations, and national differences in happiness hinge on the intangibles of culture. The Irish are appreciably happier than the Germans, the Japanese, and the British, though less wealthy than all of them."*

Over our first two decades together, our average annual income was remarkably close to that $US10,000. While the popular image of our "peasant" lifestyle is one of unremitting toil, this was far from the truth. True, we didn't drive a recent motor car, but we did have two current generation computers before they became ubiquitous. Did we feel deprived? Far from it.

Towards the end of the century I returned to the conventional workforce for 16 months managing a computer training business and training end-users myself. The job kept me from home for 12 hours a day (includes commute time), 5 days a week for $AU36,000 a year, a slightly above average income here in Tasmania at the time. Out of the $AU36,000, I was paying approximately $AU12,000 in taxes leaving $AU24,000. Commute cost was $AU2,000 using public transport. Despite pressure from the boss, I refused to buy a motor car that would have cost more than five to ten times as much as public transport. That left around $AU22,000, or approximately $US13,000 at the time. I had more than doubled my time away from home for a net increase in income of around $US3,000. The garden was neglected during this period and we had to eat tired old supermarket stuff. While the cost was probably considerably less than $US1,000 per annum, the lower quality certainly added to a decrease in contentment and overall feeling of well-being during that period.

It didn't take me too long to discover that the business was charging my time out at $AU80/hr. Returning to self-employment in the computer training business doubled my income and halved the number of hours I needed to work. More to the point, I was back in control of my life. One contract was bringing in $AU10–14,000 per month and a year of that paid for building the world-famous House of Steel.[3] To my great delight I also took up gardening again.

Recent time has seen my health rapidly deteriorate for mainly genetic reasons. I have congestive heart failure, am in chronic pain from

---

3 See http://sturmsoft.com/ House/house01.htm

osteoarthritis in my spine and need a walking frame to get around. As well I have been busy publishing books for friends and decided to write this much-improved gardening book I have promised for so many years. This is it. I hope you have enjoyed reading it and that it proves useful.

A couple of flitches of bacon are worth fifty thousand Methodist sermons and religious tracts. They are great softeners of temper and promoters of domestic harmony.
   —William Cobbett

Recommended Reading

"The Albrecht Papers", Dr William Albrecht, Acres USA 1975
Dr William Albrecht was a prolific writer of papers and this is a compendium of many that he delivered. They canvas his ideas on soil fertility, stock and human health. An essential read if you want to understand some of the science underpinning organics.

"The Living Soil and the Haughley Experiment", Lady Eve Balfour, Palgrave Macmillan 1976
Following the introduction of Howard's ideas to Britain after the Second World War, he and Eve Balfour started an organisation, the Soil Association, to test his ideas in the cooler climate of southern England. This is the subject matter of "The Haughley Experiment". Earlier, Balfour had come to her own conclusions regarding the relationships between biological activity in the soil, diet and human health. This is the subject of "The Living Soil".

"The Gift of Good Land", North Point Press 1981
Wendell Berry writes of the importance of good farming to a healthy culture. By health he means not merely the absence of disease, but of a balanced, nondestructive way of life.

"Compost for Garden Plot or Thousand Acre Farm", F H Billington, Faber 1943
Foundational. Good for historians and those who seek a deeper understanding.

"The New Organic Grower" Eliot Coleman, Chelsea Green 1989
I was delighted to be able to attend a workshop with Eliot and his wife, Barbara Damrosch in October, 1993. This book explains much of what Eliot shared with us over those two days.

"The 7 Habits of Highly Effective People: Powerful Lessons in Personal Change", Stephen Covey, Simon & Schuster 1992
"Stephen R. Covey presents a holistic, integrated, principle-centred approach for solving personal and professional problems."

"The Practicing Stoic", Ward Farnsworth, David R Godine 2018
The great insights of the Stoics are spread over a wide range of ancient sources. Uniquely, this book systematically presents what the various Stoic philosophers said in a form more easily understood than by reading the original sources alone. Above all, it's a *practical* manual, not merely a book *about* Stoicism.

"Man's Search for Meaning", Viktor Frankl, Touchstone 1970
Lessons for spiritual survival. Best read in conjunction with Covey's *7 Habits* that he largely inspired.

"The One-Straw Revolution", Masanobu Fukuoka, Rodale 1978
Many inspiring ideas in this book though he perhaps goes too far in the direction we all need to be travelling in.

"Chaos", James Gleik, The Making of a New Science, Viking 1987
Covers the discovery of chaos theory in layman's language. When I was taught physics, we were only introduced to the easy to solve equations. Chaos deals with what happens when there are no precise solutions to such things as the gravitational interaction of more than two bodies. Weather, climate, ecology are all chaotic systems.

"The Farming Ladder", G Henderson, Faber 1947
The Henderson brothers weren't organic farmers as such, but they had a deep and keen appreciation for many organic and Stoic principles. They were also excellent business managers. Many important life lessons in this book.

"An Agricultural Testament", Sir Albert Howard, OUP 1949
This book is a foundation stone of organic agriculture. In it, Howard describes his discoveries about the role of humus and mycorrhizal fungi in the soil while living in India.

"How to Grow More Vegetables" John Jeavons, 10 Speed Press 1979
John Jeavons is a follower of the late Alan Chadwick, who taught many gardeners in California his own peculiar mix of Biodynamic and French intensive gardening. This book is quite exhaustive in the area of crop yields under this regime. A "must have".

"Handbook for Vegetable Growers", James Edward Knott, John Wiley & Sons, New York, 1957
The leading one-stop reference for commercial vegetable growers for more than 50 years.

"Gaia: A New Look at Life on Earth", James Lovelock, OUP 2000
Explains the Gaia hypothesis: that the earth's living matter air, ocean, and land surfaces forms a self-organising complex system that has the capacity to keep the Earth a fit place for life.

"Recycle Your Garden—the essential guide to composting", Tim Marshall, ABC Books 2003
Everything the gardener needs to know about composting. Very practical.

"Living the Good Life", Helen and Scott Nearing, Schocken Books 1970
I'm not at all sure when I first read this, but it ignited a small flame that eventually grew into a fierce fire. While most people's lives are defined by their job, Helen and Scott promoted the idea of revenuing for half the day and engaging in personal development for the other half. The writer began this very early on in life when he was in his early twenties.

"The Climate Caper", Garth Paltridge, Quartet 2009
Quoting Rafe Champion: "Emeritus Professor Garth Paltridge is an atmospheric physicist, previously a Chief Research Scientist with the CSIRO Division of Atmospheric Research and more recently Director of the Institute of Antarctic and Southern Ocean Studies." Along with my near neighbour Mike Pook and A Arkin, they wrote a paper "Trends in middle-and upper-level tropospheric humidity from NCEP reanalysis data" that took several years to find a publisher (Theoretical and Applied Climatology). An articulate account of the actual position of the many scientists who disagree with climate alarmism.

"Carrots Love Tomatoes: Secrets of Companion Planting for Successful Gardening", Louise Riotte, Storey Books 1976
This gardening classic was first published in 1975 for gardeners who prefer pest-resistant planning to pesticides.

"Complete Guide to Self-Sufficiency", John Seymour, Faber 1976
If Michael Plane's account of meeting the man is accurate, John was a bit of a dreamer. His wife was the hands-on farmer. Nevertheless, this and Seymour's many other books are well worth reading. This particular book made our move back to the land imperative.

"Landscapes & Cycles: An Environmentalist's Journey to Climate Skepticism", Jim Steele, Amazon Digital Services 2013
Jim "compares the effects of landscape changes, natural cycles and climate change on polar bears, whales, walruses, penguins, frogs, pika, butterflies and marine ecosystems. Although it is wise to think globally, all wildlife reacts locally and all regions of the earth have been behaving very differently from what a globally averaged

statistic might suggest. Despite media horror stories, many species have benefited from recent climate change."

"Culture and Horticulture" Wolf Storl, Biodynamic Literature 1979
I believe Wolf Storl's book is the most accessible introduction to the concepts underlying Biodynamics.

"The Chilling Stars: a New Theory of Climate Change", Henrick Svensmark and Nigel Calder, Icon Books 2007
A lucid account of how clouds influence climate by modulating sunlight. Unlike CAGW, the predictions of Svensmark's theory have been discovered to be true.

"Humus", Friend Sykes, Faber 1947
Friend Sykes was an early member of the Soil Association, and in this book describes his conversion of a sick, run down farm to health and fecundity by the application of Howard's organic principles.

"Changing Agriculture", Jim Wilson, Kangaroo Press 1988
This is a book about how to apply Systems Thinking to farming. Systems thinking is a way of dealing with the world. Jim's approach is simple to understand and well worthwhile implementing.

A garden to walk in and immensity to dream in — what more could he ask? A few flowers at his feet and above him the stars.
— Victor Hugo

Resources

Seeds — New Gippsland Seeds
PO Box 1 Silvan,
VIC 3795

I have been purchasing almost all of my seeds from Peter and Sue de Vaus for nearly 40 years. These are high quality seeds, far better than from garden shops, hardware stores or "alternative" suppliers. Only suppliers to commercial vegetable growers achieve the same level of seed quality. The service is excellent also.

Fertiliser — Terra Firma
Phone: (07) 5541 2322
Email: info@tff.com.au

I've rarely used commercial fertilisers since we were producing copious amounts of compost from locally available ingredients. Many years ago I was asked to trial Terra Firma's *Organic Life* and *Dynamic Lifter* pelletised poultry manure. The best by far from the point of view of smell and results obtained, was from Terra Firma's product.

Vitec Organics
Free Call: 1800 622 345
Business Hours
Monday – Friday 8am till 4pm

Far and away the best fish emulsion I have used.

Organic Certification
National Standard for Organic and Bio-Dynamic Products:
https://www.agriculture.gov.au/sites/default/files/sitecollectiondocuments/aqis/exporting/food/organic/national-standard-edition-3-7.pdf

Picture Credits
AS = Adobe stock, GT = Gundaroo Tiller, JS = Jonathan Sturm, NC = Newscorp, PD = Public Domain

Tools

Gundaroo Tiller
Joyce Wilkie & Michael Plane
Phone: 02 6236 8173
International: 612 6236 8173
International Fax: 612 9383 8894
Email: GT@allsun.com.au

This is where I purchased my Coleman hoe, claw hoe and GR wheel hoe. "If we sell it we use it on the farm ourselves" says it all really. First class hand tools.

Weedwakka
Phone: (03) 9844 4512
Email: info@weedwakka.com.au

If you use a brushcutter, the *Weedwakka* is an indispensable substitute for nylon cord. Peter Thorne also makes tools for Gundaroo Tiller.

Acknowledgements

I am extremely grateful to a number of people for making this book possible:
Ian and Caryl Cairns for providing a home away from home;
Michael Plane for his excellent garden tools;
Eliot Coleman for his practical advice;
Helen and Scott Nearing, John Jeavons, Alan Chadwick, and John Seymour for inspiration;
Boney Cragg for free beer;
Tim Marshall for proofreading and being a great friend and colleague;
Ted Sloan for his first-rate fish fertiliser and wisdom;
Neil Jordan for encouraging me to share my discoveries while market gardening;
Allan Moult for encouraging me to write and greatly improving my writing;
All the WWOOFers and other willing workers who helped keep my garden tidy while I wrote;
Lionel Pollard for making WWOOF possible;
Susan Young, and Sonja Cook for proof-reading.
And most especially my wife Marguerite and sons Thomas and Kieron for their patience and love.

www.ingramcontent.com/pod-product-compliance
Lightning Source LLC
Chambersburg PA
CBHW052017290426
44112CB00014B/2278